Clinical Interpretation of Objective Psychological Tests

Clinical Interpretation of Objective Psychological Tests
Second Edition

CHARLES J. GOLDEN, Ph.D.

Director, Neuropsychology
Head Injury Recovery Center at Hillcrest
Head Injury Recovery Associates
Milford, Pennsylvania

ALLYN AND BACON
Boston   London   Toronto   Sydney   Tokyo   Singapore

A Division of Simon & Schuster, Inc.
160 Gould Street
Needham Heights, Massachusetts 02194

ISBN 0-205-12522-0

Library of Congress Cataloging-in-Publication Data
not available at press time.

Printed in the United States of America

10 9 8 7 6 5 4 3 2 1   95 94 93 92 91 90

Contents

Acknowledgements

TO THE FIRST EDITION

In an undertaking of this size it is difficult to fully acknowledge all those who helped prepare the manuscript. Specific thanks are due to Dr. Fred Strider, Mary Ann Strider, and David Osmon for wading through the early drafts and making appropriate comments. I owe an immense debt to numerous secretaries at the University of Nebraska Medical Center for providing typed copies of many drafts. A final acknowledgement is due to the psychologists who put together and provided the basic research on the instruments described in this book. In each case, their efforts represent many hours of detailed analytic work as well as many hours of drudgery. Their contribution to the field of psychological testing and to clinical psychology as a whole is not reflected in their listing in the references. Without their work and their inspiration, there could have been no book.

TO THE REVISED EDITION

I must acknowledge the help and support of Drexel University (and especially Drs. Canavan, Glasscock, and Hewett) for allowing me the time and freedom to finally complete this revised edition. Thanks are due as well to the readers of the original edition whose comments made this revision worth doing.

Preface

Despite extensive changes in the attitudes of psychologists toward testing, the use of psychological testing in the evaluation of psychiatric, medical, and normal individuals remains a major skill expected of the thoroughly trained applied psychologist in clinical, school, or industrial work. Psychological testing, in addition, remains the primary function of many psychologists trained at the master's level. Changes in attitudes toward testing, however, have brought about substantial modifications in the clinical interpretation of psychological tests. This has resulted from a more complete understanding of the role of psychological tests, their limitations, and their advantages. Such changes also reflect the increasingly sophisticated research that has appeared in the area.

Although many psychologists are aware that such changes have taken place, there does not exist any single source that presents the status of the clinical interpretation of the major psychological tests. One can turn to books concerned with single tests, but these are generally disappointing in the area of clinical interpretation and often inappropriate to the teaching of the clinical interpretation. One can turn to the literature itself, but one is faced with countless thousands of articles of varying validity and usefulness. These, too, suffer from an em-

xi

phasis on the psychometric and experimental properties of tests rather than on their clinical usefulness with the single patient.

The present volume is an attempt to remediate this problem in the area of adult objective psychological testing. The emphasis throughout the volume is to present the basic clinical knowledge and strategies necessary for the competent use of the most widespread and important tests in adult clinical psychology today. The tests have been selected from the four major areas of psychological testing: intellectual evaluation, achievement, personality, and organic brain dysfunction. The tests chosen are those most frequently used in each area, as well as those that promise to be useful in a significant clinical area likely to be faced by the average psychologist. The references chosen have been limited to those that would be the most useful to the reader looking for a more in-depth evaluation of a given test beyond that presented in this volume.

The book has been written so it can be understood by the individual without any specific background with a test or with psychological testing in general. As a result, the book can be used profitably with a number of different populations: as an introduction to the clinical interpretation of psychological tests for the undergraduate major or psychology graduate student, as an update for the professional psychologist at the master's or doctoral level, and as a survey and introduction for the professional outside psychology who is interested in psychological testing. In the latter capacity, the book should be of particular interest to psychiatrists, social workers, physicians, and rehabilitation professionals.

It is hoped that the book will give the reader a respect for the complexity of clinical interpretation, an understanding of the possibilities of each of these tests in a clinical situation, and a basic introduction to the way in which the clinical interpretation is accomplished. In this way, the volume can contribute to the training of better clinicians as well as provide the nonpsychologist with a better understanding of the clinical foundations and methods associated with objective psychological testing.

TO THE REVISED EDITION

In the decade since the release of the first edition of this book, we have seen a growing interest in psychological test instruments. Classic books in the field written in the 1950s were used for 20 years without our worrying that they were out of date. The last 10 years, however, have been marked by the first updating in many years for instruments such as the Wechsler Adult Intelligence Scale (WAIS), the Wechsler Memory Scale, and the Minnesota Multiphasic Personality Inventory, which have become standards in the field. The changes, minor in some cases and major in others, have increased the accuracy and usefulness of these instruments. The present revision is an attempt to incorporate these changes, as well as to describe changes in the way some of the instruments are used. The reader will note that there are new sections in the WAIS chapter (incorporating the revised WAIS); minor changes in chapters 2, 3, and 4; the introduction of the new (and improved) Wechsler Memory Scale-Revised in chapter 6; and nearly a completely new chapter on the Luria-Nebraska Neuropsychological Battery (taken from the new manual and other sources) in chapter 10. I hope that this revision will be as useful to readers as was the original.

Clinical Interpretation
of Objective
Psychological Tests

CHAPTER ONE

The Wechsler Adult Intelligence Scale

The original version of the test that was to later become the Wechsler Adult Intelligence Scale was devised in 1939 by David Wechsler at the Department of Psychiatry in Bellevue Hospital (New York) The test was intended to serve as an alternative to the Stanford-Binet, which was primarily designed as a test of children's intellectual functioning. The original Wechsler-Bellevue scale did away with the concept of mental age, which was so prominent in the assessment of children's intelligence, and introduced the concept of a deviation IQ, which measured an individual's standing relative to his or her peer group.

In 1956, the original Wechsler-Bellevue scale was replaced by an extensively altered test called the Wechsler Adult Intelligence Scale (WAIS). The WAIS corrected deficiencies in the original test, such as a restriction of item difficulty that made it difficult to assess certain intellectual characteristics, and replaced poor items difficult to score or interpret. In addition, the new WAIS had a much more extensive standardization sample which included a wider geographical representation and a wider representation of nonwhite individuals. Within five years the WAIS was one of the most used instruments in the U.S. At present, it is the most frequently administered adult intellectual test and is used in nearly all mental health and educational settings.

The Wechsler Adult Intelligence Scale – Revised (WAIS-R)

1

was released in 1981. The primary reason for this revision was to update the normative data (average IQ as measured by the WAIS had steadily increased over the years from 100 to about 107) and the ways in which responses were scored. Attempts also were made to make the stimuli more applicable to the American multiracial population. In current clinical practice, both the WAIS and the WAIS-R are being employed in various settings. Unless specifically excepted, statements in this chapter apply to both the WAIS and the WAIS-R.

PURPOSE OF THE TEST

The major purpose of any intellectual examination is to assess the individual's level of intelligence. The initial purpose of such tests was to identify individuals who were mentally retarded or who possessed very high intelligence in order to offer them appropriate educational or work placement or type of therapeutic approach. The WAIS, however, offers the examiner the possibility of analyzing scores on different subtests and allows for the identification of particular areas of strength and weakness in the individual. These resulting patterns can be used to provide vocational training, or to make diagnostic decisions in a more refined and specific manner than can a general IQ score.

Diagnostic decisions aided by the WAIS include the diagnosis of brain damage (McFie, 1975), the diagnosis of psychiatric disorders (Rapaport, Gill, & Schafer, 1970), and the assessment of such conditions as chronic alcoholism (Gudeman, Craine, Golden, & McLaughlin, 1977). In each of these cases there is more reliance on the pattern of subtest scores than on the overall IQ's generated by the test.

It should always be remembered that intelligence tests, including the WAIS, do not measure intelligence per se, but rather the ability to perform specific tasks that require intellectual abilities. These tasks can also be influenced by other factors, such as environment, practice, motivation, and interest, that influence a given individual's score. Thus, one can infer a given individual 's intellectual capacity only after taking these other factors into account. Many mistakes have been made with these tests when clinicians fail to discriminate between the test score and the person's real intellectual capacity: although they are related in many cases, they are not identical and should never be treated as identical.

ADMINISTRATION

The WAIS and WAIS-R consist of 11 subtests, six of which are classified as verbal and five of which are classified as performance. (When the WAIS-R was standardized, 2 new subscales were considered but not included in the final version.) Each subtest is administered according to detailed instructions offered in the WAIS manual (Wechsler, 1955). Wechsler emphasized the importance of sticking to the instructions as they are presented in the manual. Thus, proper administration requires extensive familiarity with the test manual, test materials, and testing situation.

Several general considerations are appropriate to all the WAIS subtests (as well as most of the tests described in this book). Testing should be done in a well-lighted, well-ventilated room. Furniture appropriate to the size of the individual to be tested should be available, and the individual should be able to remain comfortable for the full testing time. Optimal seating arrangements place the examiner on one side of the table and the examinee on an adjacent side so that they sit at a 45 degree angle (Delprato & Jackson, 1975).

The examiner and examinee should be comfortable with one another; general introductions, discussions about the subject's occupation and reason for testing, an explanation of the testing and its purpose, and a relaxed, unhurried atmosphere can often serve to do this. The testing situation should be one of general unconditional positive regard. No performance attempted by the subject is "wrong," and all performance, whether right or wrong, should be followed by encouragement and praise to motivate the subject to do his or her best; however, specific feedback that provides information, such as saying "good" only after correct items, should be avoided as it tends to increase most test scores (Isenberg & Bass, 1974, Kratochwill & Brody, 1976; Sattler, 1969; Willis & Ehrlick, 1975). With this limitation, the examiner should do all he or she can to make the testing situation a positive and rewarding experience.

Wechsler (1955) suggested that test material should not be available for the examinee to touch or see until the proper time in the test. This can be generalized to include all distractions, whatever their source. Testing should be done in a quiet room, one that does not have sudden loud noises nearby. The room itself should be tastefully decorated but free of any serious visual distractions, such as moving sculptures. Telephones and any bell systems should be disconnected if present. A sign on the door should instruct others to avoid intrusions.

In general, all tests should be administered in the order given in the manual (and discussed here). The order may be changed, however, for specific reasons. An individual with a poor educational background, for example, who is very sensitive about his or her lack of knowledge might be very agitated if the tests began with the Information subtest. Beginning with a performance subtest might be more effective in establishing the subject's cooperation.

The WAIS is generally begun by telling the subject, "This is a test of your abilities and skills. It is used to determine your IQ, but I am more interested in what information about your skills we can derive that will be of use in (whatever the purpose of the examination). There will be both difficult and easy questions on the test. Don't be upset if you feel you've missed any questions because no one is expected to get them all right." These instructions, of course, can be amended or revised to fit individual preferences and to make the testing situation as acceptable as possible to the examinee.

SUBTESTS

Information

This is the first subtest of the WAIS. Test questions should be read directly from the manual, starting with Item 5. If the subject gets either Item 5 or Item 6 correct, credit is given for Items 1 through 4. If both 5 and 6 are missed, Items

1 to 4 must be given. If Items 2 through 4 are missed, the test should be discontinued. Zimmerman and Woo-Sam (1973) suggested that one should also consider discontinuing the entire test, as subjects with performance at such a low level are not offered an adequate evaluation by the WAIS.

All the items concern specific questions of fact. As a result, the test is fairly easy to score. The reader should note that several questions (e.g., on U.S. population, height of women, and number of senators) have answers that change from year to year. In general, population estimates should be within 30 million of the correct answer (about 220 million at this time), the average height of women should be within about two inches of the current value, and the number of senators should be exact (currently 100).

Questions may be repeated if necessary. If subjects ask about guessing or state they are unsure, they should be encouraged to guess or give their best answer. Spontaneous corrections to answers are acceptable, unless the answer is accidentally given by the examiner or the subject returns with the answer after a break. All answers to this and the other verbal tests should be recorded verbatim, as the subject's verbalizations, whether right or wrong, may add some additional qualitative information to an understanding of the person.

The test should be discontinued after five incorrect answers. The examiner may "test the limits" by administering the test beyond this point in order to ascertain if the subject has additional knowledge. Additional correct answers, however, cannot be included when determining the patient's IQ. This technique should not be used with subjects likely to be embarrassed or upset by a continuing inability to answer.

If a subject gives more than one answer, one that is correct and another wrong, the subject must be made to choose between them. If several answers are given, but all are generally correct and not contradictory, the examiner may choose to score the best answer.

Comprehension

This subtest is an attempt to establish the degree to which the subject understands basic social customs and situations.

In the more advanced items, ability to interpret proverbs is also included.

The test administration begins with Item 3. If any one of Items 3 through 5 is missed, however, Items 1 and 2 are administered as well. All questions should be read directly from the manual. They may be repeated but only as they are written; the examiner is not allowed to paraphrase or change the question. Since many of the items require judgment, answers may be ambiguous. In these conditions, subjects should be encouraged to give more information by being told, "go ahead," or "tell me more about this" (Wechsler, 1955). The test is discontinued after the subject misses four questions in a row.

The Comprehension subtest (along with Similarities and Vocabulary) can be very difficult to score. Even experienced test users, for example, may disagree over borderline responses in this subtest. For this reason, it is very important for the examiner to be very familiar with the scoring criteria and to ensure that a scorable answer is elicited. Examiners must also be careful to use the scoring criteria objectively. Donahue and Sattler (1971) found that examiners tend to give higher scores on Comprehension items if they like the subject.

Testing the limits may be done by continuing the test after four wrong answers, or by asking more specific questions into the nature of ambiguous answers. Since such questions may be leading, the answers cannot be used in determining how many points the subject earned but can be useful in forming an impression of the subject. Testing the limits may also involve paraphrasing questions to see if different answers are elicited. Answers to this test should be recorded verbatim as they are often as revealing as the answers to some projective test items.

Arithmetic

Wechsler (1955) specifically warned examiners not to introduce this test as a test of arithmetic. The words "arithmetic" or "mathematics" often cause patients to expect severe failure. Wechsler suggested simply saying, "Now, let us try these" (Wechsler, 1955, p. 37). The test is begun on Item 3. Items 1 and 2 are administered only if both Items 3 and 4 are missed.

Subjects can get credit for a question only by giving the correct answer within the time limit shown. Hence, all items must be timed. Timing is begun when the examiner finishes reading the question. A question may be repeated exactly as written, if necessary, but the timing is not stopped. Answers not given within the time period are counted as wrong. Paper and pencil are not allowed.

Spontaneous corrections are allowed if they are given within the time period. Testing is discontinued after four consecutive failures. Testing the limits may also be used with this subtest. This can include allowing longer time for items on which the subject is actively working. This has the secondary effect of allowing the subject to feel that a correct answer has been reached, although it is not credited on the test. Additional items may also be given beyond four consecutive failures. Again, these cannot be included in the scoring.

Similarities

This subtest involves finding similarities between two objects. The test is begun with the first item. The format for each question is, "in what ways are a (object one) and a (object two) alike." If the first question is missed, the answer is given to the patient to illustrate what is wanted. Thereafter, no additional help is offered the subject, although he or she can be encouraged to expand on an ambiguous or borderline item, as in the Comprehension test. Questions may also be repeated. The test is discontinued after four consecutive failures. In this test, the inexperienced examiner may have difficulty telling immediately whether a borderline response is scorable; in these cases, the answer should be counted as scorable and not as a failure. This may result in the subject's being given too many questions, which is preferable to too few questions. When the test is scored, no credit is given for answers given after four consecutive failures. This general procedure is applicable to Comprehension and Vocabulary also.

Testing the limits consists of asking additional questions or encouraging the subject to give more answers, even if he or she is not sure how good those answers are. The subject may often know better answers but may not recognize that they are better. As with the other subtests, however, such answers may not be used to increase a subject's score.

Digit Span

This test consists of two sections: Digits Forward and Digits Backward. For Digits Forward, the subject is told that the examiner will say some numbers, which the subject should repeat afterward exactly as they were given. The first item involves three digits. The most difficult item involves nine digits. If the subject correctly repeats a series, the examiner goes on to the next longer series. If an item is missed, a second item of the same length is given. If this is repeated correctly, the examiner moves on to the next longer series. If the second item of a given length is missed, the test is discontinued.

Digits Backward is given in much the same way. In this subtest, the subject must repeat the given numbers in the reverse order rather than exactly as stated. Item difficulty varies from two to eight numbers, and the administration is otherwise identical to Digits Forward. The test is ended when the subject misses two items of the same length.

On both Digits Forward and Digits Backward, additional items may be given in a testing the limits analysis. If a subject has missed all items, one may also attempt a two-digit or one-digit item to determine the severity of disorganization in the patient and to see if the instructions were understood.

Vocabulary

This is the last of the verbal tests. It consists of 40 items that are presented verbally as well as on a written card presented to the examinee. The subject is told that the test requires the subject to give the meaning of some words. In general, each word is presented with the statement, "What does (word) mean?" The test starts with the fourth word. If any of the Items 4 though 8 are missed (zero score), the first three items are also given. If an answer is ambiguous or incomplete, the examiner should encourage the subject to tell him or her more. The test is discontinued after five consecutive failures. Much of the discussion regarding scoring and questioning discussed under the Comprehension and Similarities subtests is applicable to Vocabulary as well. As with the other tests, additional items or questioning may be used in a testing the limits procedure to further evaluate the subject's competency in this area.

Digit Symbol

Digit Symbol requires the subject to match empty spaces under the symbols 1 to 9 with symbols assigned to those numbers in a table at the top of the work page. An example of a Digit Symbol-like task is shown in Figure 1-1. The subject is first shown the task, the examiner states that each number is associated with a symbol, and then the examiner instructs the subject to place the appropriate symbol in the empty box below each number. The examiner then goes over the first 3 items verbally and shows the subject what to do. The subject is then allowed to do 7 additional sample items. These 10 items serve as the practice portion of the test. At this point, the subject is told to fill in as many squares as he or she can without skipping any items (Wechsler, 1955). After the examiner says "begin," the subject starts and is allowed to continue for 90 seconds. If the subject skips an item, the examiner instructs him or her to do them in order without skipping any. At the end of the 90 seconds, the subject is told to stop. No additional

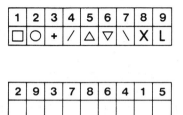

Figure 1.1. Example of a Digit Symbol task. The upper table is used to fill in the lower items.

items that may have been done by the subject are counted in the score.

Special instructions are provided for left-handed clients whose writing hand covers the table that gives the association between the numbers and symbols. In this case, a second key (from another record form of the WAIS) is placed before the subject so that the key can easily be seen.

The examiner should stress for all subjects that perfect reproduction of figures is not necessary, especially if an inordinate amount of time is spent on such activities. If the subject stops at the end of the first line and does not immediately go to the second line, the examiner should instruct the subject to "Go to the next line and continue until I tell you to stop." Subjects should not be allowed to erase; if they find an error, they can simply write over it.

Testing the limits may involve a readministration of the test if the examiner suspects that an initial low score was due to not understanding the task. The examiner also may ask the subject to read or write the numbers (to ensure that he or she knows them) or to write the symbols in order (to be sure that the symbols are visually perceived). These techniques can help clarify the source of the subject's problems when there is a poor performance.

Picture Completion

This task involves a set of pictures included in the WAIS kit, each of which has an important detail missing. The subject must identify the missing detail in each picture. All items on the test should be administered regardless of failures. For the first and second items, failure is followed by an explanation of what is wrong. For one additional item, if the subject finds some essential part missing, the examiner should say, "Yes, but what is the most important thing missing?" (Wechsler, 1955). This, however, can be done for only one item. Answers should be given within 20 seconds, a more than ample time period if the subject is aware of what is missing.

The subject need not identify the missing detail in verbal terms. The subject may describe the use of the piece, or point to where the detail is missing. The examiner may question the subject to determine if an answer is correct. The major scoring criterion is that the subject recognizes where something is missing and what it is. If a nut were missing from a screw, for example, the subject could say "the thing that holds the screw on," or point to the end of the screw, or say "nut" or "the square thing that goes there," or make any other similar answer and still get credit.

Testing the limits is less appropriate with Picture Completion. One can see if the subject has missed items because he or she does not understand what the picture is. The subject may be asked to list all missing elements if there is a tendency to concentrate on unimportant details. None of this information, however, can be used in scoring.

Block Design

This task employs nine blocks, all of which are painted identically with all red sides, all white sides, and sides that are half red and half white, divided along the diagonal. The task requires the subject to duplicate 10 designs in the Block Design booklet using the blocks. The task is similar to that used in many children's block toys. If the subject mentions this and is upset about it, it is useful to point out the strong relationship of Block Design performance to engineering skills (Zimmerman & Woo-Sam, 1973).

The initial designs use four of the nine blocks that are provided (blocks not in use should be left in their box). The first design is done in blocks by the examiner without showing the card with the design on it to the subject. The subject is given four additional blocks and allowed to copy what the examiner has done. If the subject fails, the examiner makes the design again out of the subject's blocks, mixes them up, and asks the subject to try the design again. The examiner then goes to the second item whether the subject succeeds or not. The examiner shows the subject the design on Card 2, then tells the subject that he or she will make the blocks match the picture. After this is completed, the blocks are mixed up and the subject is instructed to do the design from the picture. If the subject fails, the demonstration is repeated and the subject is given a second chance to do it.

After the first two trials, no additional help is given the subject. Design 3 is presented, and the subject is told to copy the design and to tell the examiner when he or she is finished. This procedure is followed for each design, except for Design 7. Here the subject is told that the design requires nine blocks, all of which are placed before the subject. The test is discontinued after three consecutive failures. Failures on Items 1 and 2 require that the subject fail both chances to do the item.

There are definite time limits for all items (60 seconds for each item through Design 6, 120 seconds for Designs 7 to 10) that must be adhered to by the examiner. If a subject is nearly finished, however, the examiner may allow the subject to continue, although a correct answer is not scored. Spontaneous corrections within the time limit are allowed. In some cases, a subject may forget to tell the examiner when he or she is ready. If this occurs during the early cards, which do not give a time bonus, the subject should be reminded at the end of 60 seconds that the examiner is to be told when the item is finished.

Testing the limits can involve telling a subject after he or she finishes that there is an error and asking him or her to correct it. Allowing extra time can often give valuable information about the subject.

Picture Arrangement

This subtest involves the arrangement of pictures so that they tell a logical, coherent story. Most people find the task interesting and challenging. The test materials consist of eight sets of cartoon pictures varying in length from three to six pictures. On the back of each card is a number denoting the sequence in which the pictures are to be laid out and a letter indicating the sequence in which the pictures are to be arranged by the subject.

When the first item is presented to the subject, he or she is told that the pictures tell a story about a bird building a nest and that he or she is to place the cards in the correct order. If the subject's sequence is incorrect, the examiner shows and explains to the subject what the correct sequence is. Then the pictures are placed in the mixed-up order, and the subject is given a second chance to sequence Item 1. Item 2 is then presented with the instructions to put those cards in the right order. If this sequence is missed, the examiner again demonstrates and tells the correct story (about building a house). The subject is then given another chance on Item 2. If both Items 1 and 2 are never correctly done, then the test is discontinued. The subject is otherwise given all the Picture Arrangement items. Each item is simply presented to the subject, who is told to put the cards in the right order.

There are definite time limits for each item. The examiner may allow the subject to exceed the time limits as a testing the limits procedure; however, such performances get no credit in the scoring. It is important to keep an accurate time since two items (7 and 8) offer time bonuses and no credit is given for overtime performances.

Testing the limits may also involve getting the subject to tell the story he or she is laying out; this can serve as a projective test and a measure of the subject's social competence. If there is a basic error in the subject's analysis of what the pictures represent, correcting this and then allowing another attempt can also be a way of evaluating the subject's social and intellectual skills.

Object Assembly

Object Assembly serves as the last Wechsler subtest. It consists of four jigsaw puzzle items that the subject must complete within specified time limits (two minutes for each of the first two items and three minutes for each of the last two items). Timing is extremely important on this test as time bonuses are available for each item. A screen is set up between the examiner and examinee for each item. The items are laid out behind the screen as detailed on the examiner side of the screen. This can be time-consuming if the examiner is unsure of the order and the pieces; hence, previous practice is recommended so this can be done efficiently without undue waste of time.

For the first item, the subject is told that if the pieces are put together correctly, they will make something. Then the subject is told to go ahead and put the pieces together as quickly as he or she can. For later items, the instructions are simply to put the pieces together as quickly as possible. For all items, the subject is given credit only for performance under the time limit. If he or she fails to finish by that time, it is necessary to score from the final configuration. Since scoring can be somewhat difficult initially, this may entail stopping the subject at the end of the time period so that partial credit may be given.

Scoring for partially finished figures involves the number of correct juxtapositions as defined by the WAIS manual. This involves placing together any two pieces in the correct way. The pieces need not be in the correct place overall, however. Thus, the scoring can take some time, especially for an inexperienced scorer. Testing the limits by giving extra time is an allowable procedure, but only when scoring has been finished.

SCORING THE WAIS

Each subtest is scored according to specific rules given in the manual. For Information, Picture Completion, and Digit Symbol, the raw score is the number of items correctly answered. (It is important to remember that five of the verbal tests do not begin with Item 1 and that credit is given for the skipped items.) For Arithmetic, it is the number of correct answers plus two possible points for fast performance on the last two items.

Three subtests, Comprehension, Similarities, and Vocabulary, employ a scoring system that rates the quality of each answer. A high-quality answer scores a two, a low-quality answer a one, and an incorrect or unacceptable answer zero. The criteria for judging quality on each answer are given in the manual; it is extremely important that the examiner be familiar with these criteria and stick to them as closely as possible. It is also necessary that the examiner be aware when an answer is borderline or incomplete so that the subject may be encouraged to expand or explain the answer. Proper questioning during testing makes scoring of these items much easier. For all three of these subtests, the final raw score is the sum of the scores on each item.

Digit Span is scored by simply summing up the number of digits forward and the number of digits backward that the individual can remember. On Object Assembly, Picture Arrangement, and Block Design, scoring is a combination of the number of correct answers and time bonuses. On Picture Arrangement and Block Design, each correct answer is worth four points. If a person gets a correct answer after first missing the item on Items 1 and 2, the correct answer is worth two points. For Items 7 through 10 of Block Design and 7 and 8 of Picture Arrangement, additional points are given for fast performances according to Wechsler's tables in the manual. In addition, Picture Arrangement gives partial credit (two points) for nearly correct answers listed in the manual for Items 6, 7, and 8. Partial credit answers, however, are not eligible for time bonuses.

Object Assembly offers partial credit and time bonuses for each item. Time bonuses are available only for fully correct answers. Partial credit is given for any pieces correctly placed together at the end of the time period, as defined in the manual. This test is easily the most difficult performance test to score. For all three tests, Block Design, Picture Arrangement, and Object Assembly, the total raw score is the sum of the scores on the individual items.

DETERMINING SCALED SCORES

After raw scores have been calculated, scaled scores are determined. All scaled scores are based on the performance of 500 subjects between the ages of 20 and 34. The mean score of this group has been arbitrarily defined as 10, the standard deviation as three. All scaled scores are based on this group, no matter what the age of the subject. Raw scores are changed into scaled scores by using the conversion table available on all WAIS record sheets.

Because of the scale transformation used, the scaled scores give direct information on a patient's level of performance in relation to the reference group. Fifty percent of all subjects will get scores from 8 to 12, 16 percent of all subjects will get scores below 7, 16 percent will score above 13, and 2½ percent will score above 16.

DETERMINING IQs

Scaled scores on the six verbal tests (Information through Vocabulary) are summed to give a *Verbal Weighted Score*. Similarly, scaled scores on the five performance tests (Digit Symbol through Object Assembly) are summed to get a *Performance Weighted Score*. These two scores are summed to give a *Full Scale Weighted Score*. These three scores are then found in the appropriate IQ conversion table for the patient's current age. In these tables, the IQ equivalent of each weighted score is given.

There are situations in which the complete WAIS is not given. In these situations, weighted scores must be estimated. The estimation formulas are as follows:

Verbal Weighted
$$= \frac{\text{Sum of Scaled Scores of Tests Given}}{\text{Number of Tests Given}} \times 6$$

Performance Weighted
$$= \frac{\text{Sum of Scaled Scores of Tests Given}}{\text{Number of Tests Given}} \times 5$$

BRIEF FORMS OF THE WAIS

Short forms of the WAIS are usually given in situations in which only an IQ estimate is needed or the abilities reflected in only certain subtests are of interest. Short forms are often used in psychiatric settings in which a quick screen is desired so that subjects who need more extensive testing can be identified and given the entire WAIS. The accuracy of these versions differs with the number of tests used. For example, Maxwell (1957) and Silverstein (1970) found that any combination of five tests could be used to estimate overall IQ with a .95 or better correlation. They also found similar accuracies for many different combinations of four tests, the best being a combination of Information, Vocabulary, Block Design, and Picture Arrangement. A combination of only Vocabulary and Information or Vocabulary and Block Design can correlate greater than .9 with full scale IQ. As a result, many different forms of an abbreviated WAIS can be used with confidence, especially if four or five scales are involved; the tests employed can be chosen on the basis of a clinician's needs in a given situation. For smaller batteries, however, it is recommended that the Maxwell and Silverstein articles be consulted.

One disadvantage of brief forms is the restriction of information available. As discussed below, there is only little interpretive value in the size of most IQs; much more information comes from subtest patterning and from observing the subject's performance on different tasks. Such tests are at best screening devices from which no definite conclusions can be reached. As long as these objections are kept in mind and the abbreviated form is used for a logical, psychologically reasonable purpose that aids in the evaluation of patients, there is no reason to avoid such forms. Care must be taken in such situations to ensure that others who see the test results (e.g., teachers, psychiatrists) are aware of the limitations of a short battery.

CLINICAL INTERPRETATION: THE INDIVIDUAL SUBTESTS

Each subtest of the WAIS is hypothesized to measure certain major intellectual skills. As a result, analysis of how a patient performs on each subtest can yield valuable information for understanding a patient and for answering applicable referral questions. One important caution must be recognized, however: no subtest is a pure measure of any simple intellectual skill. All subtests represent combinations of skills, with some skills more heavily weighted on some tests than on others. It is important to recognize when interpreting test results that low scores may be due to a variety of reasons, ranging from very obvious to more subtle dysfunctions. For this reason, many users of the WAIS place a great emphasis on observing the patient while he or she does a subtest. Testing the limits is frequently used as a way of separating alternate theories about why a patient did badly.

As a result, an analysis of individual subtests does not give final answers, but rather enables a clinician to generate hypotheses about the subject's performance. These hypotheses can then be tested by looking at the manner in which the subject performed the other subtests, the qualitative indices gained from observing the patient, and the results of testing the limits. If one hypothesizes that Block Design is performed poorly because of poor spatial skills, for example, one would expect that the designs generated would be rather bizarre, including significant rotations. If, in fact, an individual was slow but accurate, this hypothesis might have to be modified or dropped. Similarly, a poor spatial ability would show up in the performance on Object Assembly, and if this score is above normal, again the hypothesis would have to be reexamined.

In this way, hypotheses generated by each subtest can be confirmed or altered. This enables the clinician to form a picture of the individual's strengths and weaknesses. When this is combined with other analysis techniques, the clinician can then accumulate extensive information on a patient's performance.

Information

The Information subtest serves primarily as a test of an individual's fund of general knowledge. It represents information to which an average individual with an average educational background would be expected to have access. The test measures long-term, remote memory and the ability to assess and use that memory. In general, it is also related to an individual's reading background. Poor performance may be associated with a poor educational or cultural background as well as with low intelligence. Significantly low Information scores in an individual who was once normal or near normal suggests severe deterioration in intellectual function, which may be related to severe psychosis or degenerative brain disorders. The score will also be low in individuals suffering early brain damage of the left hemisphere or of both hemispheres. In such individuals, the score may reflect the individual's attainment at the time of the injury. In adults with deterioration late in life, the Information subtest may be the highest score. In these cases, it suggests the person's earlier IQ level. This can serve to help measure the amount of deterioration a person has suffered for cases involving insurance compensation for injury.

Schizophrenics will typically do less well on items involving reasoning than on those involving simple recall (Norman & Wilensky, 1961). Individuals from alternate cultural backgrounds are also likely to do poorly, as are individuals from poor educational backgrounds (Finlayson, Johnson, & Reitan, 1977).

Comprehension

The Comprehension subtest evaluates an individual's ability to understand common social customs and situations, and to provide for appropriate activities as well as the reasons behind such activities. It assesses one's awareness of social norms and practices and one's ability to abstract the reasons behind them. The test also evaluates long-term memory and experience and the ability to verbalize these factors. The test also involves the individual's judgment: to select from alternative answers and to provide those that are most acceptable and logical (Rapaport et al., 1970).

Poor performance on Comprehension can be associated with long-term dysfunction, such as early brain injury or childhood psychosis. A poor or alternate cultural background can also cause low scores. (In such cases, one must assess whether the answers given are reasonable for the individual's cultural and educational background.) Comprehension is in general less affected by educational background than is Information.

There is some evidence that socialization is a strong factor in Comprehension. As noted above, one must be able to view the logical choices and select those most reasonable, a process that implies knowledge of one's culture. In addition, Hunt, Quay, and Walker (1966) reported correlations between Comprehension and socialization. Wechsler (1958) found that adolescent sociopaths performed at the mean or lower on Comprehension, suggesting general agreement with this hypothesis.

Comprehension will generally be relatively high in brain injured adults, serving in the same manner as does Information. It can also be used to estimate premorbid level of functioning and, except in severe deterioration, is among the highest scores. Psychotics will generally score lower on Comprehension than on Information and Vocabulary because of the judgmental decisions more inherent in Comprehension. Comprehension as the highest score is not unusual in intelligent adults, especially if educational levels do not match their intellectual levels.

One advantage of the Comprehension subtest over the other subtests is its ability to elicit a number of important qualitative remarks from individuals. Otherwise hidden pathological conditions may show up in a bizarre response or responses on Comprehension. For example, an individual may say we register marriages so that the government can keep track of children who are to be sent to secret camps. A particularly antisocial youth suggested that when one sees a fire, one should watch carefully so one can see the people die. Such responses may almost be diagnostic in and of themselves. Preoccupation with bizarre ideas may result in lowered scores, or may show up in only one or two items so that the individual has a normal or even superior score overall.

Good scores on the test suggest someone in touch with social reality and with the day-to-day world. These scores are particularly important in individuals with otherwise poor profiles. For example, the mentally retarded individual with a higher Comprehension score can probably operate on a higher social level than suggested by the person's overall IQ and may be an excellent job candidate because of this ability. Poor scores, however, may not mean the opposite. Testing the limits is useful in attempting to isolate the causes for a given Comprehension score.

Arithmetic

The understanding of number concepts is an important part of intellectual development, especially in a highly numerical, science-oriented civilization. The Arithmetic subtest provides a basic measure of an individual's ability to work with arithmetic problems in logical and daily problems. In addition to measuring obvious arithmetics skills, the test also requires verbal understanding (translating the verbal problems into arithmetic operations and back again), memory (especially in older and brain injured patients), and concentration. Educational background and experience with arithmetic appear to be the important aspects of performing well on the test.

Before discussing this test, it is necessary to consider the problem of an individual's reactions to the test. Many individuals react quite dramatically to the problems, often stating that they are stupid and cannot do such things, and even refusing to try what are otherwise simple problems. Such a strong emotional reaction in what are otherwise normal individuals lowers scores, often to the lowest score on the WAIS. In many cases, these scores must be discounted in determining the individual 's intellectual capabilities. The score is important, however, in making vocational choices for the person; such an individual would not do well in college math or as an engineer without a good course in how to relax when doing arithmetic. The reactions also may be a clue to how the individual handles strong frustration.

Arithmetic may result in a low score in mentally retarded individuals as well as in brain injured persons. Individuals with concentration problems may also do poorly. Transient high-anxiety states may cause low scores on this test and on Digit Span (Firetto & Davey, 1971; Keiser, 1975; Knox & Grippaldi, 1970). Digit Span, however, appears to be more sensitive to this general anxiety than is Arithmetic (Rapaport et al., 1970).

It should be emphasized that Arithmetic is not a particularly good measure of arithmetic skills (the ability to add and subtract and so on). Individuals often do better on a pure test of mathematical skills, such as the Wide Range Achievement Test (discussed later), than they do on Arithmetic where they lack paper and pencil and there is greater emphasis on memory, concentration, attention, and verbal skills. If one is interested in actual grade level skills, such tests as the Wide Range Achievement Test are much more appropriate.

Arithmetic scores will often be poor in organic disorders of many kinds, with particularly low scores achieved in left hemisphere injuries. The test involves such a wide range of skills, however, that low scores may be found in almost any kind of injury.

Similarities

Similarities relates to an individual's ability to form verbal concepts — specifically generalizations — when given two members of a specific verbal class (e.g., tools or clothing or living beings). The test requires memory, concentration, and the ability to relate the two objects to a common class. These relations may be done at two levels: concrete (you wear them) or abstract (clothing). The more abstract a person's associations are, the higher the score on the test. The individual must be able to concentrate on the essential details of the objects compared, and must have the verbal skills to form the relevant verbal concepts.

Similarities provides a measure of higher cognitive skills. The individual who does well is often able to work well with verbal abstract ideas and to handle simple reasoning. The impaired patient is often one who has low verbal skills or who is able to respond only in a concrete fashion. In the poorest cases, the individual is not able to see any relationship at all, even in the simple items. This implies an individual operating at a very low, reactive level with few generalizations to link things together. Low scores may also suggest low emotional control (Rapaport et al., 1970).

Generally, the Similarities score varies little from a subject's mean score in most diagnostic groups (Zimmerman & Woo-Sam, 1973), although there is considerable individual variation. One exception to this is a brain injury in the left temporal lobe or left parietal lobe that may interfere with an individual's ability to form categories. The test also has characteristics similar to Vocabulary, Comprehension, and Information, however, which tend to keep the scores up because of prior experience and learning (long-term memory). This skill is generally not affected except by long-term deterioration or extremely severe brain dysfunction. On the other hand, the test requires new learning and abstracting, especially in the more difficult items. These complex skills are quite sensitive to deterioration in brain damage and in emotional disorders. Thus, Similarities represents a "swing" test that may stay up or go down depending on the severity of the injury and the nature of the disorder. As a result, comparison of Similarities to the more stable, long-term memory tests (Vocabulary, Information, and Comprehension) and to the more abstract, deterioration-sensitive tests (Digit Span, Block Design, and Digit Symbol) can provide a good barometer of actual deterioration as opposed to simple anxiety effects. For example, McKeever, May, and Tuma (1965) found that high Similarities scores were good prognostic signs in predicting early release in schizophrenic patients.

It is rare that answers to Similarities questions will indicate a specific pathology. As a result, such answers should be attended to closely. Zimmerman and Woo-Sam (1973), in a review of the Similarities literature, suggested that schizophrenics tend to deny the presence of similarities between objects more so than brain damaged individuals who simply have no answer. This result has not been generally confirmed, however. Such denials appear to be more common in paranoid schizophrenics with current acute exacerbations rather than in all schizophrenics. Similarly, the performance of the brain damaged differs considerably with type and extent of lesion (see section on Organicity).

Digit Span

Digit Span is a measure of immediate auditory memory. The test requires the ability to attend and concentrate as well as to remember. In Digits Backward, there is the additional skill of reverse sequencing, which appears to be largely spatial rather than verbal in nature. Digit Span is not a general measure of memory skills. Other memory skills—delayed auditory memory, visual memory of all kinds, logical memory, and the like – are not measured by the test, and there is not necessarily a correlation between Digit Span performance and other measures of memory.

Digit Span is very sensitive to both anxiety and brain deterioration (Firetto & Davey, 1971; Golden & Anderson, 1978; Keiser, 1975; McFie, 1975; R. E. Walker, Sannito, & Firetto, 1970; R. E. Walker & Spence, 1964). Scores are quite depressed in patients with anxiety states, but are relatively normal in schizophrenics without cognitive deterioration (Wechsler, 1958). Digits Forward and Digits Backward are affected by left hemisphere brain damage, especially in the temporal lobe, whereas localized right hemisphere injuries, especially the right frontal lobe, might affect Digits Backward alone.

Rapaport et al. (1970) suggested that extremely low Digit Span scores, relative to all other scores, may indicate a depressive psychosis or deteriorated schizophrenia, whereas a good Digit Span score, relative to all other scores, in a schizophrenic suggests an absence of anxiety.

Vocabulary

Vocabulary is generally recognized as the best single estimate of intelligence. In making this statement, it is assumed that all individuals have had an equal chance in terms of education, cultural background, and verbal interactions. To the extent that this assumption is true, it has been found that Vocabulary alone can correlate up to .9 with Full Scale IQ. Vocabulary measures one's ability to learn words and express their meanings. It is one of the primary "hold" tests among the Wechsler subtests that resist change with mental deterioration and aging.

Low Vocabulary scores are often the result of poor general intelligence, poor educational background, different cultural background (especially where standard English is not an individual's first language), or early brain injury. Brain injury (especially in the left hemisphere) will not affect the individual's level of vocabulary at the time of the injury, but will affect future learning. Thus, Vocabulary can often be used to evaluate premorbid intelligence in the individual injured in adulthood and to estimate the age of injury in an individual injured as a child. The exceptions to this rule are general deteriorating disorders such as Alzheimer's disease (Golden & Anderson, 1978).

High Vocabulary scores may reflect high verbal intelligence and good education in an inquisitive, curious individual who likes to read and has a sensitivity to new verbal experiences. Since Vocabulary is not affected by many pathological conditions, however, a high Vocabulary score does not necessarily imply a currently intact individual. A low score, in contrast, generally implies mental retardation or a serious pathological condition in individuals with an adequate cultural and educational background.

Digit Symbol

Digit Symbol measures a wide variety of skills. It is the most sensitive of the WAIS subtests in detecting motor problems in the dominant hand. It also measures the ability to associate a symbol with a number. The test involves visual memory as well as the ability to maintain a course of action in a speeded, sometimes tense race against the clock. As a result, the test is also sensitive to high levels of anxiety. Because of its sensitivity to memory and motor deficits, the test is also useful in detecting brain dysfunction.

Consequently, low scores may suggest a number of conditions ranging from anxiety to brain damage. The test is generally sensitive to age effects as well. Unlike most of the verbal tests, this test can be administered to culturally and educationally deprived individuals. (This is also true for Block Design.) Testing the limits, as described earlier, and close observation can be useful in identifying specific problems, although in some cases the problems may be so intertwined that only a general dysfunction can be recognized. Extremely good scores on Digit Symbol are rare in most pathological conditions.

The correlation with anxiety is best seen with current, situational anxiety rather than with a general trait of anxiety.

Thus, attempts by the examiner to keep the testing situation and the examinee relaxed can be useful in producing better scores.

Picture Completion

Picture Completion is a measure of an individual's ability to perceive and visually organize a sketch and then recognize that an essential element of some kind is missing. In addition, one must be able to avoid distractions and inessential details. Since familiarity with the objects pictured is necessary, there is a strong cultural component in the test. For example, while I lived in Hawaii, I found many subjects who did poorly, simply because the items were foreign to their experience.

Of all the performance tests, Picture Completion is the least sensitive to focal brain disorders. Thus, in serious left hemisphere injuries, which affect the traditional scores that measure premorbid intelligence (Comprehension, Vocabulary, Information), the Picture Completion score becomes the best estimate of that premorbid intelligence.

Paranoid patients may frequently express the belief that nothing is missing from the pictures. Weiner (1966) suggested that schizophrenia can be recognized in Picture Completion by the type of errors that are made. For example, when responding to a picture of an animal with a missing tail, a schizophrenic might answer that udders, tongue, or sex organs are missing. To a picture of a violin without a string peg, the schizophrenic might say the violinist was missing, whereas a normal might answer the bow or strings. Rapaport et al. (1970) suggested that extremely poor performance is suggestive of deteriorated schizophrenics and depressed psychotics. Moderate impairment suggests schizophrenia in general, whereas normal performance is suggestive of neurosis in a psychiatric population.

Block Design

Block Design is the purest measure of spatial (nonverbal) reasoning in the WAIS. As a result, it is an excellent measure of nonverbal intelligence and general spatial skills necessary for such tasks as engineering. The subject must begin with the picture presented, break it down in some manner so that the placement of blocks can be determined, and then place the blocks in the correct manner. This task requires strong visual analysis skills and visual-motor coordination. In the more difficult items, speed, concentration, and attention are also demanded for a maximum score. The test also allows the examiner to observe how the subject goes about problem solving: with impulsiveness, with great planning, in a hit-and-miss manner, or with a combination of these techniques.

Organic impairment often affects Block Design performance extensively. This is especially obvious in diffuse injuries and injuries involving either parietal lobe. In most brain injuries, the Block Design score will be below the subject's mean score and often will be the lowest of all the performance tests. In schizophrenics, however, the Block Design score tends to stay at or above the subject's mean score (Wechsler, 1958). As a result, Block Design is an excellent measure for discriminating schizophrenic from brain damaged performance, as was demonstrated by Golden (1977).

One disadvantage of Block Design is its difficulty for low-intelligence subjects, as the test does not have any really easy items. On the other hand, several very difficult designs help the test to discriminate among individuals with high nonverbal intellectual skills. A second major advantage lies in the qualitative impressions about the subject that can be gained by attentively watching the subject's performance, something sometimes missed by many examiners.

Picture Arrangement

Picture Arrangement enables the evaluation of several major skills: visual perception of individual pictures, organization of a series of pictures, awareness of social sequences, planning skills, ability to form and test hypotheses (possible stories), flexibility, and general ability to sequence material in a logical order. One drawback of the test is its dependence on social sequences, which may differ from culture to culture; consequently, a cultural bias is possible on the test and must be considered in any evaluation.

Picture Arrangement is considered by many to be a measure of what Wechsler (1958) called "social intelligence" (Edinger, 1976). Wechsler found that adolescent sociopaths did very well on this test, but that schizophrenics varied considerably. Brain injured patients do not show as great a loss on Picture Arrangement as they do on the other performance tests (except Picture Completion). Test scores can be affected by injuries to the right frontal areas, however, and may be affected more than the other performance tests in certain left hemisphere injuries that disrupt social or verbal skills.

Some insight into a subject's manner of thinking may be gained from having the subject explain incorrect stories, as this may indicate some defects in social competence or the understanding of cause and effect relationships. This information can be valuable in a qualitative evaluation of a subject.

Object Assembly

Object Assembly requires visual analysis and visual-motor skills from a subject. The subject must recognize what the object is from the pieces presented, or at least their interrelationship. Then the subject must put the pieces together in a manner that creates the object involved. As in Block Design, an examiner is able to watch how a patient faces a relatively difficult problem solving task.

Both organic and schizophrenic patients may do poorly on Object Assembly. The Object Assembly score is often one of the higher scores in mentally retarded subjects, however. Wechsler (1958) reported that neurotics show impairment on Object Assembly, but Ladd (1964) failed to find any deficit. Rapaport et al. (1970) suggested that depressed individuals tend to do poorly on the test, maybe because of the heavy emphasis on time bonuses in scoring Object Assembly.

INTERPRETING PATTERNS OF SUBTEST SCORES

Interpreting differences between subtest scores is often important in the analysis of a WAIS profile. For example, a clinician may be interested in whether a person's ability to interpret visual information and to find inconsistencies (Picture Completion) is significantly different from the person's ability to analyze a visual configuration and to reproduce it in blocks (Block Design). Such a comparison might allow the clinician to infer that the patient can visually analyze what is put before him or her, but is unable to perform the motor skills necessary to reproduce the pattern (construction dyspraxia, a major symptom of many organic brain disorders). Similarly, a clinician might ask if a score on a test not sensitive to anxiety (Vocabulary) is stronger than a score on a test sensitive to anxiety (Digit Span). This allows the clinician to infer the presence of a significant amount of anxiety or other similar disorder.

Such comparisons lie at the heart of interpreting the pattern of scale scores. The comparisons allow a clinician to infer the source of the problem in a lower scaled score on one of the tests. The process basically involves comparing the two or more tests involved and attempting to identify which skills are measured by one test and not the other. These are the skills that are then likely to be impaired or, conversely, the skills that are strong. When such comparisons are made over all of the scales that significantly differ from one another, a pattern will usually emerge, giving the clinician a strong idea of the individual's relative strengths and weaknesses. This pattern of skills can then be used to predict and to diagnose approximately for the referral question.

These comparisons have some difficulties associated with them. The major problem is that the subscale scores are not all reliable; that is, one cannot be sure that the score the patient received is his or her real score. Thus, when two subtests differ by only one point, it may be that there is really no difference at all, and that the apparent difference was created only by chance events and the unreliability of the subtests.

As a result of this problem, scores on each pair of tests must differ by a certain number of scale scores before the difference can be considered significant. Specifically, scores must differ anywhere from three to five scale points before the difference is significant at the .05 level. The size of the difference depends on which two subtests one is comparing. This, however, is a rather burdensome arrangement, as the user would have to consult a table every time he or she wanted to know whether the difference between a given pair of scores was significant. In actual practice, most clinicians simply work from the assumption that all differences of a given size are likely to be significant, a practice that appears to work well. More conservative clinicians will generally assume that a four-point difference is necessary for significance, while many others simply assume that a three-point difference is sufficient to establish a clinical difference.

INTERPRETING IQs: THEORETICAL ISSUES

Interpreting the meaning of an intelligence quotient has become one of the more controversial issues in clinical psychology. This controversy has centered around biases in the test against individuals with certain cultural and educational backgrounds. As noted earlier, several of the subtests are performed more poorly by individuals with poor education or from different cultures in the absence of any reasonable expectation of an intellectual difference between two groups. The mere fact that education and culture affect a test result does not make it a bad test, however. The problem arises when the test is misinterpreted. If an individual with a poor educational background gets a low score on Information, for instance, we may conclude that the individual has had little educational opportunity (which in this case is true). If we were to conclude that the person was brain damaged, however, we would be in error because our interpretation of the test score was wrong.

Thus, in interpreting any IQ score, several factors must be considered. These can be best expressed as an equation: IQ score = Actual Intelligence + Environment + Motivation. This simply means that any IQ score calculated is a combination of an individual's actual intelligence plus or minus a factor for the person's environment (culture, education, language, experience) and a factor for the individual's motivation. Note that this equation makes no assumption about the nature of actual intelligence. The equation applies whether one believes that intelligence is an interaction of environment and biological skills, is an effect of biological skills alone, or is determined by background alone.

Environment includes all the exogenous factors that influence intellectual development. Psychometric theories assume, in general, that each individual taking the test has had average chances to gain an education, to interact with other people, to learn standard English, and to generally experience life as a child and adult in the dominant American culture. To the extent that this assumption is not true, then the obtained IQ on the WAIS (or any other test) will deviate from the actual IQ of the individual. If the total experience of the individual has been greater than that offered others, the obtained IQ will be too high; if the total experience has been smaller, the obtained IQ will be too low. In both of these circumstances, the obtained IQ will have to be adjusted if we contend that we are measuring "actual IQ" instead of how well one performed on the test.

Motivation is also an important factor. Again, we make the assumption that an individual has an average level of motivation to do the test. This, of course, is not true. Some cultural groups or other subgroups do not place an importance on IQ tests or test performance in general. Some individuals with psychiatric disorders may not be motivated to do anything, let alone take an intelligence test. On the other hand, the child from a home that places a strong emphasis on education may be highly motivated to do well and perform higher as a result. Minor deviations from average motivation do not affect test scores greatly. Individuals whose motivations are seriously deficient, however, or those who may be motivated to deliberately do badly will get much lower scores than they are capable of achieving. In these cases, the test results must often be rejected as generally uninterpretable (except for the observation that the patient is unmotivated). Patients with high motivation may do somewhat better than expected, and the results must be regarded as an example of the person's achieving at his or her best. One exception to this must be noted: if the person is too highly motivated and concerned about his or her performance, the anxiety generated by the individual's concern may actually lower performance. This can often be seen most dramatically in the Digit Symbol and Digit Span scores.

Thus, we interpret any IQ (or any scale score) by looking at the actual score on the test, estimating the person's environmental background (through interview, as a rule), estimating the individual's motivation (by observation during the testing), and estimating the patient's actual IQ from these factors. Which of these factors is of importance in interpretation of a given case differs considerably depending on the situation. If we are asked, "Which person of these two will do better in a school situation today without any additional training?" the person with the actual higher Verbal IQ would probably be the best bet. If we were asked, "Which person who is doing badly now would benefit by additional training?" we would ideally pick the person with a high actual IQ (discounting cultural effects) and a high motivation, since he or she would more likely be interested in such education. If we are asked, "Can this person take care of herself?" we might look at actual performance, since that is where the individual is now. Each situation must be approached on the basis of the parameters of that situation.

INTERPRETING IQs: PRACTICAL FACTORS

All Wechsler IQs have a mean of 100 and a standard deviation of 15. Thus, 50 percent of all people have an IQ in the range from 90 to 110, the range of average or normal intelligence. Sixteen percent of the population have an IQ below 85, and about 2½ percent have IQs above 130. IQs at or above normal do not generally have the behavioral implications of low IQs. At these levels, a person's desire, personality factors, creativity, and emotional factors have more of a behavioral influence than does IQ. Thus, the individual with 105 IQ may become a success, whereas the person with 130 IQ may be a failure.

For reference, however, the average high school graduate will have a WAIS IQ of about 100, the average B.A. an IQ of 110, the average M.A. an IQ of 117, and the average Ph.D. an IQ of 124. On the WAIS-R, however, these expected average scores are probably some 7 points lower, as will be discussed in the comparison section on the WAIS and WAIS-R. Thus, it is highly unlikely that the individual with 95 IQ would get a Ph.D., but well within possibility that such an individual would get a B.A. Such predictions, however, must be tempered with the recognition that some individuals with 95 IQ probably do have doctoral degrees.

Performance and Verbal IQs can be interpreted in much the same way as Full Scale IQs. Higher Verbal IQs predispose individuals toward careers with high verbal content (psychology, most other social sciences, law, etc.), whereas higher Performance IQs predispose them to such careers as engineering, mathematics, architecture, or surgery. Since most individuals have Performance and Verbal IQs that are relatively close together, however, such differences usually are not major in determining a career; such factors as interest, vocational aptitude, and parents' occupation are much more significant determinants.

Low IQ

The lower an IQ is below normal, the more important it becomes in limiting an individual's choices. At extremely low levels, the person has no choice and little ability; he or she must be cared for continuously. At the higher levels, IQ plus a number of social factors determine the extent and independence of a person's adjustment.

Individuals with IQs in the range of 70 to 84 are generally considered marginally intelligent (Maloney & Ward, 1976). Such individuals are able to achieve reasonable social and vocational competence if they are given proper education and training and have sufficient job opportunities. Many are never recognized by others as being lower in intelligence because of the ability to interact with others at a normal level (social competence). In general their intellectual attainments limit their socioeconomic status. Sometimes they drop out of school because of frustration, but they are capable of finishing most American high school programs. The lower level of intelligence, along with lower socioeconomic status, may dispose these individuals to a higher degree of stress and lower level of medical care, which may lead to more frequent hospitalizations and serious physical and mental problems.

IQs in the 55 to 69 range are typically defined as mild mental retardation. Since 1973, however, the American Association of Mental Deficiency has defined mental retardation as an IQ below 70 along with a significant deficit in adaptive behavior, both of which developed before the age of 18 (Grossman, 1973). Thus, in addition to the IQ deficit, the person must show an inability to adapt to his or her environment. In the adult, this is usually defined as the ability to achieve social and economic self-sufficiency (Maloney and Ward, 1976). Using this double definition, the rate of mental retardation is significantly reduced.

It is important to recognize that social adaptability depends a great deal on both the individual and the society to which he or she must adjust. A highly stressful, technological society would thus create a larger number of mentally retarded individuals than would a more agrarian, less stressful environment. As a result, the incidence of mental retardation varies from locale to locale and country to country. The urban psychologist must recognize that the individual living in a rural setting may be perfectly adapted there even if a problem arises when the person comes into the city.

Individuals with IQs in the 55 to 69 range, as well as those with lower IQs, are more likely to develop psychiatric disorders than others. This is theoretically due to their inability to handle as much stress or complexity as a person of normal abilities because of a lack of adequate cognitive skills to handle the problems. In such cases, disorders may range from neuroses to acute psychotic-like problems. It is necessary for the psychologist and other professionals working with the person to take into account the role of IQ and transient situational stress in the development of these disorders, rather than to assume a long-term underlying psychotic disorder.

In working with the person with an IQ in this range, it is also necessary to assess such factors as motivation, attitudes, and past experience in addition to intelligence when making recommendations for training or other types of disposition. The consideration of any secondary deficits, such as motor dysfunction, perceptual problems, and health disorders are also important, as these additional strengths or weaknesses can make a big difference in prognosis. Individuals with higher scores in such tests as Comprehension and Picture Arrangement should be considered better risks because of a higher understanding of social and practical situations. In suggesting training or job opportunities, a careful analysis of skills, by carefully examining subtest patterns, is imperative.

IQs in the range below 55 are variously described as moderately retarded (40 to 54), severely retarded (25 to 39), or profoundly retarded (24 or below). IQs below 40, however, must be estimated on the WAIS because Wechsler did not provide tables for such IQs. In addition, easy items on the WAIS for measuring lower IQ are practically nonexistent; as a result, the accuracy of IQs below 55 is questionable. If one needs to know how far an IQ is below 55, the test of choice is the Stanford-Binet (see chapter 2 in this volume).

Individuals with moderate mental retardation may be able to hold jobs, but many have difficulty in learning self-help skills. Individuals with severe or profound retardation are generally severely brain damaged and unable to care for themselves. Special help from trained professionals is necessary for the care and teaching of these individuals.

THE PIQ-VIQ DIFFERENCE

Much has been written about the significance of differences between performance IQ (PIQ) and Verbal IQ (VIQ) In general, however, little has been learned. One of the problems of looking at this difference is the assumption that the PIQ and VIQ measure different things. Even a casual analysis of the test, however, reveals this to be false. For example, nearly all the performance tests involve verbal components. Instructions are primarily verbal, although some demonstrations are given. Social competency as measured by Picture Arrangement usually has a strong verbal component. Digit Symbol involves numbers and symbols that are similar to letters and offers a clear advantage to the literate individual. Picture Completion must be understood purely through verbal instructions. On the other hand, arithmetic skills are strongly spatial in nature, as educators have tried to show with the "new math." Reversing digits in Digits Backward is a spatial skill. An overlap arises when one tests brain injured patients; the left hemisphere controls verbal skills, which causes low VIQ scores, but it also controls right hand motor skills necessary to do Digit Symbol, Block Design, Picture Arrangement, and Object Assembly. Finally, all the tests are influenced to some degree by the assumed general underlying intelligence factor that many biological and neurological theories of intelligence define. The overall relationship between the scales is shown by their high intercorrelation (.77) and the high correlation of both scales with Full Scale IQ (.96, .93) (Wechsler, 1955).

Despite these factors that act to keep the PIQ and VIQ alike, there are generally differences between them in almost all individuals. In general, these differences are small (less than 10 points), and probably due largely to chance variations in scores and rounding errors in translating from raw to scale scores. In some individuals, however, these differences are considerably larger. In some cases, this may be due to one very poor score, such as in Arithmetic, which lowers an otherwise high IQ. In these cases, the difference is due to a specific problem in one area. In other cases, large differences (greater than 10 points) may reflect differential aptitudes that may arise because of environment or culture (individuals from alternate cultures may average as much as 15 points lower in VIQ than in PIQ), teaching (an educational curriculum may have emphasized one skill over the other, usually verbal skills in bright individuals), or simply an inability to do better in one sphere of endeavor than in another.

One extensive area of research has attempted to relate PIQ-VIQ differences to brain damage. As can be recognized by the reader, the presence of significant differences in normals for the reasons cited above make it difficult to ascribe large differences only to brain damage. Many researchers have attempted to prove, however, that there are greater differences in brain damaged groups. Although some studies have been reported supporting this contention, in general no definitive pattern or highly reliable diagnostic sign has been found (e.g., see Golden & Anderson, 1978; Todd, Coolidge, & Satz, 1977). Although it can be said that strong PIQ-VIQ differences may be associated with brain damage in some cases, such differences are often not present. Golden and Anderson (1978) indicated that the differences are more likely in acute, focal brain disorders and less likely in both chronic and diffuse brain disorders. Since most brain damage seen by psychologists falls into the latter group, the sign is of limited value.

Given that the difference is not a good indication of brain damage versus normality, other researchers have looked at the ability of the difference to predict right versus left brain damage. These studies have hypothesized that since the left hemisphere controls verbal functions, individuals with left hemisphere injuries should have lower verbal scores than performance scores. Similarly, since the right hemisphere controls nonverbal functions, individuals with right hemisphere injuries should have lower performance (nonverbal) scores. An impressive number of studies have supported this contention (Balthazar, 1963; Balthazar & Morrison, 1961; Black, 1974; Dennerll, 1964; Doehring, Reitan, & Klove, 1961; Fields & Whitmyre, 1969; Goldstein & Shelley, 1973; Russell, 1972). Despite this support, an equally imposing list of studies has failed to support the use of the PIQ-VIQ difference in lateralization (Heilbrun, 1959; Meyer & Jones, 1957; Pennington, Galliani, & Voegele, 1965; Reed, Reitan, & Klove, 1965; Smith, 1966).

An examination of the studies supporting and contradicting the PIQ-VIQ hypothesis reveals some basic problems in the difference score. It appears to work only in localized lesions rather than in extremely massive lesions (as these will tend to disturb the function of the brain as a whole), and works better with acute than with chronic injuries. Individuals with lesions in the parietal-temporal area of both hemispheres tend to have higher difference scores. Frontal lesions may indeed even fail to affect average IQ at all (Smith, 1966).

Reasons for the failure of the test in many situations suggest that the PIQ-VIQ difference can be used only as a general indicator that suggests a hypothesis to the clinician. Such hypotheses must be confirmed by closer examination of the test results and the nature of the errors made by the patient. If PIQs are lower than VIQs, for example, because the right (dominant) hand is paralyzed, one is much more likely to have a left hemisphere injury, as the left hemisphere controls the right hand. Similarly, left frontal lesions that are massive may disturb an individual's ability to follow directions and will cause both IQs to be equally low. A subtle right frontal injury may affect Digits Backward alone, causing the PIQ to be higher than the VIQ.

WAIS PATTERNS AND THE DIAGNOSIS OF BRAIN DAMAGE

Many advocates of the WAIS recognized quite early that simple differences in PIQs and VIQs were not sufficient for the diagnosis of brain damage, noting many of the same problems cited above. These researchers attempted to find alternate ways to diagnose brain dysfunction. The most famous of these advocated the "hold" and "don't hold" tests. The theory behind this approach suggested that some tests on the WAIS were very sensitive to brain damage, and that they would be affected every time a brain injury was present. Other tests, the theory said, were hold tests. These scores would not go down in brain damaged subjects. Thus, if one would compare the hold and don't hold tests, one could tell if there was a relative decrease in the don't hold tests. If there was a decrease, then there was brain damage. Numerous combinations of hold and don't hold tests were suggested for these formulas. All ended up with one basic result: the theory did not work (Golden & Anderson, 1978).

The reasons for this failure were numerous. First, tests sensitive to brain damage (e.g., Digit Span or Digit Symbol) are the same tests sensitive to anxiety, psychiatric disorders, distraction, lack of motivation, and nearly every other disorder that interferes with the assessment of intelligence. As a result, there is no way to tell the brain injured from the anxious from the psychotic patient using these formulas. The formulas did work relatively well with normals, however. The problem is that the psychologist never has to say whether a normal control is brain damaged; he or she is almost always working with a choice of diagnoses such as brain damage or schizophrenia.

A second major reason for the failure is that each of the don't hold tests is unaffected by a great number of brain disorders. Originally, the don't hold tests were developed from populations consisting primarily of diffuse organic brain syndromes. In these individuals, scores on all the don't hold tests were down. In focal injuries seen in general hospitals or neurological settings, however, only one or none of the don't hold tests (e.g., Digit Symbol) may be impaired. In essence, the problem boiled down to the observation that the hold and don't hold tests differed considerably depending on the type and focus of the brain damage.

From the recognition that the WAIS is differentially affected by different lesions has come research looking for patterns of WAIS scores that signify different lesions. With this method one determines the pattern of impaired test scores. This pattern can then be matched against patterns expected in different kinds of brain injury. If the pattern matches what would be expected in a given brain injury, then the subject is likely to be brain injured in that part of the brain.

The most ambitious use of the WAIS in this manner was reported by McFie (1975), who outlined the basic patterns expected in different types of localized brain injuries. Left frontal lesions are characterized by a loss on Digit Span and a mild or no loss in VIQ. Such injuries also are accompanied by a deficit in verbal associative learning. Right frontal lesions are characterized by deficits in Picture Arrangement, on memory tasks involving designs, and sometimes in Digits Backward (Golden & Anderson, 1978). Left temporal lesions produce losses in Similarities and Digit Span; right temporal lesions cause a drop in Picture Arrangement and in design memory. (Tests for design memory are discussed later.) Meier and French (1966) suggested that a loss in Object Assembly also may be seen with right temporal lesions. Left parietal injuries cause losses on Arithmetic, Digit Span, Block Design, and sometimes Similarities (Mahan, 1976). Right parietal lesions affect memory for design, Block Design, and Picture Arrangement.

Diffuse injuries generally cause a loss on most of the tests sensitive to brain injury: Digit Span, Arithmetic, Picture Arrangement, Object Assembly, Block Design, and Digit Symbol. (Digit Symbol tends to be down in all brain injuries, as well as in many intact individuals.) Injuries to subcortical areas generally affect tests with strong motor components: Digit Symbol, Block Design, Object Assembly, and Picture Arrangement, in this order. Injuries that involve more than one of the areas discussed above produce various combinations of the test deficits, depending on the precise location of the injury.

Deficits that are caused by brain injury early in childhood, especially before age two, show a considerably different pattern of scores from that of adults. As a rule, the individual has an IQ below 80 and often in the range of mental retardation. The tests traditionally referred to as hold tests (Information, Comprehension, and Vocabulary) generally are the lowest tests in the record. This is due to the inability of the early brain injured child to take full advantage of educational opportunities and day-to-day learning. Often the highest scores in these subjects are on Digit Span, Picture Completion, Arithmetic, and Block Design. Recognition of this pattern allows the psychologist to differentiate between relatively early brain damage and brain damage occurring later in life.

As a test of organicity, the WAIS is not accurate enough to be used alone. Combined with a test of visual memory, such as the Benton Visual Retention Test, the WAIS can be useful as a screening instrument for deficits in individuals known to be brain damaged. It is not diagnostically effective enough to be used to make a confident diagnosis of brain damage; however, it has been shown to be a highly useful instrument to add to a more extensive neuropsychological test battery such as the Halstead-Reitan (see chapter 9 on this test).

ESTIMATING PREMORBID INTELLIGENCE

Another way of using the WAIS for estimating the presence of brain damage is to compare current IQ with an estimate of premorbid IQ. This is in many ways like the hold/don't hold formulas (with many of the same problems) except that it allows clinicians to estimate premorbid IQ either from the WAIS subtests or alternately from other sources of information.

When working from WAIS subtests, clinicians are obviously looking for hold tests that indicate where the patient's IQ fell prior to an injury. However, the use here is more limited, which allows for better results. First, the person must show evidence that there was no premorbid evidence of a psychiatric or neurological condition (before an accident or other condition occurred that is thought to have lowered the IQ). Behavior and performance in school and work must have been within normal limits. Second, if no difference is found between premorbid IQ and current IQ, the clinician should not conclude that the person has no damage; he or she should simply conclude that the comparison is "noncontributory" to an understanding of the patient's problem. Under these conditions, IQ estimates from combinations of hold tests such as Vocabulary, Comprehension, Information, and Picture Completion (prorated as discussed earlier) can be employed. When substantial differences are found (i.e., when premorbid IQ is higher by 15 or more points), this is evidence of a deterioration in IQ.

An alternate method (which can be used at the same time) is to estimate scores from premorbid group intelligence tests taken in school or in the armed services, premorbid achievement test taken at almost all schools, or college entrance examinations. In all of these cases, the clinician is interested in the individual's percentile score, which can be converted through appropriate tables in statistics books to a standard z score. The z score is then initially converted to an IQ score by multiplying the z score by 15 and adding 100 to the result.

This converted score is then further modified depending on when the score was achieved and whether the WAIS or WAIS-R is being used. For scores on tests normed before 1975, a direct comparison can be made with the WAIS IQ without further modification. However, if the comparison is to the WAIS-R, the score should be lowered by seven points. For scores on tests normed after 1975, seven points must be added before the test is compared to the WAIS; however, for the WAIS-R, no further modification is made.

When estimating from a test that yields multiple scores,

the best procedure is to average the percentiles from all of the available scores before going to the z score conversion. When the person has had multiple tests usually the most recent test before the individual's injury or disorder is the most useful, if the test is seen as reliable and well standardized. It should always be remembered that group tests tend to underestimate individual IQ. Thus, if there are several tests given and one or more have substantially higher scores than the rest, these tests may be more accurate except when they occurred before the age of 15, since the younger the person is at the time of testing, the less accurate the test is in predicting adult IQ. Thus, if all tests were given before age 15, one usually relies on the latest administered test unless there are clear clinical reasons to distrust the score.

In addition to making estimations based on prior tests, many clinicians have attempted to estimate scores from demographic information. I have not been impressed by most such formulas: they appear to gain little over a simple conversion on the basis of education, as discussed previously. Indeed, a guess that everyone who is not mentally retarded or identified as a genius or a psychiatric patient would have an IQ in the 85 to 115 range would result in an accuracy rate of over 70 percent, a finding in line with the accuracy of the more complex formulas that have been presented. The problem here is that there are simply too many individual factors. In nearly all cases, using an estimate from the WAIS itself or using outside school or job related testing is preferable to using such formulas at the present time.

PSYCHIATRIC DISORDERS: DIAGNOSTIC APPROACHES

It is questionable whether the WAIS, or any other intelligence test, should ever serve as a primary diagnostic instrument for psychiatric disorders. Diagnostic inferences made from other tests such as the Minnesota Multiphasic Personality Inventory, which is discussed later, can be confirmed or supplemented, however, with information gained from the WAIS. If a clinician has diagnosed a psychosis, for example, an analysis of WAIS performance is useful in determining the degree to which the psychosis interferes with the person's cognitive skills. Knowledge of cognitive skills (or their lack) can also aid in the understanding of a potential psychiatric disorder and its possible relationship to intellectual rather than emotional problems. Finally, unsuspected psychiatric disorders can occasionally be recognized during an intellectual examination.

In evaluating psychiatric disorders, it is particularly important to focus on signs of emotional disorders that are spontaneously offered by the patient in terms of bizarre answers to questions on tests such as Comprehension and in terms of ineffective learning strategies on Block Design or Object Assembly. Observation of high anxiety states may also be made, especially on Digit Symbol and Digit Span. In addition, especially poor performance on Vocabulary, Similarities, Information, and Comprehension, in the absence of a history of mental retardation, may also imply a serious psychiatric disorder. In determining the possible meaning of symptoms observed on the tests, testing the limits for the subtests, as described earlier, can be a useful additional feature.

COMPARING THE WAIS AND WAIS-R

An important issue caused by the release of the WAIS-R is its relationship to the WAIS and the vast body of clinical literature, practice, and lore that have grown up around the WAIS. In the WAIS-R manual, Wechsler (1981) reported that WAIS-R IQs were about seven points lower than WAIS IQs in the same population. Prifitera and Ryan (1983) reported similar results using a clinical rather than a normative sample.

In a major survey of the literature, Ryan, Nowak, and Geisser (1987) evaluated 15 studies in which the WAIS and the WAIS-R were given to samples of subjects. Overall, these studies found an average difference of about 6.5 points between the WAIS IQs and the WAIS-R IQs, with the WAIS IQ higher; however, the size of the difference dropped off with higher IQ subjects. Urbina, Golden, and Ariel (1982) found larger differences in elderly than in younger individuals (up to 20 points in groups over age 75). Simon and Clopton found that the WAIS-R yielded higher IQs in mild and moderately retarded individuals. So, although the idea of a Seven-point difference is reasonably correct, it does not necessarily hold for all populations.

Other studies have suggested that the WAIS and WAIS-R are basically similar. Ryan, Prifitera, and Rosenberg (1983) found that the WAIS and the WAIS-R showed similar relationships to the Halstead-Reitan Neuropsychological Battery (see chapter 9 for a description of the Halstead-Reitan). Ryan and Rosenberg (1983) found correlations between the WAIS-R and the Wide Range Achievement Test (see chapter 2) similar to those reported for the WAIS. Ryan, Rosenberg, and Heilbronner (1984) found similar relationships for both the WAIS and WAIS-R with the Wechsler Memory Scale (see chapter 6).

The results of these studies suggest that, except for the IQ level these two tests are largely interchangeable (not surprising considering that many items are identical on both tests). However, IQ scores should be viewed with caution when comparing the two tests.

ADVANTAGES AND DISADVANTAGES

There are a number of significant advantages in choosing the WAIS as a measure of intellectual ability. First, it offers an IQ that is the standard against which all other IQ tests are currently measured. Consequently, the use of nearly any other test is validated on the observation that it correlates with WAIS IQ. Under these conditions, use of the WAIS itself seems to be logical whenever this is possible. Second, unlike most other adult intelligence tests, the WAIS yields more than a Full Scale IQ. It also provides subtest scores that yield significant information about adult functioning that can be used to help answer numerous referral questions. Third, the test remains the most comprehensively normed adult intelligence test available today. Finally, the WAIS is one of the most heavily researched instruments available to the psychologist. Normative data and validity studies are available for numerous psychological service settings, patient populations, and administration conditions. Although only a small part of this literature is relevant to any one setting or population, the information is available for the psychologist who needs it.

The WAIS does have distinct disadvantages, however. Perhaps the greatest problem at present is the confusion over whether to use the WAIS or the WAIS-R. The research to date has clearly shown that WAIS-R IQs are, on the average, seven points lower than WAIS IQs. The reason for this is simple: the WAIS-R normative group, 25 years later, did substantially better on many questions than the WAIS group, causing the norms to be elevated. Thus, the same performance on the two tests yields different IQs because they are compared with different standards. The reason for this is not clear: whether it reflects better education, the effects of television, more motivation, or a host of other possibilities cannot be determined.

Because of this difference in achieved IQ, many clinicians have complained that the WAIS-R is resulting in IQs lower than the person's real IQ (real IQ being defined as performance on the WAIS). This is a misleading argument because, as discussed previously, there is no such thing as real IQ based on a test score. Both tests represent samplings of performance compared with performance of normative groups. The only real question is which test is the better normed and more representative of current behavior: there is no question that the WAIS-R is the better normed and more appropriate test.

Another related problem is the issue of whether the WAIS-R can be analyzed in the same way as the WAIS. There is no question that most of what is discussed in this chapter is derived from the 25 years of experience with the WAIS and the prior experience of psychologists with the Wechsler-Bellevue. At present, evidence is scant on this issue, but the generally high correlations between the WAIS and the WAIS-R, as well as the very similar item content in the two versions suggests that the clinical rules work as well or better with the WAIS-R. Unless evidence to the contrary is clearly generated, the general interpretation rules can be used with the WAIS-R with as much confidence as with the WAIS.

Finally, there is the question of the elderly. In my own clinical experience, WAIS-R IQs are often as much as 20 points lower than WAIS IQs in the normal elderly. Again, this is the result of a much better selected normative group in the WAIS-R standardization, which elevated the norms substantially in some cases. Thus, there must be extra caution in comparing WAIS-R IQs and WAIS IQs in this population. This does not suggest that the WAIS-R misrepresents the IQs of the elderly, but rather that the WAIS severely overestimated such IQs.

Another disadvantage of the WAIS is that it is unsuitable for large group testings. Its individual administration format makes it difficult to screen large numbers of patients in psychiatric and other settings that process numerous patients. In these situations, a briefer screening test of some kind, usually designed to correlate with the WAIS, is employed (see chapter 2).

Another drawback is the problem of administering the WAIS to black, Chicano, and other cultural groups in the U.S. The test remains heavily influenced by cultural and language concepts that reflect the life of the average American, but not that of most minority groups. Although the WAIS-R's design and normative procedures are much more sensitive to these issues, there is still no way the test can be considered culturally fair as an estimate of real IQ capacity, although it still remains a good measure of achievement in each of the areas tested. As a result, many minority educators and psychologists have suggested that the WAIS is biased against minorities, and they advocate the use of so-called "culture fair" tests, or tests designed specifically for a minority culture (see chapter 2). For example, Williams (1975) suggested the use of the BITCH (Black Intelligence Test Corrected for Honkies), a test specifically designed for the black culture.

Another drawback of the WAIS is its susceptibility to the improvement of scores with retesting. Since no alternate form of the test exists, this makes it difficult to use the WAIS in situations in which frequent reevaluation is indicated. It should be noted, however, that this drawback is true of many of the intelligence tests that currently exist.

The final problem is the tendency of the original WAIS to

overestimate low IQs when compared with the Wechsler Intelligence Scale for Children (WISC) and its 1976 revision, the Wechsler Intelligence Scale for Children-Revised (WISC-R). The problem lies in the fact that there are far too few easy items on the WAIS. An individual given a score of zero, the lowest possible, may actually be operating at a level much lower than that. Such lower levels are not tested on the WAIS, however. For example, a 15-year-old child may test at an IQ of 65 on the WISC, making the child eligible for special classes. The same child, at 16, may take the WAIS and earn an IQ of 75. Although the child has not changed at all, he or she is no longer eligible for special classes. Although the range problem still exists with the WAIS-R, the tendency of the WAIS-R to yield lower IQs in general has mitigated this problem to a great extent.

Consequently, users of the WAIS must be cautious in interpreting scores of adults who test below an IQ of 80 on the WAIS, especially if those individuals have scores of zero on any subtest, as this suggests individuals operating at a level lower than 70 IQ. In these cases, the user may estimate the correct IQ at about 10 points lower than that actually achieved. If further testing is needed for legal or other purposes, it is suggested that the Stanford-Binet be used (1972 norms), because it provides the most accurate estimate of a low IQ in an adult.

CASE EXAMPLES

Case 1. This case was referred to me because of a "psychotic episode" in which the patient apparently threatened his family and employer. Because mental retardation was indicated in the patient's history, the patient was evaluated using the WAIS (Table 1-1). As the reader can see, the patient earned a VIQ of 50 and PIQ of 48. There were no signs of psychosis on the test. The patient was highly cooperative but able to respond only slowly and on a very concrete level. Discussion of the case with the staff social worker indicated that the patient's problem began when he was expected to master a new job, one that was clearly above the patient's learning potential. It was hypothesized and later confirmed that the patient was probably reacting to extreme frustration due to the expectations of his parents and employer, both of whom assumed he was smarter than he actually was. (One reason for this may have been the patient's Comprehension score, which was significantly higher than his other scores.) The patient was transferred to a job more in keeping with his skills and was able to adapt without problems.

Case 2. This patient was referred by a neurosurgeon for investigation of possible changes in the patient's cognitive skills related to a suspicion of generalized cerebral atrophy due to presenile dementia (Alzheimer's disease). As can be seen in Table 1-1, the patient's scores were quite variable. Vocabulary, Comprehension, Arithmetic, Similarities, and Information were uniformly high, while Digit Span was extremely low. There were significant drops in the performance tests on Digit Symbol, Picture Arrangement, and, to a lesser extent, Block Design. The PIQ was significantly below the VIQ. The patient was cooperative but tended to be somewhat apathetic; however, she did everything that was asked of her.

The analysis of the test results revealed a pattern inconsis-

TABLE 1-1   Scores for WAIS Cases

	Case 1	Case 2	Case 3	Case 4
Information	1	14	6	12
Comprehension	4	14	6	13
Arithmetic	1	12	4	6
Similarities	0	13	3	6
Digit Span	0	6	5	5
Vocabulary	1	15	5	14
Picture Completion	1	14	7	10
Digit Symbol	0	6	6	4
Block Design	0	10	7	8
Picture Arrangement	0	7	4	8
Object Assembly	0	12	5	9
Verbal IQ	50	116	72	100
Performance IQ	48	110	73	102
Full Scale IQ	< 48	114	71	101

tent with generalized cerebral dysfunction. On the verbal tests, only the very poor score on Digit Span stood out, as did the Picture Arrangement and Digit Symbol scores on the performance tests. The pattern as a whole was more consistent with bilateral impairment of the frontal lobes, which was suggested to the neurosurgeon, who referred the patient to a neurologist. A CAT scan and subsequent surgery later confirmed a bilateral, slow-growing tumor involving both frontal lobes.

Case 3. The patient was referred for determining eligibility in a program designed for adult, mentally retarded individuals. As the reader can see in Table 1-1, the patient earned an IQ of 71, somewhat above the 69 cutoff. Since the WAIS is known to somewhat overestimate these scores, however, it was suggested to the agency that the patient was still eligible. Retesting on the Stanford-Binet yielded a score of 66, which was low enough to qualify the individual for the program.

Case 4. This case represents a fairly typical profile of an individual six months after a tumor was removed from the left parietal area. There remained significant but small deficits in Arithmetic, Block Design, and Similarities, with a slightly lower score on Digit Span. The person's overall IQ is about 100 at present. If his premorbid IQ is estimated from the Comprehension, Vocabulary, and Information subtests, however, the patient's prior IQ is determined to have been about 115, suggesting a drop of 15 points or one standard deviation. Thus, although the individual's IQ is normal, his current level of functioning reflects a large and serious decline.

CHAPTER TWO

Alternate Tests of
Intellectual Performance

Although the WAIS is unquestionably the major test of intellectual performance in use today, a number of other tests are available which can be useful in specific circumstances. These tests will be discussed briefly in this chapter along with indications for their use. It should be noted that each of these tests offers approximations, not exact equivalents, to the WAIS IQ.

STANFORD-BINET

The Stanford-Binet preceded the WAIS as the major measure of child and adult intelligence. The Binet was originally designed as a test of children's intelligence, but was later extended to assess adult intelligence. The original Binet used the concept of mental age to assess intelligence. Briefly, this approach attempted to establish the age at which the skills possessed by the individual would be considered normal (defined as 50 percent of an age group having a given skill). When the mental age of the individual was divided by the chronological (true) age, the resulting quotient would be an IQ. An IQ over 100 would indicate a brighter than average individual, whereas an IQ below 100 would indicate a duller than normal individual. Recent editions of the test, however, have adopted the deviation

IQ approach pioneered by Wechsler. Binet's IQs have a mean of 100 and a standard deviation of 16.

Administering the Stanford-Binet

The Binet tests are arranged in year levels ranging from two years to superior adult. The first problem facing the examiner is to establish where to begin the test in order to determine a basal level, a year grouping in which the examinee can pass all the tests. Beginning too low will lengthen the test and often insult the patient. Beginning too high may convince the patient that the test is very difficult and cause undue anxiety. One useful way to establish the starting point is to administer the Vocabulary test; this generally provides a good basal level. This method is best used with adults who are suspected of possible mental retardation. Adults with normal or better intelligence may be started at the average adult level as a rule.

If the individual does not pass all the tests at the level chosen, it is necessary to administer the levels previous to the one chosen. If the individual only missed one test at the level chosen, it is generally necessary to go back only one level. If the examinee missed all or most of the tests at a given level, however, it may be necessary for the examiner to go back more than one level depending on the examiner's assessment of the examinee's abilities. After a basal level has been established, testing at higher levels is continued until all the tests at a given level are failed. Administration instructions for each subtest can be found in the Stanford-Binet manual. Readers may also find Pedrini and Pedrini (1970) of use.

A general rule in administering the Binet is to make sure that all tests are administered and scored as directed. As the test can be long with some patients, there is a tendency to skip tests or administer them incorrectly, which invalidates the Binet IQ. Some minor alterations in test procedures may be used with physically handicapped individuals, although IQs generated from such procedures must be viewed with caution. The reader interested in such modifications is referred to Sattler (1974).

After completing the test, the examiner must allot credit

for each test. The individual is given full credit for all years up to and including the basal level year. Thereafter, credit is given for each test passed at each level according to the values for tests at each level, which differ from one month value for tests at the initial two-year-old level to six months value for tests at the highest (Superior Adult III) level. The months credit earned at each year level are summed to get a total score. This is then located in the appropriate table in the Binet manual to yield an overall IQ.

Interpreting the IQ

The Binet IQ can be interpreted much as the WAIS IQ, except for the use of a standard deviation of 16 rather than 15. Thus, at IQ levels of 70, the Binet IQ is two points lower than the WAIS IQ; at 52, the difference is three points; at 36, four points; and at 20, five points.

Comparability of the WAIS and Binet IQs

The median correlation between the WAIS IQ and the Binet IQ is about .78, suggesting a high degree of relationship. The tests tend to deviate at the high and low ends of the scale: Binet IQs tend to be significantly lower in individuals with IQs less than 70 and significantly higher in individuals with IQs higher than 130. As a rule, the Binet correlates higher with the WAIS verbal tests because of a greater emphasis on verbal functions than is seen in the WAIS.

Pattern Analysis

Although the Binet was not specifically designed for a pattern or scatter analysis, as was the WAIS, the success of the procedure with the WAIS has encouraged many authors to develop systems for doing scattergrams or pattern analyses of the Binet. Several major systems of this type are described for the reader in Sattler (1974). These systems are applicable to the mentally retarded population not best served by the WAIS.

Advantages and Disadvantages

The primary advantage of the Binet is in establishing an IQ for adults suspected of mental retardation. As noted in the last chapter, the WAIS tends to overestimate low IQs, a serious problem in a borderline individual of about 66 IQ who may have a WAIS IQ greater than 70. In these cases, and in cases of all lower IQs where an exact IQ is desired, the Stanford-Binet is the test of choice.

On the negative side, despite the attempts to develop scattergrams and the like for the Binet, pattern analysis with the Binet in adults is considerably more difficult and tentative than with the WAIS. As a result, the Binet is rarely the test of choice for normal adults. The Binet is also somewhat more difficult to administer and score than the WAIS, a factor that also contributes to the popularity of the latter.

AMMONS FULL RANGE PICTURE VOCABULARY TEST

The Ammons Full Range Picture Vocabulary Test consists of pictures representing complex scenes or situations. The patient is given a word and must select the picture that best represents the word. The test covers a wide age range, with norms from age two to adult. The patient is given a stimulus word orally or reads it in written form. The test is able to evaluate the full-range of intelligence. Two forms are available, each with a separate set of four pictures. The same pictures are used for all items, making the test easy to give and score. Of the studies currently available, the correlations range from .49 to .92 with WAIS IQ (e.g., Granick, 1971; Sydiaha, 1967), with the majority of studies yielding correlations in the range between .7 and .9.

QUICK TEST

A related test is the Quick Test. The Quick Test consists of three sets of picture plates, each with four pictures representing complex scenes or situations. Each plate has a series of 50 words associated with it. The words are presented to the examinee orally or in a written form. All words are given to all subjects, with total administration time for all three sets averaging around 50 minutes. The three sets are highly intercorrelated, however, and one may choose to administer only one 50-item word list in a time of 10 to 15 minutes. Tables provide transformations to IQs, but the test is appropriate only for individuals with average or below average IQs rather than for individuals falling in the full range of IQs. Tables provide equivalent IQs for age six through adult levels.

Interpretation

IQs on the Quick Test correlate with full scale WAIS IQs from .34 to .88, with the lower correlations occurring in brighter populations for which the Quick Test is inappropriate. Among psychiatric patients, the correlations average about .80 (e.g., see Borgatta & Corsini, 1960; Davis & Dizonne, 1970; Ogilvie, 1965; Quattlebaum & White, 1969).

Although IQs based on vocabulary give the best estimate of any test in determining Full Scale IQs, these Quick Test scores are not as sensitive to pathology as are WAIS scores. They tend to estimate premorbid intelligence rather than determine the impaired intellectual performance in organic brain injured patients and other severely pathological groups. IQs tend to be higher, as a consequence, than the WAIS equivalent, and considerably higher in some cases than the person's level of adaptive functioning. Thus, the IQs provide a weak measure of current adaptive skills. When the Quick Test is used as a screening test, any IQ below 80 should be an indication for a full WAIS, as should any historical or neurological signs of organic brain dysfunction.

SHIPLEY-HARTFORD SCALE

The Shipley-Hartford Scale consists of two subtests. It was originally developed to screen for mental retardation in psychi-

atric patients, and also has been used for the diagnosis of organicity. A major advantage of the test lies in the fact that it can
be group administered rather than administered as an individual test. The test also can be easily administered by technicians
and other nonprofessionals.

The first part of the test consists of a multiple choice vocabulary test in which a meaning must be selected from one of
four alternatives. The second part of the test consists of items
in a series, such as "EFGH———." The patient must fill in the
last part of the series. Intelligence scores may be determined
by taking the patient's raw score and using tables to determine
an equivalent IQ. An organic deterioration index is derived
by comparing the IQ derived from the verbal test with an IQ
derived from the series test which theoretically measures abstract skills in the patients. These latter skills are hypothesized
to be sensitive to brain damage, whereas the vocabulary test
is theoretically insensitive to brain damage. Thus, the ratio
between the two scores is a measure of the probability of
organicity. When the ratio is below 70, the patient is said to be
brain damaged.

Interpretation

Correlations between the WAIS and the Shipley-Hartford
IQs range from .73 to .86 in numerous studies, averaging
around .80 (see Bartz, 1968; Mack, 1970; Monroe, 1966; Pringle
& Haanstad, 1971). One of the most serious problems with the
Shipley-Hartford, however, is its low correlation with the WAIS
at IQs below 93. Watson and Klett (1968) reported that at this
level, the two IQs were correlated at a level of only .23, far too
low for any kind of clinical interpretation. Since most screen-
ings are aimed at recognizing low intelligence, the Shipley-
Hartford is not applicable in most clinical uses. If used, one
would have to give full WAIS evaluations to all the patients
with IQs under 93. If the Shipley-Hartford is used, the reader
is referred to the conversion tables of Paulsen and Lin (1970),
who present conversion tables with age corrections not available in the standard table.

There are also questions about the Shipley-Hartford as a

test of organicity. A number of studies have reported that the test fails to discriminate between organic, psychiatric, and normal patients (Aita, Armitage, Reitan, & Rabinowitz, 1947; Parker, 1957; Savage, 1970). In general, the percentage of patients identified as organic increases greatly with increasing severity of a psychiatric disorder (Yates, 1954). Overall, the test does not appear to be useful in most circumstances, even as a gross screening test of organicity (Golden & Anderson, 1978).

RAVEN'S PROGRESSIVE MATRICES

The Raven's Progressive Matrices was intended as a culturally fair test of intelligence based on purely nonverbal and noncultural items. The test consists of a design with a piece missing. The examinee must select from six choices the correct design that is the missing piece. An example of a Raven's type item is seen in Figure 2-1. The test requires such abilities as spatial skills, recognition of design, abstract skills, ability to recognize numerical and spatial relationships, and concentration and attention skills. The overall performance on the test has been found to relate to educational level (Colonna & Faglioni, 1966).

The Raven's Matrices may be administered by anyone, even nonprofessional technicians. The instructions are easily explained. For each of the 60 items, the patient simply points to the piece that fills in the missing hole. Two sample items are included, and few subjects, except very deteriorated individuals, have difficulty in grasping what is necessary. The test has no time limit, but rarely takes over an hour. The patient may mark his or her answer on an answer sheet, or this may be done by the examiner. An alternate version is available for children and for use with severely retarded adults.

Norms for the test are available for ages 8 through 65. The norms are scanty, however: equivalent scores are presented for seven percentile levels rather than for direct conversion to IQ equivalents. Peck (1970) presented more extensive percentile norms for age groups from 25 to 65. These percentiles may be changed into IQs by converting the percentiles into standard z

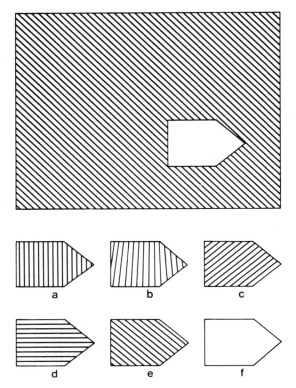

Figure 2.1   An example of a Raven's item. The proper piece to fill in the upper drawing is chosen from the six alternative pieces at the bottom.

scores (using tables available in many statistics books), multiplying the z by 15, and adding the result to 100.

Interpretation

Raven's IQs and WAIS IQs have been reported to correlate from .43 to .93 in populations including organic and psychiatric patients. In general, the Raven's is more sensitive than the VIQ to pathology and less sensitive than the PIQ. Thus, the degree of deterioration in a population greatly influences the reported correlations. In addition, the Raven's has a low ceiling, so equivalent IQs are difficult to estimate for bright individuals. Correlations tend to be higher in populations with lower mean IQs.

Poor performance on the Raven's is associated with brain dysfunction, which also causes difficulty on such tests as Block Design. Thus, scores tend to be lower than overall WAIS IQs in individuals with specific losses in these design skills, but who retain verbal and verbal conceptual skills. This underestimation may cause the examiner to expect less of the patient. The difficulty in estimating Raven's IQs because of the lack of extensive normative data, especially in American populations, is also a major problem in using this test.

PEABODY PICTURE VOCABULARY TEST

One of the more common brief tests of intelligence is the Peabody Picture Vocabulary Test (PPVT). The PPVT is easily administered and requires only a pointing response from the patient. The examinee is told a word and shown four pictures representing simple objects or concepts. The examinee must point to the picture representing the word to be defined. The test consists of 150 words and 150 sets of four pictures. A second word list (form B) can be used with the same 150 pictures. The test has the potential use of estimating IQs of individuals with severe speech or physical handicaps, although this has not been extensively researched. Test administration can be fast, because the examiner need only administer items above the subjects basal level. If the basal level (highest level with six consecutive items correct) is determined accurately (by estimating the individual's IQ), the test can be completed in under 15 minutes. Even when this is not done, the test rarely takes more than 30 minutes to reach a ceiling (missing six of eight consecutive items).

Interpretation

The PPVT IQ correlates about .75 to .80 with the WAIS IQ (Bonner, 1969; Ernhart, 1970; Pool & Brown, 1970). PPVT

IQs tend to overestimate WAIS IQs, especially in lower IQ ranges. Thus, if the PPVT is used as a screen, subjects with IQs lower than 80 should receive full WAIS evaluations. As noted earlier, vocabulary scores tend to be stable in brain damaged adults. As a result, the IQs of organic patients may be seriously overestimated by the PPVT. The test does offer a useful measure of premorbid IQ, however, when this is necessary to determine degree of disability or for diagnostic purposes.

A revised version of the PPVT, the PPVT-R, was released recently. Although the format and other features remain the same, the new test has updated norms that are more comparable to the WAIS-R. Thus, as the WAIS-R should be used instead of the older WAIS, the PPVT-R should be used in all clinical settings instead of the PPVT.

CONCLUSIONS

The alternate tests of intellectual function are often employed in situations in which the time and personnel required for the WAIS are not available or are economically unreasonable because of the small amount of return for the effort involved. The brief tests enable the clinician to identify those subjects who can benefit most from further evaluations with such tests as the WAIS. In addition, the tests offer an alternative to the WAIS in situations in which the WAIS is inaccurate, such as in patients with very low IQs for whom more exact IQ scores are needed. The tests can also serve as substitutes in testing physically or speech handicapped individuals who are unable to take the WAIS.

When substituting an alternate test for the WAIS in a desire to save time, a number of considerations must be involved. First, the limitations of the brief tests must be considered carefully. For example, the Shipley-Hartford, probably the easiest and fastest alternative test, is inaccurate with low IQ patients. Thus, the group-administered Shipley-Hartford might serve only as an initial screen to differentiate normal individuals (greater than 93 IQ) from individuals with lower IQs. At this point, an individually administered screening test, such as the Quick Test or PPVT, might be necessary to further identify individuals who need more extensive examination. Use of these alternatives for all clients could eliminate the Shipley-Hartford entirely, but they are difficult to give to large numbers of individuals since they are individually administered. In some settings, the initial screening is done simply by contact with the person rather than by giving a test such as the Shipley-Hartford. With an experienced psychologist, psychiatrist, or other skilled professional performing the initial screen, this can be as effective as a group screening test.

As the reader can see, a number of alternatives are possible in any given situation. Before adopting any of these tests, the clinician should carefully consider the advantages and disadvantages of each approach, analyzing such factors as staff availability, present screening procedures, purpose of the exam, type of population (organic, psychiatric, normal), and needs of the population. The use of a procedure or set of procedures that is inadequate for the person being tested is rarely justified, and overly extensive testing (which the patient must pay for) is not likely to be of benefit to the patient. A balance of these factors can provide professional and practical uses of these alternative examinations.

CHAPTER THREE

Tests of Achievement

Tests of school achievement have long been used by the clinical psychologist to evaluate the role of education in symptoms demonstrated by the patient. There are, however, few achievement tests that fit into the testing requirements of the psychologist. Ideally, such a test would be comprehensive, yet short enough to fit into a larger test battery; easily administered without an extensive background in education; scorable in an objective and consistent manner; and applicable to a wide range of individual adults, ranging from those with little or no educational skills to those with advanced postgraduate degrees. At present, there are two primary tests that meet these requirements: the Wide Range Achievement Test and the Peabody Individual Achievement Test.

WIDE RANGE ACHIEVEMENT TEST

The Wide Range Achievement Test (WRAT) was first presented in 1936 as a standardized assessment of educational skills. The authors of the test stated that it was designed to be an adjunct to tests of intelligence and other psychological characteristics. The test was immediately accepted by numerous clinicians in education and psychology. Two subsequent revisions (1946, 1965) served to keep the test up to date. All three versions of the test examined three major areas of educational achievement: reading, spelling, and arithmetic. The 1965 version was set to evaluate individuals from the prekindergarten level to the college graduate. Two forms of the test (one for above 12 years, one for below 12 years) were devised to provide maximum speed in the testing situation. Altogether, the test takes about 30 minutes to administer. In 1984, the WRAT-R, a revision of the WRAT with updated norms, was released. Other than the norms, the two versions are practically identical, with the appropriate subtests correlating between .91 and .99. It is recommended that the WRAT-R be used in place of the WRAT because of its more up to date norms and more detailed development and attention to such issues as culture.

Administration

Each version of the WRAT (Level I and Level II) consists of tests for spelling, arithmetic, and reading. For each level the Spelling Test is administered first. Initially, the individual is shown a series of figures (lines, circles, triangles, etc.) which they are told to copy. The subject is allowed 60 seconds to copy 18 marks. Then the individual is asked to write his or her name on a line on the answer sheet. The first part of the test is given to anyone who fails to get at least five words correct on Level I spelling. As a result, these sections are skipped when testing the adult until the third part of the spelling test is given.

For both levels of the test, the third spelling section consists of words that are said by the examiner and written by the client. For each word, the examiner says the word and then uses it in a sentence. The subject is allowed 15 seconds to write the word unless he or she has a motor handicap that impairs writing speed. The examiner may allow sufficient time to compensate for the handicap in these cases. The test is discontinued after 10 consecutive errors. In general, subjects should be encouraged to guess if they hesitate in writing a word.

The words for Level I and Level II differ in that Level I has many more easy words and Level II many more hard words. All adult subjects are given Level II, unless a poor performance is elicited where it was not expected; then it is often useful to follow up with Level I to gain more information.

The Reading Test consists of three prereading tasks that are not generally administered to adults: identifying 2 letters in the subjects own name (written in the spelling section), identifying 10 letters, and naming 13 letters of the alphabet. These tests are administered only when the individual fails one of the first 11 words in Level I (most difficult word: *how*), reading pronunciation, or one of the first 10 words in Level II (most difficult word: *form*).

In the reading pronunciation section on both levels, the subject reads from a list of words presented in a test booklet. For convenience, we have usually given the subject a clear list from which to read while marking his or her answers on the subject's form. The subject is given 10 seconds for each word. The subject may be asked to repeat a word if the examiner is unsure what the subject said or if it is a borderline response listed in the test manual (J. F. Jastak & S. R. Jastak, 1965). The subject should also be encouraged to guess when he or she is unsure. The test is discontinued after 10 consecutive errors. As with the other tests, Level II is administered unless an unusually low score is expected. The manual provides the allowable pronunciations.

The Arithmetic Test consists of a basic oral part and the written mathematics section. The oral part consists of counting 15 dots, reading five digits, showing three and eight fingers, comparing two numbers, and performing three oral addition and subtraction problems. If a score of less than five points is achieved on the written part, the oral questions are given. Credit for these items is otherwise automatic.

The written section contains problems ranging from simple addition to advanced algebra. The subject is told to do the problems as quickly as possible. The subject is also informed not to spend too much time on one problem as skipping is permitted. The subject is given 10 minutes. As a rule, most subjects reach their upper limit by the end of 10 minutes. In cases where there is a suspicion that overly slow and meticulous performance has prevented the subject from reaching the limits of his or her skills, extra time can be allowed but should not be included in the standardized score. Any additional items solved correctly, as well as the subject's manner of performance, can be used in making recommendations in the case. As with other tests, Level II is normally given the adult subject.

Scoring

Scoring is relatively simple for the WRAT-R. For each level, there are points assigned for each correct item. One simply counts up the number of correct items to obtain the total score. After the raw scores have been determined, these may be translated directly into grade level equivalents by using tables printed on the test form. Separate tables are printed for Level I and Level II. The grade level scores may be translated into a standard score equivalent to the WAIS IQ by using tables in the test manual. Thus, the standard scores have a mean of 100 and a standard deviation of 15. Tables are available through all adult age levels, ranging up to age 74. The tables in the manual may also be used to determine age appropriate percentiles.

Scoring Issues

Grade level scores can be rather misleading in the adult. Low scores, representing primary and junior high school levels, tend to indicate levels of performance in school that are somewhat standard across the nation. Any given school may, however, teach the material included as a given grade level in the WRAT-R as many as two years before or after the grade suggested by the WRAT-R. Scores in the high school or college level are much more questionable. For example, if an individual takes no math after the 9th grade, as is allowed at many schools, a math score at 8th or 9th grade level might be regarded as normal. In a recent sample collected by the author, a group of midwestern high school graduates had only a 10th grade average, rather than a 12th grade average concurrent with their years of school. In many adult education programs, the levels required for graduation are at the 9th grade level in some subjects, depending on state requirements. Thus, a 10th grade average on one section might be perfectly adequate for the individual.

Given the problems in interpreting grade level scores, standard scores would appear more meaningful. They do not entirely take care of the problem of educational opportunity, but they do give a standard reference group against which the subject can be measured. Moreover, the scores are comparable to IQs. Thus, we can compare whether achievement levels for the individual are comparable to the individual's intellectual level. J. F. Jastak and S. R. Jastak (1965) showed that there is a high level of correspondence between WAIS IQs and WRAT standard scores. In general, differences of 10 points or more appear to be clinically meaningful. If the IQ is higher, the person is performing at a level significantly below expectations. In these cases, one must consider the possibility of learning disabilities in the adult (see Learning Disabilities, below). If the educational level is higher, the scores suggest either a late brain injury (see Brain Damage, below) or a person able to take maximum advantage of his or her skills. These individuals are often highly motivated, but may also be under a great deal of stress to perform at levels above their capabilities. In either case, where there are large discrepancies, one must seriously consider the possible role they may play in any presenting psychiatric disorder.

In evaluating differences between IQs and WRAT-R standard scores, differences on Spelling and Reading should be given more weight than differences on Arithmetic. As noted in the chapter on the WAIS, many individuals are adversely affected when asked to do mathematical problems. This can create wide swings in scores due to anxiety rather than intellectual factors. This is reflected in the somewhat higher correlations between Reading, Spelling, and the WAIS (about .85) than that between Arithmetic and the WAIS (.75). As might be expected, VIQs offer much better correlations with the WRAT-R scales than do PIQ.

Educational Interpretations

As noted above, the WRAT-R can give the psychologist a rough idea of the individual's standing in terms of school grade level and in comparison with other individuals his or her age. While grade level scores are only approximate, they may be combined with the standard score and IQs to make educational recommendations. Individuals with low grade level scores but greater ability as implied by the IQ are often good candidates for adult education courses leading to a high school degree if the patient does not possess such a degree. Areas where the individual is outstandingly low (compared with ability and in absolute terms) might indicate where remediation is needed. The patient with normal intelligence, for example, who has trouble reading might be helped in vocational placement if such training was offered. These are also individuals for whom a learning disability evaluation is indicated (see Learning Disabilities, below).

In other cases, individuals with low grade level scores and standard scores might not be encouraged to attend college. For example, one patient with an acute anxiety disorder in her first year of college was found to be reading at a substantially low level (seventh grade) despite good grades in a rural school. It was clear that the stress of going to college when she did not have the educational skills had led to her problem. Returning her to school would only have resulted in the return of the problems. The psychological report suggested either remedial training prior to college or the patient's forming goals more consistent with her abilities to avoid future problems.

Learning Disabilities

The diagnosis of learning disabilities is and has been a controversial and unclear area. A person is defined as having a learning disability if he or she is at least two grade levels behind age-expected grade level in a specific area. The individual must have normal intelligence, and the disability cannot be due to poor motivation, poor cultural background, blindness, or loss of hearing.

In adults, the definition requires several facts to be established: (1) The person must have an IQ in the normal range (85 or greater). (2) The person must show a specific deficit in some educational skill below that expected by the person's intelligence. For the skills measured by the WRAT-R, this means a standard score at least 15 points below the individual's IQ. In addition, the grade level achievement of the individual should be at least two grade levels below the person's final grade level in school. (3) The deficit cannot be due to cultural problems, emotional disorders, blindness, loss of hearing, or unwillingness to study in school.

The first point is most easily established by the WAIS. In individuals whose problems are verbal, however, only the performance tests or a test such as Raven's Matrices may be employed to estimate IQ. The second point requires a significantly low score on one or more of the subtests of the WRAT-R or on another standard measure of specific learning areas. The requirement that the standard score be at least 15 points below the IQ ensures that the deficit is not due to intellectual loss alone. For example, an individual of 40 with an IQ of 85 would be expected to earn a grade level of 5.9. Although this is obviously low, it is consistent with the IQ and not a surprising deficit. Such an individual would have to have a grade level of 3.1 before being considered learning disabled. This avoids classifying many performances that are normal for the individual as learning disabilities. Similarly, an individual with an IQ of 126 would possibly have a learning disability at a grade level of 10.7, which is usually a "normal" performance. The grade level requirement is made so that inadequate schooling is not diagnosed as a learning disability. No matter what an individual's IQ, he or she cannot be expected to show educational performance above the actual training that person has received.

The third requirement is inherent in the basic definition of learning disabilities. This criterion needs to be established through an examination for emotional problems (as discussed in later chapters), a thorough history, and appropriate evaluations for sight or hearing if they are suspect. Any emotional disorder must be evaluated carefully to determine if it caused the learning problem or if it was the result of the learning problem and the subsequent stress and frustration engendered by such problems. A good history and interview are the best tools in establishing those relationships. Ancillary tests, such as the Minnesota Multiphasic Personality Inventory, are also useful in establishing such disorders.

It is necessary to evaluate carefully the nature of the disorder for those individuals in whom a learning disability is diagnosed. This can be done by more extensive testing. Neuropsychological testing aimed at identifying specific deficits is often helpful in this regard (see Golden & Anderson, 1978). Referral to an educational specialist is usually appropriate for educational programming or vocational training, when appropriate, unless the clinician is experienced in designing such programs.

It should be emphasized that learning disabilities may play a major role in the development of psychiatric disorders. Such disabilities can lead to extreme frustration and stress, which in turn can lead to failure, acting out behavior, depression, anxiety, and other psychiatric symptoms. Thus, when they are found in individuals with such problems, their possible etiological role must be closely evaluated. As noted above, a careful history from the individual and collateral sources can be useful in making such a connection. In individuals in whom this is found to be the case, psychotherapy is strongly recommended to allow the patient to gain insight into the nature of his or her problem.

Brain Damage

Achievement tests are used by a variety of clinicians interested in the diagnosis of brain damage. The most common role of the achievement tests is as indicators of the patient's past status. In the individual with a normal premorbid status, his or her achievement level should be consistent with the individual's IQ, especially if normal or above normal educational background is present. When an individual receives a brain injury as an adult, the IQ goes down, the degree depending on the severity and the location of the lesion (see the WAIS chapter). Achievement scores remain remarkably stable, however, except in very severe and obvious disorders. Thus, in most brain injuries, there will be a gap between IQ and standard scores on the WRAT-R that can be used to estimate the degree of impairment. Deficits on such tests as the Halstead-Reitan can be used similarly.

Achievement tests may also be used to diagnose specific types of brain injury. For example, some parietal-occipital injuries are characterized by losses in spelling skills, even of relatively simple words (Golden & Anderson, 1978; Luria, 1966).

Losses in the ability to carry in multiplication and subtraction may be associated with right hemisphere injuries when all other mathematical skills are intact. Disorders of reading may be associated with temporal-occipital injuries in the left hemisphere. Using these signs, the WRAT-R can be a useful adjunct to other tests in the assessment of brain dysfunction.

Advantages and Disadvantages

The WRAT-R has a number of advantages as a test of achievement. It can be given quickly, without difficulty. It has been standardized on a large normative population and has been shown to be useful in clinical practice over a number of years. It is generally accepted as a standard measure of achievement by others, both in psychology and in education.

The test also has some significant disadvantages, however: The only measure of reading skills requires intact motor skills and an "American" accent. Individuals with physical disorders that interfere with speech and individuals with foreign accents are not able to take the Reading subtest. The Mathematics subtest measures basic skills, but not whether the person can use them in day-to-day situations. (In this regard, it is often useful to compare this score on the WRAT-R with the Arithmetic score on the WAIS-R.) When these issues are significant, one can consider the Peabody Individual Achievement Test as an alternate test of achievement.

PEABODY INDIVIDUAL ACHIEVEMENT TEST

The Peabody Individual Achievement Test (PIAT) was published in 1970 by Dunn and Markwardt as a wide range screening instrument in the areas of reading, spelling, mathematics, and general information. Unlike the WRAT-R, only two of five subtests require the subject to select from one of four multiple choice responses printed on frames enclosed in two hard-cover, loose-leaf-notebooks. The test shares several advantages with the WRAT-R: it can be administered quickly by nonprofessionals; it offers an easy to use, attractive format; and it is appro-

priate for a wide range of ages and levels of functioning. Norms
are available through age 18.

Administration

The five subtests of the PIAT are given in a nearly identical manner and scored in an identical manner. For each subtest,
the examiner starts at an item representing the highest difficulty that the subject should be able to complete without trouble. In the first subtest (Mathematics), this level is determined
by what the examiner knows of the individual: his or her age,
grade level completed, IQ, and performance on other tests. In
later subtests, this level can be estimated by assuming performance equal to that on the previous subtest.

After the first item is determined, the examiner tests in a
forward direction until the subject misses an item. If five items
have been correctly answered in a row at this point, then the
examiner continues forward. If five consecutive items have not
been answered in a correct manner, the examiner works backward from the initial item until five consecutive items have
been correctly answered. At this point, the examiner returns to
the most advanced item completed so far and continues forward until five of seven consecutive items are missed. At this
point, the subtest is completed and the examiner should move
on to the next subtest.

The subtests are given in the following order: Mathematics, Reading Recognition, Reading Comprehension, Spelling, and General Information. For three of the subtests –
Mathematics, Reading Comprehension, and Spelling – the subject must choose from one of four possible answers presented.
For mathematics, an oral problem is given, as well as presented
graphically or written verbally depending on the question. For
Reading Comprehension, a statement is read by the subject,
who must then match it to a collection of four drawings, one of
which represents the statement the subject has read. For spelling, the subject is given a word (included in a sentence as well)
and must select the correct spelling from among four choices.

The Reading Recognition Test requires subjects to read
words and pronounce them correctly, as in the WRAT-R reading

test. The General Information Test presents questions similar to those in the Information subtest of the WAIS. The subject must answer the questions verbally. The examiner may ask for clarification of answers in this test when the scoring is unclear or when one is directed to do so by the scoring criteria that accompany each item.

The questions may be repeated for all items if the subject asks. Spontaneous corrections by the subject are allowed. The last answer given is the one scored. The examiner, however, should never indicate whether an answer is correct either verbally or nonverbally. All questions, directions, and other material read to the examinee must be read verbatim from the materials provided in the PIAT kit rather than recited from memory. At no time may the examiner embellish or abbreviate the instructions in any manner, even when repeating an item.

Scoring

To score each subtest, one must first determine the basal and ceiling items. The basal sequence is the five highest numbered consecutive items that the subject got correct in the entire protocol. Thus, if the five highest consecutive correct items were items 55 to 59, these would be the basal items. If the subject got items 55 to 59 correct and 65 to 69 correct, then 65 to 69 would be the basal items even if the subject missed one or more of the items between 60 and 64. The ceiling sequence is determined by the lowest set of seven consecutive items in which the subject missed five items. Again, if the subject missed five items in the sequence 43 to 49 and in the sequence 53 to 59, the lower sequence, 43 to 49, is considered the ceiling sequence even if items 50 to 52 are all correct.

The *basal item* is the lowest of the basal item sequence, and the *ceiling item* is the highest item missed in the ceiling item sequence. The *critical range* includes all of the items from and including the basal item up to and including the ceiling item. To obtain the raw score for any subtest, the number of errors made in the critical range is subtracted from the number of the ceiling item.

Once the raw scores are determined, they may be changed

into grade level scores, percentiles, and standard scores, as with the WRAT-R, on the basis of the individual usage. For adults, the highest age level presented, 18 years, is used. In addition, percentile ranks are presented for grade level. These are useful with individuals who did not complete school. The tables help adjust for the lack of schooling to some degree, although not for differences in age between an adult subject and a youngster at a given grade level.

In addition to the individual test scores, the examiner may calculate a total score (sum of the raw scores on all five tests) and its percentile, grade, and standard score equivalents.

Interpretation

For the adult subject, a difference of more than 15 raw score points between any two subtests is likely to indicate a significant advantage or disadvantage for a given subject. This is useful in categorizing the subject's strengths and weaknesses. Of particular interest are findings that indicate a significant difference between the Reading Recognition and Reading Comprehension subtests. A difference in favor of Recognition suggests an individual whose reading is primarily by rote, and who has difficulty understanding things he or she might be expected to understand. A difference in favor of Comprehension suggests either someone with a motor speech impairment, someone from a foreign background, or someone who has learned primarily by reading rather than by speaking and interacting with others. The latter explanation is useful to explore with high-IQ psychiatric or other patients who may tend to isolate themselves and use books as an escape.

Differences in favor of General Information over the other tests may suggest an individual whose learning has primarily been outside a formal school setting. As with the WAIS Information, this subtest can give a good estimate of intellectual skills.

Other interpretations made with the PIAT alone are generally equivalent to those outlined for the WRAT. For the PIAT Reading Recognition and WRAT Reading, correlations on the order of .9 or better have been reported, as have similar correlations for PIAT and WRAT Spelling. PIAT Reading Comprehension correlates highly with WRAT Reading (.9), as does PIAT Reading Recognition (on the order of .7). The relationship between PIAT and WRAT Arithmetic is questionable, however. A review by Kieffer and Golden (1978) found that the two tests correlate about .5, a substantially low correlation for two tests purporting to measure the same thing. There is no equivalent in the WRAT for General Information.

The difference between the WRAT and PIAT mathematics tests is important to examine. Kieffer and Golden (1978) suggested that this difference may be due to the emphasis in the PIAT on daily problem solving skills rather than the emphasis on pure math in the WRAT. In this case, it would appear that the PIAT is more useful as a measure of an individual's ability to use math in a day-to-day situation than in planning possible placement in a school situation. The WRAT, on the other hand, would probably predict school placement well but not the ability of the child to use the knowledge. Thus, a difference in scores between these two subscales could have significant meaning depending on the referral questions and goals for the patient.

The user of the PIAT should pay particular attention to the Spelling Test as well. As the PIAT requires spelling recognition rather than spelling ability, there will be children for whom the spelling score on the PIAT would be substantially higher than the WRAT-R score, although in general these two skills correlate highly. In cases where some of the WRAT-R/PIAT differences are suspected, it is sometimes useful to administer both tests to the same child.

Advantages and Disadvantages

The primary advantage of the PIAT lies in its applicability to a handicapped population. The Reading Comprehension subtest, in particular, offers an excellent measure of reading skills in the speech impaired individual. This ability is particularly important because of the significance of reading skills in many jobs and educational placements. This advantage also extends to the Mathematics and Spelling subtests, but is less important since additional time may be given on those tests to correct for motor impairment. The advantage is quite important, however, in individuals with significant paralysis or any other disabling motor or sensory condition affecting the dominant hand. In addition, norms are provided for grade level as well as age.

There are several disadvantages with the PIAT as well. First, the test provides norms only through age 18 and the 12th grade. This is a handicap with adults, especially those with a college education. In these individuals, the WRAT-R is usually the test of choice. A second disadvantage is the interpretation problems with the Mathematics subtest in situations where one wishes to make an educational placement rather than evaluate the individual's ability to function in common situations. Finally, the General Information Test is redundant with the WAIS Information test. As a result, many clinicians do not administer it.

CASE EXAMPLES

Case 1. LC, a 36-year-old man, was evaluated after a significant industrial accident which resulted in a gross motor disability. He had worked as a lugger in a meat packing plant, a job that required considerable physical strength but little education as he had dropped out of school in the eighth grade. Testing indicated an IQ of 115 and achievement scores of 100, 103, and 95 on the Reading, Arithmetic, and Spelling subtests of the WRAT-R, unusually high scores given the individual's poor schooling. It was felt that the individual had considerably greater talent at school-type work than was indicated by his past schooling. Since the patient could no longer work at his former job, it was suggested he get his General Education Degree (which was no problem given his WRAT-R scores) and go into some area of interest to him at college or a technical job training school. The patient eventually secured a degree in electronics and was employed in a situation where his disability made little difference.

Case 2.   LD, a 16-year-old female, came from a family that placed a great emphasis on education. As an adopted only child she was constantly pushed to do well in school by her mother, a college teacher, and her father, a lawyer. She was referred for evaluation because of a suspected learning disability and an increasingly difficult behavior problem at school. Initial testing revealed a 100 IQ and achievement test scores that were all normal (98 to 106). From the achievement and IQ testing, no evidence of a learning disability was found. Indeed, her performance was quite normal for her age. A further evaluation revealed that the parents considered normal progress a failure. The parents' continuing harassment (not letting her date, go to movies, or do other things she liked because of her poor school record) and pressure were leading to the behavioral problems. Family therapy was recommended to correct this problem before it got more serious.

Case 3.   HJ, a 20-year-old male, was referred because of an acute psychotic breakdown which occurred in his third year of college. The patient earned an IQ of 135 and standard scores above 130 on all the subtests of the WRAT-R. After resolutions of the acute symptoms, the patient was unsure whether he could do the academic work at college. It was suggested that his problem was not academic, but rather an inability to relate to other people (based on MMPI results). It was suggested that he return to school and continue medical and psychotherapeutic intervention on an outpatient basis. The patient was able to finish school without difficulty under this regimen.

Case 4.   AS, a 21-year-old male, was a sophomore in college who was flunking all of his classes after having a basically good record. While he had an IQ of 120, his reading recognition score on the PIAT was equivalent to a standard score of 115, while the Reading Comprehension score was 85. This suggested a severe problem in Reading Comprehension. Further testing and investigation indicated a significant problem in understanding written material. The patient was studying by reading books four or five times, rarely leaving his room except for meals as this was the only way to keep up. The testing revealed, however, fully normal skills when the material was presented auditorily. The current problem was apparently caused by an increase in required reading material and the patient's inability to continue to withstand the stress he was under. We arranged to have written material presented orally to the patient, as well as for oral administration of tests. The patient's grades increased from a near F average to Bs and As within the course of two months.

CHAPTER FOUR

Minnesota Multiphasic Personality Inventory

$\mathbf{B}$eginning in the 1930s, McKinley and Hathaway began to assemble a large pool of objective personality items for the purpose of creating a diagnostic instrument that would aid in the classification of psychiatric patients. From a final pool of about 1,000 items, a set of 504 items were selected that were considered reasonably independent of one another. These items were given to normals and to patients with various psychiatric diagnoses. The purpose at that time was to create a scale that would represent each diagnostic group tested: hypochondriacs, depressives, psychopathic deviates, hysterics, paranoids, obsessive-compulsives, schizophrenics, and manics. It was hoped that an individual with a specific diagnosis would get a high score on the appropriate scale, thus yielding a quick diagnosis.

Unfortunately, the scales did not work as expected. Individuals with given diagnoses showed high scores on several different scales, making the task of diagnosis much more difficult. Furthermore, it became recognized that the group labeled schizophrenic was not a homogeneous group, but was rather highly heterogeneous. Thus, the labels attached to the scales did not mean what they appeared to mean: a high score on psychopathic deviate, for example, does not mean that one is a psychopathic deviate.

Despite this failure, the Minnesota Multiphasic Personality Inventory (MMPI) has become the most used objective test of personality and, in recent years, probably the most used personality test, surpassing even the traditional leader, the Rorschach Inkblot Method. It has proven itself to be highly adaptable to different environments, psychiatric systems of nomenclature, and theories of personality. It has become the premiere screening instrument used in psychiatric, medical, and community mental health facilities.

More recently, an updated version of the MMPI, the MMPI-R, was released by the authors. This new version updates some of the questions, eliminates outdated or inappropriate questions, and updates the norms. Although there has been little general use of the revised version at this point, the preliminary data suggest that the interpretive strategies used with the original version are appropriate for the new version. However, it will be several years before we see the degree of complete clinical acceptance of this new version and any ways in which we will have to seriously modify interpretational approaches.

PURPOSE

The original purpose of the MMPI, as noted above, was to help establish psychiatric diagnosis at a time when there was a belief that the psychiatric nomenclature was as useful as the medical diagnostic nomenclature that has proven so useful in the treatment of physical disease. This was done by devising scales empirically found to be related to a given disorder, whether or not the item possessed face validity. It has been found that scores on the individual scales are associated with a number of traits and behaviors. The analysis of these traits has become a major thrust of MMPI research. Rather than pointing at a definitive diagnosis, the MMPI allows the psychologist to form a picture of an individual's behaviors, traits, underlying dynamics, level of adjustment, contact with reality, attitude toward the world, and characteristic beliefs. From this picture of the individual, such material as diagnosis, prognosis, likely future behavior, and other information may be determined on the basis of personality theory, clinical experience and research, and research relating to diagnostic categories. The MMPI can be used to suggest modes of treatment appropriate to an individual, whether that treatment is medical (primarily drug therapy), psychological, or social. Finally, the MMPI provides an objective measure of individuals or groups of individuals which may be used to measure behavioral change in therapy or because of environmental conditions. The MMPI is useful in both clinical work and research.

ADMINISTRATION AND SCORING

Unlike many of the personality instruments of its time and subsequently, the items in the MMPI were not determined on the basis of any single theory, but were intended to comprehensively review all symptoms and attitudes that might be of interest in psychiatric disorders. Consequently, the MMPI includes questions involving a wide range of items, many of which do not have any clear relationship to specific psychological disorders.

The scales in the MMPI were derived empirically as well. Rather than assign items to a particular scale because they belonged there, the authors administered the test to selected psychiatric groups. The items on each scale consisted of those items that differentiated the clinical group from normal control groups. Thus, while some of the items may make sense, a good number of the items do not, except in the sense that they did manage to differentiate the clinical group. As a result of this, each scale consists of items that are highly face valid (obvious items), while also consisting of items that are not face valid (subtle items).

In addition to the original 8 clinical scales, 4 validity scales were also developed which allowed for the clinician to investigate individuals who might be lying, faking bad, or faking good, or those who do not have the reading ability necessary to take the test. To these original 12 scales, 2 additional scales were later added, Masculinity-Femininity and Social Introversion, both of which became part of the regular MMPI. Beyond these scales, hundreds of additional scales can be scored and used for a wide variety of purposes.

Administration

The MMPI can be administered either as a group or as an individual instrument by any normally intelligent person with a minimum of training. Unlike most of the other instruments discussed in this book, the test need not be given by a psychologist. In actual practice, the test is given by clerks, psychological technicians, nurses, and others so as to minimize the time spent on the test by the Ph.D. In addition, scoring may be done by a minimally trained assistant or clerk.

There are four basic forms of the MMPI. Two are intended for individuals with serious disorders who are unable to take the test normally, while two others represent the forms most often used. Other forms of the test exist, but all are put together on the same basis of one of these versions.

The boxed version of the MMPI consists of 550 MMPI items on individual cards. These items are placed by the subject behind dividers labeled True, False, and Cannot Say. Most administrators emphasize that the Cannot Say category should not be used in general, and that the patient should answer simply whether True or False is most accurate. This emphasis is important as too many Cannot Say items make the test unscorable. It is often useful in this version to have the individual reconsider Cannot Say items after the test is completed. This form of the test should be used only for individuals who simply cannot fill out a normal answer sheet under any conditions, but still are lucid enough to answer the questions. The test is scored by transferring the patient's answers to an answer sheet and then using appropriate scoring overlays. As might be expected, this form is highly time-consuming for the scorer.

The second special form of the MMPI is a tape-recorded version of the test. The subject listens to the questions and then puts his or her answers on an answer sheet between hearing the questions. Alternatively, the examiner may have the subject tell him or her the answer and the examiner may mark it down. This form is for subjects who are generally alert and able to respond in a reasonable time but who are illiterate or semiliterate. (Generally, a sixth-grade reading comprehension level is considered necessary to take the MMPI.) For subjects who are not alert and do not respond in a reasonable amount of time, it is often necessary to stop the tape. For such subjects, it is sometimes more efficient for the examiner to read the test to the subjects in order to allow for variable response times. We have found this technique useful with highly labile patients who are unable to concentrate for more than a few items at a time. Answers to items are recorded on the appropriate test form and scored as described below.

The most common form of the MMPI is the group booklet form. Two alternate forms exist: one printed in a soft paper booklet and a second printed within a hardbound cover. The paper form consists of 566 items, 16 of which are repeated for scoring purposes. The most common answer sheet for this form is two sided (with questions 1 to 300 on side one) and designed to be scored by an IBM-805 scoring machine. The test may also be scored by hand-scoring templates. Several scales have two templates, however, one for the front side and one for the back side, making scoring difficult. In addition, this form of the test requires that the individual have a normal sized desk to work on.

The alternate form (form R) has hard covers enclosing the pages and is spiral bound. The covers may be opened and used as a desk; this enables one to test subjects who have no desk, such as patients in hospital beds. The answer sheet to form R fits over pegs on the cover that hold the sheet in place so that items and the proper answer column are lined up. Thus, the subject need not match items to item numbers (which are not included on the answer sheet). Another advantage of this form is its easy transformation into a short form; to score all the standard scales, one need only administer the first 399 items. In the paper booklet form, a short form of the test includes the first 360 items plus items 371, 374, 377, 383, 391, 397, 398, 400, 406, 411, 415, 427, 436, 440, 446, 449, 450, 451, 455, 461, 462, 469, 473, 479, 481, 482, 487, 502, 515, 521, 547, 459, and 564. Administering such a hodgepodge of questions is awkward at best.

The advantage of a short form capability lies in the time reduction necessary to do the test. In a psychiatric population, the test as a whole will take anywhere from $1\frac{1}{4}$ hours to $3\frac{1}{2}$

hours, while the short form may be completed in 45 minutes to 2¹/₂ hours. The short form can be administered, as a rule, within one or two sessions, while the longer form may take three or even four sessions. Thus, the short form can generate data considerably faster, an important consideration if results are desired quickly and there are limitations on the subject's time (as in an acute care medical or psychiatric facility). The disadvantage of the short form is the inability to score some of the experimental or additional scales if they are desired.

Form R is scored by templates placed over the answer sheet when the scoring is done by hand. The form may also be scored by the National Computer Systems in Minneapolis, Minnesota.

SCORING

Raw scores for the scales are determined by templates placed over the appropriate answer sheet or by computer. (Computer programs will also, as a rule, do all the additional steps to be described below.) Raw scores for several of the scales are corrected according to the size of the K score, one of the validity scales to be described below. This is done for scales measuring Hypochondriasis, Psychopathic Deviate, Psychasthenia, Schizophrenia, and Mania. The amount of K correction added to each scale was determined empirically for each group by investigating what K, if any, could be added to maximize the discrimination of clinical and control groups. The K correction formula and tables are listed on each MMPI profile form.

After the proper K corrections have been determined, the raw scores for each scale are plotted on the MMPI profile sheet. The scales are plotted in the order listed in Table 4-1. Table 4-1 also lists the name of each scale, the abbreviation for each scale, and the appropriate scale number used in MMPI profile coding.

Profile Coding

After the profile has been plotted on the MMPI sheet, the profile may be coded. The coding offers a shorthand which can

TABLE 4-1 MMPI Scale Names, Numbers, and Abbreviations

Scale	Number	Abbreviation
Lie		L
Validity		F
Correction (Bias)		K
Hypochondriasis	1	Hs
Depression	2	D
Hysteria	3	Hy
Psychopathic Deviate	4	Pd
Masculinity-Femininity	5	Mf
Paranoia	6	Pa
Psychasthenia	7	Pt
Schizophrenia	8	Sc
Mania	9	Ma
Social Introversion	0	Si

be used to describe the profile to others in an efficient manner. These profile codes are useful to know since most MMPI books and much research use these codes to describe individual as well as group research. The major system used at present (Welsh, 1948) is described here.

First, the scales are listed in order by the size of the T score on the profile sheet. Only the clinical scales (those with numbers in Table 4-1) are listed in this manner. The scales are listed by their numbers. So, for example, we might have a subject with the T scores suggested in Table 4-2. In order, we would list these scales:

    8 6 7 5 4 9 0 3 2 1

Then the symbols listed in Table 4-3 are placed after the last scale score which is equal to or greater than the number associated with each symbol in Table 4-3. For example, the symbol ′ follows the last scale score, which is equal to or greater than 70 (in this case, Scale 7). No symbol is placed after a scale with a T score less than 29, or to the left of the highest score, or to the right of the lowest score. If there is no scale between scores 80

TABLE 4-2   Scores for Sample Case

Scale	T Score
L	40
F	55
K	59
1	29
2	39
3	40
4	60
5	69
6	87
7	83
8	103
9	59
0	54

TABLE 4-3   Symbols for MMPI Profile Codes

Symbol	Scores equal to or greater than
*	90
"	80
'	70
—	60
/	50
:	40
#	30

and 70, for example, the symbol for 80 (") is simply followed by the symbol for 70 ('). Thus, for our patient:

8*67" '54 − 90/3:2#1

Underlining is used to connect all scales within one T score point of each other. After the list for the clinical scales, the validity scales are listed by their symbols (F, L, K, ?) in the order from the highest T score to the lowest. For our subject:

K F/L:?

These are put together to yield:

8*67″′ 54−90/3:2#1 K F/L:?

The reader will find that practice with these symbols will soon lead to quick coding skills.

CLINICAL INTERPRETATION

In examining each of the MMPI scales, the clinician generates hypotheses about his or her subject. These hypotheses are suggested on the basis of the research and clinical experience with the MMPI. After completing the analysis of all the scales and scale configurations, some of the hypotheses stand out because of their repetition in several places. In general, these form the major inferences that the MMPI can generate about the patient. Secondary hypotheses, consistent with these inferences, can then be drawn from the remaining hypotheses, whereas hypotheses inconsistent with the picture are either discarded or used to modify the overall impression of the patient. In turn, the picture generated can be integrated with knowledge about the patient's life, demographic characteristics, referral problems, and so on. In addition to this, the clinician may add inferences on the basis of personality theory and current knowledge about the development of specific psychological disorders. An extensive picture of the individual may be generated in this way and used to answer referral questions and make suggestions for treatment or prognosis.

In general, this process begins with the validity scales. These enable the clinician to determine whether a profile is valid or questionable, as well as to determine the test taking attitude and approach of the patient. The validity scales may also suggest some of the major psychodynamics of the patient, such as the presence of strong repressive or denying tendencies. The information from the validity scales gives one a general outlook on how to view the patient's profile. For example, if the validity scales suggest that the individual avoids saying negative things about himself or herself, then clinical scales suggesting severe psychopathology must be taken quite seriously, as such an individual may not be able to recognize that his or her responses are bizarre. Similarly, if one has the impression that the individual tends to exaggerate, a higher profile might be considered in a less severe light.

After the validity scales have been examined, the clinical scales are considered. Each of these is interpreted in order to generate additional hypotheses about the individual. Then the patient's high point pattern (those scales higher than all other scales) is investigated. This pattern is generally given a heavy emphasis because it represents the individual's predominant characteristics. The inferences from the other scales are used to modify this high point impression, or to enable the clinician to select among the possible high point interpretations. In some cases, several high point patterns may be present that must be integrated together. In this way, a picture of the MMPI possibilities is drawn, which can be integrated with the demographic, personal, and interview data.

One major aspect of this process must be kept in mind by the novice interpreter. The most common error in MMPI interpretations is for the clinician to hold to one single interpretation for a given scale or configuration. In actual practice, this is never the case. All profile scores and configurations have more than one interpretation. Thus, one must be alert to the evidence generated by all the scales, not only a single high score or high point pair. For example, while one high point pair may suggest paranoid schizophrenia, if this is combined with scores indicating good contact with reality, the enjoyment and seeking out of other persons, and a generally positive affective state, one must look for alternate explanations rather than holding to the standard interpretation. This flexibility is essential if the clinician is to gain a maximum amount of information from the MMPI.

As the reader can see, the interpretation of the MMPI is

not simply an automated process of looking up "the" interpretation of a profile. It is an important clinical task that requires insight, a good knowledge of psychopathology, a grounding in personality theory, and the intelligence to integrate these factors with the possible interpretations of the MMPI scales and configurations, and to then integrate these observations with knowledge about the patient gained from history, behavior, interviews, and the like. As a result, this is not a process that can be done by a computer. The computer is limited to standard interpretations and is neither capable of the integration necessary nor capable of combining the results with the person's individual characteristics, behavior, or history. The computer cannot recognize unique situations, nor can it adjust for differences across populations, a major factor that any clinician who has worked in such diverse settings as VA hospitals, general medical hospitals, mental health centers, and psychiatric hospitals can recognize. Consequently, despite the proliferation of computer programs and their use, the computer is no substitute for clinical judgment and interpretation of the profile.

THE VALIDITY SCALES

The MMPI has four scales used to measure the validity of the profile: ? (Cannot Say), L (Lie Scale), F (Unusual item endorsement), and K (Test Taking Attitude and Correction Factor). In addition to their role as validity scales, these scales also offer information about the patient's personality.

Cannot Say (?) Scale

This scale involves a counting of all unanswered questions or questions answered both True and False. Many clinicians emphasize to their patients that all questions should be answered either True or False, depending on which is most accurate. In this way, most Cannot Say responses can be eliminated. It is also useful to scan a subject's answer sheet after the test is completed and to have the subject go over the questions again to eliminate Cannot Say responses. All but a few can usually be removed. A profile is considered invalid if there are more than 30 Cannot Say answers. Our own experience, however, has shown that with the above techniques, few subjects should get more than 5 Cannot Say responses, making this scale relatively meaningless. In practice, we will often omit even reporting the scale, except in cases where the score is unusually high.

L (Lie) Scale

The L scale consists of 15 items to which a True answer would involve admitting a minor, but generally universal, fault. For example, one might have to admit that he or she does not read every editorial in the paper every day. Individuals trying to look especially good will often answer False to these items, causing the L scale score to rise. A high L scale score indicates that the person has not been wholly truthful in reporting symptoms and suggests a relative invalidity. In all cases, however, one must still look at the clinical profile. High L scale scores may accompany profiles that are diagnostically significant. The person may admit to some bizarre ideas and ways of adjusting, often because the person is not in touch enough with reality to recognize the items as bizarre. This, of course, has direct clinical relevance in understanding the individual.

High L scores may also indicate individuals who either are highly moralistic or wish to appear that way. In valid profiles, such individuals tend to be conforming, uncreative, repressed (especially if there are high K and H scores) unaware of others, confused, generally without guilt, and delusional (in psychiatric populations), and tend to have strong beliefs of their own grandiosity. Such individuals may also be ministers, social reformers, perfectionists, and otherwise unusual individuals who do live the life they describe. In general, L scores greater than a T score of 60 can be considered elevated; scores above 70 are both rare and highly significant.

Low L scores (especially of one or zero raw score) may indicate individuals who are trying to present a negative picture, especially if associated with low K and high F scores. They may also be seen in unconventional normal people and in highly educated individuals trying to be "believable." Low L scores may also be associated with honesty, self-confidence, independence, and willingness to admit minor faults.

F Scale

The F scale consists of 64 items that were answered in the scored direction of this scale 10 percent of the time or less. Thus, endorsement of items on the F scale in the scorable direction involves the endorsement of bizarre and unusual items, including a significant number that are shared with the Schizophrenia and Paranoia scales. The F scale was designed to detect unusual or bizarre responding. A wide variety of individuals get high F scores, ranging from the individual who answers randomly or answers everything True to the individual who is highly psychotic or otherwise disturbed.

In interpreting F scale scores, scores greater than a T score of 100 must be examined carefully as they may indicate an invalid profile. This may be due to an inability to read or understand the questions, random responding, or deliberate attempts to "fake bad." The attempts to fake bad generally involve individuals who have something to gain from a poor impression, such as the individual involved in a court case, the disability applicant, the person attempting to prove an insanity plea, or the patient who wants to use the hospital as a way to protect himself or herself from life. If the above possibilities are not true, the alternate interpretation suggests an extremely psychotic individual with strong paranoid delusions, hallucinations, speech disorders, and extreme social withdrawal, which may or may not be associated with organicity.

F scores above 80 may indicate an individual who is answering all questions False, is malingering, is careless, is asking for help, or is clearly psychotic. This range, especially from 80 to 90, may frequently be seen during acute schizophrenic episodes or acute exacerbation of a chronic psychosis. It is rarely seen in individuals who do not upon interview appear to be grossly psychotic unless the profile is faked. For individuals clearly in trouble but not extremely psychotic, the F score may suggest a person who is desperate for help. (This should usually be accompanied by a high score on scale 7 as well.)

Scores between 70 and 80 are commonly seen in valid profiles from individuals with psychosis or those who are diagnosed as borderline psychotics, especially if accompanied by scores greater than 70 on Schizophrenia or Paranoia. These may also represent individuals who are very deviant in terms of political or religious attitudes or who are seen as opinionated, complex, restless, opportunistic, or affected. Antiauthoritarian attitudes may be strong, as may be obsessive-compulsive behavior. These individuals may be very concrete and have suffered a serious brain injury affecting verbal responding. They may also be hostile, suspicious, and inappropriate. Signs of depersonalization can also be present.

Scores below 70 are rarely diagnosed as psychotic but may be diagnosed as borderline. Individuals with recent acute psychotic disturbances that are in remission may also get scores between 60 and 70. In a psychiatric setting, the F score in this stage may indicate restlessness and agitation due to a recent acute situational disorder in a neurotic individual, or an extremely serious trauma (such as rape or the murder or death of a close relative) in a normal individual.

Scores between 50 and 70 may occasionally be associated with relatively intact paranoid psychosis or paranoid schizophrenia. These individuals typically show no serious thought disorder but have delusions that are characteristically reasonable and logical within themselves. These delusions often are based on a single false assumption and built up from there into a perfectly reasonable delusional system that is difficult to break or place in doubt.

A low F score, below a T score of 60, generally indicates a normal individual who functions well in most or all aspects of his or her life. The person may be socially conforming, fully normal, or attempting to show a fake good profile (especially when the raw score is two or less and the K score is above or near 70). Normals with low F scores may be described as unassuming, sincere, honest, and calm. Such individuals are rarely social agitators and are usually happy or relaxed with their current life situation. The low F score in a person known to have serious problems but who is not faking may indicate an individual unable to confront the problems in his or her life.

K Scale

The final validity scale is the K scale, which was added to the MMPI in an attempt to detect more subtle instances of test bias than is measured by F or L. The K scale was also an attempt to provide a means of statistically correcting the clinical scales for these biasing tendencies. To determine the items on this scale, the profiles of psychiatric patients who look normal and normal patients who show psychiatric profiles were examined. The resulting K scale was intended to measure both biases against truthful answering (high K scores) and biases toward overly negative reporting (low K scores).

In general, high K scores are not associated with specific behaviors, but rather with a reluctance to admit symptoms. The high K responder may be trying to fake a good profile or may have responded False to all MMPI items (see Fig. 4-1 and Fig. 4-2). Alternately, the high K responder may be shy, lack insight or awareness of problems, be hysterical, or be very perfectionistic and conventional. High K scores in an obviously psychiatric profile may be strongly associated with an individual's lack of awareness that his or her behavior is different from the behavior of others.

Normal (average) K scores may suggest a generally normal balance and contact with reality if the remainder of the profile is consistent with such an interpretation. Overall, such Individuals are characterized by a number of positive terms, including independent, self-reliant, resourceful, versatile, clear thinking, and socially involved. When the remainder of the profile is not consistent with such an interpretation, however, these terms are likely to be misleading. For example, normal K scores are frequently found in acute psychiatric populations, in which case the score simply suggests no overt biasing in the answers to the MMPI.

Low K scores may be associated with faking bad profiles, suicidal ideation, homosexual concerns, and a generally negative orientation to the person's situation in life. The individual

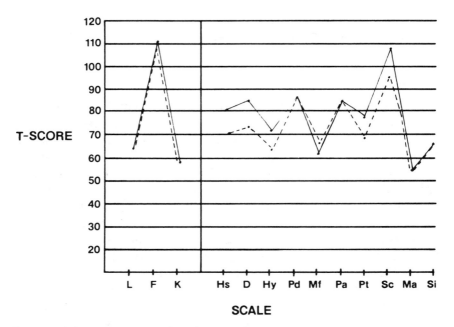

Figure 4-1. An example of a random profile. The heavy line is the plot for males, the dotted line for females.

may be asking for help, either consciously or unconsciously. The patient may have little insight and be in a state of distress and suspicious of others. Low scorers are harsh in social interactions and may come across as cynical, awkward, and shallow.

K scale scores may be associated with education and age. Individuals who are young may take a more positive outlook toward life, minimizing or failing to recognize problems. Similarly, highly educated individuals may see problems as minor and unimportant. As a result, both of these groups may often produce exaggerated K scores, especially in the young, highly educated combination.

Determining Profile Invalidity

There is no clear difference between profiles that are invalid and those that indicate a number of important psychiatric conditions. As a result, the determination of profile

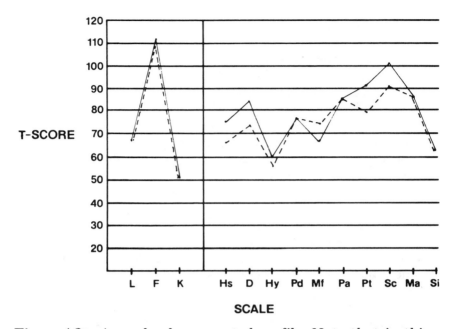

Figure 4-2. A randomly generated profile. Note that in this figure and Figure 4-1 all validity scales are elevated above 50 as are all the clinical scales.

invalidity can be difficult. The traditional method involves invalidating any profile with an F, K, or L score greater than a T score of 70 or any profile with more than 30 Cannot Say responses. Although it is true that sticking to these rules eliminates almost all invalid profiles, a large number of valid profiles also are eliminated. For example, F scores above 70 may indicate serious psychotic disorders, K scores above 70 may indicate a high level of defensiveness, and L scores above 70 may be associated with moralistic, rigid individuals.

An additional method of determining invalidity was suggested by Gough (1950), who suggested taking the difference between the raw F and raw K scores (F−K). Gough indicated that a score greater than 9 would mean that the individual was faking bad, and a score less than −9, on the other hand, would indicate a faking good profile. Carson (1969) suggested that the cutoffs should be at 11 rather than 9, whereas others have suggested alternate cutoffs for different populations. Unfortunately, the problems with this score are much the same as the problems with the basic validity scales. Any rigid cutoff generally excludes a number of valid cases as well. High $F-K$'s may merely reflect individuals who are psychotic and severely disturbed, while low $F-K$'s (negative) may reflect highly defensive, rigid individuals. Thus, while one can look at $F-K$ much as one looks at the other validity scales, this still does not solve the problem of determining invalidity without losing valid results.

The first step in determining invalidity is for the clinician to be aware of and recognize typical response patterns associated with invalid profiles. Figures 4-1 to 4-8 present a wide variety of responses associated with random responding, all true responding, all false responding, faking good, and faking bad. As the reader can see, random response patterns generally create F scores above 100 and K and L scores above 50. These can be easily distinguished from a highly psychotic profile which would (generally) have lower scores on all three scales. The presence of a random profile can also be determined by observing the patient. If the profile is valid, the patient should be overtly and severely psychotic. Random profiles are also associated with patients who take the test in a quick and careless manner.

In determining the reason for a random profile, the clinician should interview the patient and confront him or her with the results if that is possible, or request the patient to tell how he or she took the test. Random profiles may result from a lack of reading skills, which can be determined from a reading comprehension test (chapter 3). Patterning may be seen in the answer sheet of the random responder. All true or all false profiles often may be generated, or the answers may be in a pattern, such as two true, then two false, and so on. These patterns may often be detected by looking at the answer sheet.

Faking bad responses are similar to those seen in extremely severe psychotic disorders: F greater than 100, L and K less than 50. Typically, Scales 6, 7, and 8 are highest. Since this is such a severely psychotic profile, it is often easy to compare the patient's behavior to the psychotic, deteriorated behavior that would be expected. Faking good profiles are characterized by high Ks and Ls (greater than 70) and most

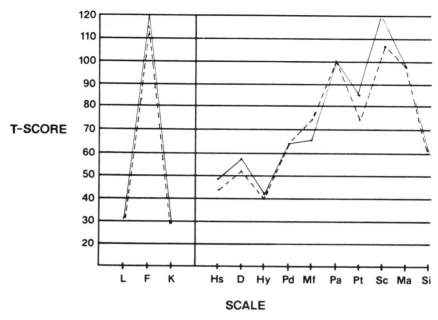

Figure 4-3. Profile generated by all true answers. Solid line is male profile. Dotted line is female profile.

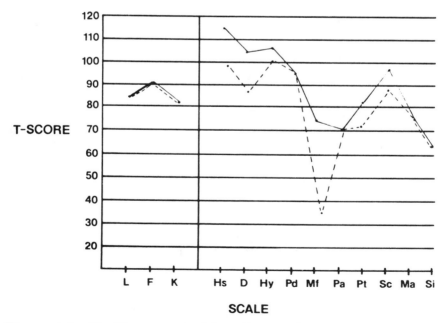

Figure 4-4. Profile generated by all false answers. Solid line represents male profile while dotted line is female profile.

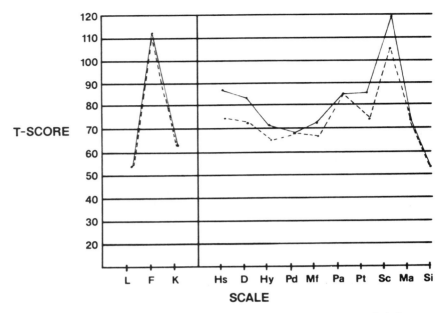

Figure 4-5. Profile generated by alternating true and false answers. Solid line is male profile, and dotted line is female profile.

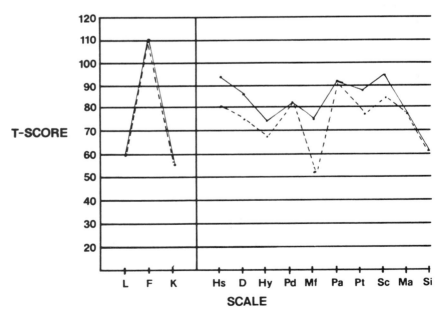

Figure 4-6. Profile generated by pattern of TTFF answers. Dotted line is female profile, and solid line is male profile.

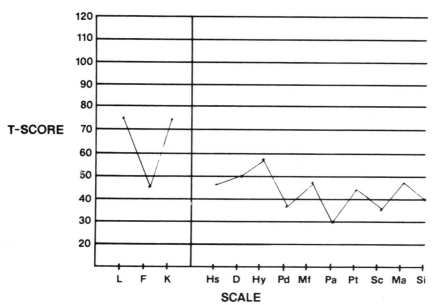

Figure 4-7. Example of one possible faking good profile. Note the high L and K scores along with the low F score. The general low scores on all the clinical scales (except Hysteria) are also common to these profiles.

clinical scales below 50. F scores will also be below 50, often with raw scores of two or less. In diagnosing both faking good and faking bad responses, the clinician should investigate to determine the motivation for such a response. In our practice, we have found it useful to discuss this with the patient and point out the advantages of taking the test honestly. While this does not always get the patient's cooperation, it has been successful in a significant number of cases.

Among the most difficult faking responses to detect is the malingering profile. Such individuals do not try to show themselves as being patently bad, as do those individuals who overtly fake bad profiles. There still is, however, an elevated F score (above 70 or 80), along with clinical peaks on Scales 2, 4, 6, and 8 that give the profile a saw-toothed appearance. Since this is also a profile that suggests severe maladjustment, as well as the presence of psychosis, the matching of the patient's

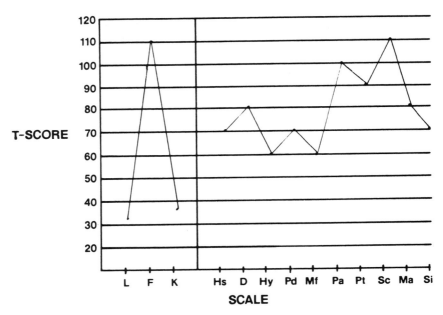

Figure 4-8. Overt faking bad profile. Note the high F and very low K and L scores with the typical high points on the Schizophrenia (Sc) and Paranoia (Pa) scales.

behavior against the profile and discussions with the patient can be useful in diagnosing this pattern (see Figure 4-9).

THE CLINICAL SCALES

There are 10 basic clinical scales to the MMPI, although some clinicians exclude the Masculinity-Femininity and Social Introversion scales. In evaluating the importance of each scale, several factors must be kept in mind. First, when high scores on a scale are discussed, the meaning is relative to the profile. Thus, a score that is both high (greater than 70) and high relative to all the other scales should be taken as much more significant than a high score that is only the fifth or sixth highest in the profile. Similarly, a score in the 60s might assume greater im-

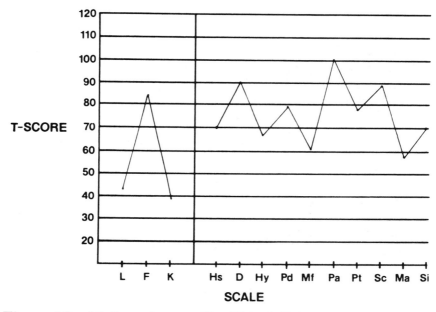

Figure 4-9. Malingering profile. This differs from the faking bad profile in its generally lower scores and the sawtoothed peaks on Scales 2, 4, 6, and 8.

portance if it is the highest score of the profile, especially in an individual with a high K score. One must also be aware of the importance of the lowest score or scores in the profile, no matter what the actual elevation may be.

A second important factor is to recognize that several scales have a significant number of items that are repeated on a second scale. Thus, two scales such as Hypochondriasis and Hysteria tend to move up or down together. The degree to which one is high and the other low often suggests specific interpretations important to the scale and pattern analysis.

Finally, the role of the validity scales must be considered. Interpretations should be adjusted according to whether a person minimizes problems, exaggerates them, or tends to be open and reasonable about the responses.

The material for the descriptions of the clinical and validity scales came from a number of major sources, including Boerger, Graham, and Lilly (1974); Dahlstrom, Welsh, and Dahlstrom (1972, 1975); Drake and Oetting (1959); Gilberstadt and Duker (1965); Golden, Sweet, and Osmon (1979); Good and Brantner (1974); J. R. Graham (1977); Hathaway and Meehl (1951); Hedlund (1977); Marks and Seeman (1963); Osmon and Golden (1978); and Welsh and Dahlstrom (1956); as well as from my own clinical experience.

Scale 1 (Hs)

The Hypochondriasis scale serves as a measure of an individual's concern about somatic functions. High Hs scores are associated with abnormal concerns over bodily functions and vague hypochondriacal complaints. Complaints by high scorers may include diarrhea, loss of appetite, insomnia, and general fatigue and depression. High scorers may be passive and tend to withdraw from others. Patients with true medical complaints may also tend to score higher on Hs, but scores over 65 in younger individuals and over 70 in older individuals almost always suggest a strong psychological component. In many people with high Hs scores, there are at least some real physical symptoms, ranging from the symptoms we all feel from day to day to more serious disorders, such as ruptured disks or diabetes, which are exaggerated by the patient's psychological status. This is important to emphasize as all the complaints of the high Hs patients cannot be dismissed as psychosomatic.

High Hs scorers are also likely to report general listlessness, psychomotor retardation, depression (often with a high score on the Depression scale as well), anxiety, irritability, lack of self-confidence, ambivalence, and lack of aggression with hostile feelings usually turned inward, and they often appear very defensive and unable to deal with negative emotions on any level. A high Hs score accompanied by a significantly lower Depression score suggests that only the general complaining and overconcern are present without the symptoms related to depression.

Low Hs scores are common in young people and individuals who are free of somatic complaints and generally positive and optimistic about life. Such individuals may be described as sensitive, alert, cheerful, and sociable. Overall, this suggests that low Hs scorers tend to be free from most neurotic patterns and able to interact with others in an efficient and pleasant manner.

Scale 2 (D)

The Depression scale is associated with depressed mood, poor self-concept, suicidal thoughts, psychomotor retardation, mild anxiety, and agitation. Somatic symptoms, loss of sleep, and loss of appetite are common in high scorers, especially if there are elevations on the Hypochondriasis and Psychasthenia scales. Scale D is also correlated with feelings of helplessness, poor morale, dejection, distress, apathy, and a denial of positive feelings. Scale D scores are quite variable, depending on an individual's mood when the test is taken.

Individuals with high Depression scores may report an inability to feel positive emotions. They are generally very pessimistic about themselves and others, and express guilt over past behavior or thoughts. They may show symptoms of obsessive-compulsive disorders, especially when they also have a high score on Psychasthenia. High scorers feel useless and may attempt to withdraw from social contacts and business responsibilities, often spending excessive time sleeping. They are usually ambivalent, especially if scores are above 80, and unable to make decisions even in minor matters. They are often motivated to seek help, but offer little active cooperation. Individuals with chronic high Depression scores frequently have symptoms that interfere with daily life and cause serious somatic symptoms, such as a refusal to eat; they often need treatment with antidepressive drugs. Patients with acute depressive episodes and without somatic scores (usually with high Psychasthenia scores) are more likely to recover on their own, as long as the remaining clinical scales are below 70.

Low scores on Scale D are highly suggestive of a happy, relaxed individual who may show signs of high levels of activity depending on the Mania score. These individuals are cheerful and pleasant, comfortable in social situations (also note the score on Social Introversion), responsible, clever, and likely to assume a leadership role. Combined with a rise on the Psychopathic Deviate scale, they may also be impulsive, uninhibited, and antiauthoritarian. These individuals generally do not have strong guilt feelings. A low Scale 2 (lowest score in the profile except for Scales 5 and 0) in a profile with high Scales 8 and 9 can suggest a manic-depressive disorder, manic phase (see also the discussion of high point 29 patterns).

Scale 3 (Hy)

The Hysteria scale is a measure of the tendency to develop conversion problems, the substitution of somatic complaints for anxiety. The scale is also highly related to depressive symptoms such as psychomotor retardation. Scale Hy contains a number of items about physical complaints that it shares with Hypochondriasis. As a result, a high Hysteria score alone is not sufficient to suggest the presence of an hysterical disorder of either the conversion or the dissociative type, which may be characterized by amnesia, feelings of depersonalization, multiple personality, and the like. In some two-point combinations (see next section on two-point patterns involving Hysteria), such individuals tend to show a variety of somatic symptoms, including headaches, stomach pains, backaches, and, in women, menstrual disorders. Such individuals occasionally develop more dramatic symptoms, such as psychogenic blindness, paralysis, or loss of sensation. These individuals are seen most often in hospitals or doctors' offices rather than psychiatric clinics, although a psychologist or psychiatrist may be called in to consult on the case after medical evaluations have failed to find significant physical correlates of the patient's complaints.

The presumed, underlying deficit in the high Hy individual is the inability to handle hostility and stress. Such individuals appear to be very friendly, sociable, talkative, and enthusiastic; however, they also can be egocentric, childish, immature, narcissistic, and lacking in psychological insight. Hysterical individuals may act out sexually, often acting seductive toward physicians of the opposite sex, and may be promiscuous if there is a high point 34 combination. A low point 6 in these patients is very suggestive of severely repressed hostility that can come out in a cyclic manner in the form of temper tantrums or suicide threats and attempts. High point 3s are likely to have unhappy marriages, be resentful of anyone in authority (although pleasant to them in a face-to-face visit), and resentful of physicians and psychologists. Typical high 3s may tell each physician they see that they have had trouble with past doctors, but that the current doctor is obviously much smarter (more skillful, more attentive, knowledgeable, etc.) and that things will go very well now. High 3s rarely have insight into their own behavior and resent suggestions that they have psychological problems. High Scale Hy patients are often extremely repressed, as seen in concomitant high K and L scores.

Low Hy scores are associated with individuals who are conforming, unfriendly, and suspicious, and who have a narrow range of interests (especially if associated with significantly higher Paranoia scores); low scorers may also be content with their life, realistic, and level-headed.

Scale 4 (Pd)

The Psychopathic Deviate scale was intended to measure asocial or antisocial tendencies in an individual. These can include lying, stealing, promiscuity, drug abuse, and a general disregard for social rules and conventions. High Pd patients may have assaultive thoughts, acting out behavior, hostility, irritability, and general antisocial ideas. In Freudian terms, these are individuals with little or no effective superego: they have been unable to incorporate the standards of society into their own consciences. High Pd individuals often are rebellious, underachieve in school, have a history of acting out before age 15, are unable to form close relationships, have difficulties in marriage and at work, show poor judgment, act impulsively, and demonstrate narcissistic and egocentric tendencies. Such an individual under stress may turn to suicidal gestures, not out of real depression, but as a way of getting revenge on others or manipulating them to support his or her own goals.

High Scale 4 scorers may seem highly sociable and interested in others, but this interest basically extends only to what can be gotten from the person. Goals may be short-termed and vary on impulse. High 4s may be intelligent, cynical, aggressive, and prone to worry, especially when not in control of a situation or the events directly affecting their lives.

On a more positive side, the more socialized high 4 individual may turn the aggressiveness, energetic, and sociable characteristics of the personality type to more positive goals, especially when a person's intelligence is high enough to control the more antisocial tendencies in the personality type. Such people make highly successful physicians, psychologists, salesmen, and other professionals who have to deal with people. It should be noted that one cannot diagnose the antisocial or dissocial personality from this typology alone, but only on the basis of a history of antisocial activity.

Low 4s are generally conforming, submissive to authority, passive, noncompetitive, moralistic, security conscious, uncreative, disinterested in sex, and pliable. Such individuals are afraid of accepting responsibility for their own behaviors and may have strong guilt feelings over minor infractions.

Scale 5 (Mf)

The Masculinity-Femininity scale is the only MMPI scale scored differently for males and females and interpreted separately. The scale is discussed separately for each sex.

In a male, a high score on Scale 5 indicates someone who may be confused about sexual identity and insecure in the masculine role. One important exception to this is the highly educated, culturally oriented male who values cognitive pursuits and creativity. Such individuals are creative, imaginative, individualistic, tolerant, and sensitive to the feelings of others. Thus, while high Scale Mf scores in the male may suggest sexual confusion and even homosexuality, the examiner must be careful not to confuse this with the more positive traits suggested by the profile. A low score in a male, especially a score below 40, may suggest a man who sees himself as overly masculine, the traditional macho stereotype. Such individuals will place a strong emphasis on physical strength, aggressiveness, adventurousness, and thrill seeking. These individuals may be coarse and vulgar, and often have deep-seated doubts about their own masculinity. The doubt of masculinity is most strongly seen in individuals with a macho image of themselves who very clearly do not fit that image. Alternately, low Scale 5 males may lack insight, and be jolly, relaxed, and conforming.

In females, a high Scale Mf score suggests the rejection of the typical feminine role. These women have strong interests in the so-called masculine areas of sports, work, and hobbies. These females may be aggressive, competitive, coarse, rough, outgoing, uninhibited, unemotional, and unfriendly. Such women may see themselves in active competition with men, attempting to show they are equal or better. A low Scale 5 score in a female suggests a woman who describes herself in typical female stereotypes: she is passive, submissive, yielding, defers to males, and may have doubts about her femininity. These doubts may be strong in women professionals and women with high Scale 4 or 6 codes, especially when associated with high Scale 3 scores as well. Low scoring females may be sensitive, modest and idealistic or constricted, complaining, and self-pitying.

Scale 6 (Pa)

The Paranoia scale suggests suspiciousness and oversensitivity, and may indicate paranoid delusions when the score exceeds 70, especially in patients with high F and Schizophrenia scores as well. High scores on Scale Pa are associated with formal thought disorders as well as depressive feelings, but without the feelings of guilt or responsibility that are typically projected onto others. High Scale Pa patients may have strong sexual concerns and preoccupations. Delusions may be centered around threats of rape or homosexual rape either overtly or on a symbolic level.

Extreme elevations on Scale Pa (greater than 75) are almost always associated with psychotic behavior in a valid profile. The individuals may have delusions of reference, grandeur, or persecution. Thinking disorders are almost always present (although in their incipient stages, the paranoid delusions can exist without a thought disorder). Patients are often angry or fearful and may plot revenge on others. They may be dangerous to others or even to themselves as a result. (One patient, for example, jumped out of a second story window while escaping from imaginary pursuers.) Diagnoses of paranoid schizophrenia are most common in this group, with occasional diagnosis of paranoid state.

High scores on Scale Pa that are less than 75 are less associated with psychoticism unless there is a rise on Schizophrenia as well. These individuals are excessively sensitive, hostile, resentful, and eager to blame others for their own failures. They may be suspicious and guarded and lie in interviews, giving different stories to different investigators. They are rigid individuals and poor risks for psychotherapy.

Low and moderate Scale Pa scores, in normal individuals, are generally associated with sensitive, trusting, energetic individuals who have a wide range of interests and values. Such individuals are found to be intelligent, poised, rational, and cooperative but may lack self-confidence or be submissive and prone to worry.

In psychiatric or maladjusted patients, a Scale Pa score in the range of 35 to 50 may suggest guardedness, self-centered behavior, high sensitivity, underachievement, and undependability. These patients may feel little guilt (especially in association with a high Psychopathic Deviate score). These individuals are unlikely to be psychotic, however.

A score less than 35, especially in a psychiatric patient, may indicate someone who is overtly paranoid, delusional, defensive, and evasive. It is the defensive and evasive qualities that cause these patients to deny their symptomatology on the test and results in the extremely low Scale Pa score. Extremely low scores in what appear to be normal individuals may suggest people unable to handle hostility or even face the fact that they have hostility toward others. Such individuals may be prone to temper tantrums as pressure builds up because of their continuing denial and repression. The low Scale 6 score may often be associated with high K and high Hysteria scores.

Scale 7 (Pt)

The Psychasthenia scale was devised to identify individuals with obsessive-compulsive traits or strong phobias: In other words, individuals with high levels of anxiety. High Scale 7 scores correlate with obsessive thinking (more so than with compulsive behavior), with strong feelings of anxiety or tension, with depression (with frequent concomitant highs on Depression), and with phobias of all kinds (the type depending on the experiences of the patient or the symbolic meaning of the specific phobia for that patient).

High scorers are seen as high-strung and jumpy and may show overt physiological signs of anxiety such as sweating. Because of the great tension they are under, high Scale 7 scorers show difficulty in concentration, thinking, planning, understanding, and recognizing environmental cues that could rationally reduce the anxiety state. High 7 patients are guilty, depressed, perfectionistic, and lacking in self-confidence. They may be overly organized, neat, orderly, and meticulous but lack creativity or ingenuity. They may be indecisive and may vacillate, worrying over everything numerous times without reaching a decision of any kind.

High 7s may have physical problems centering around the heart, intestines, and stomach (e.g., ulcers); insomnia (because of obsessive thinking); tension headaches; and exhaustion. Such disorders as bronchial asthma may be brought about by anxiety in such individuals. High 7s need long-term psychotherapy as these are often life-long patterns: brief psychotherapy is ineffective or of short-term benefit. High 7s may use rationalization and intellectualization as defense mechanisms, making them hard to reach in therapy.

Low scores on Scale 7 are associated with calm, capable, well-adjusted individuals without neurotic tendencies (although they may show character or personality disorders). These individuals are generally realistic and able to handle stress effectively. They may value success, recognition, and status.

Scale 8 (Sc)

Scale 8, Schizophrenia, is a measure of thought disorder in patients with psychiatric disorders. The scale correlates with such symptoms as unusual thought contact, psychosis, delusions, hallucinations, depersonalization, inappropriate affect, refusal to speak, peculiar posturing, peculiar mannerisms, bizarre behavior, bizarre dress, withdrawn behavior, dependent behavior, and emotional lability. It is also associated with poor memory, conceptual disorganization, disorientation, inability to concentrate, inability to understand proverbs, poor hygiene, and intellectual deterioration.

High Scale 8 scores (above 100) are not usually produced by psychotic subjects, but may indicate a random or faking bad profile. T scores of 80 and above are suggestive of extreme confusion that interferes with the test as well as with the patient's life. Scores between 70 and 80 are associated with chronic schizophrenic conditions, whereas scores above 80 more likely represent acute episodes or acute exacerbations. High scores on Scale 8 (above 70) along with high scores on F (above 70) are nearly always associated with a current psychotic condition, while lower scores or high 8 scores without high F scores may be associated with a schizoid personality.

Individuals with schizoid personalities typically feel alienated from life. They have few friends, are isolated, feel misunderstood, and are rarely acceptable to others. They avoid situations that are new or that bring them into emotional contact with others. The prognosis in psychotherapy for any high scores on Scale 8 is generally poor because of the typical chronicity of the disorder and the pervasiveness of the problem. Some help, however, can be offered individuals with initial, acute psychotic breaks that are characterized by elevated scores on both Scales 7 and 8 (see the discussion for the 87 two-point code). These individuals are generally best treated by a combination of psychotherapy and medication, especially in chronic disorders.

Low scores on Scale 8 are associated with mature, adjusted individuals who are described as well-balanced, adaptable, and responsible. Such individuals may be cautious, practical, and conservative. They may avoid competitive situations, and be concerned about status and power.

Scale 9 (Ma)

Scale 9, Mania, measures the presence of hypomanic behavior, including such symptoms as overproductivity in thought and behavior, expansive (grandiose) self-concept, elevated mood, loud or excessive speech, impulsive acts, flights of ideas, increased motor activity, elation over sad things, and lability of mood. High Scale Ma scores are also associated with psychotic symptoms such as confusion, delusions, suspiciousness, paranoid thoughts, depersonalization, poor memory, disorientation, and inability to concentrate. These symptoms are especially serious in patients with T scores over 80 and are often accompanied by high Schizophrenia scores as well. Hallucinations may also be present, especially when scores exceed 90. These high manic states are often associated with the manic phase of a manic-depressive disorder or with a schizoaffective disorder. These patients often respond to drug treatment with lithium while in the manic phase.

Individuals high on Scale Ma also tend to be friendly, sociable, and gregarious. They like to be around people, and often joke and have a good sense of humor, unlike individuals with other forms of psychosis. The manic may also have periods during which he or she is irritable, is aggressive, and shows strong paranoid delusions. The manic may make unrealistic plans for the future and claim to have high connections and power. The manic may also be reacting to a depressive episode in an attempt to deny a current depression by showing manic behavior. Such individuals may show the interesting elevated 29 pattern (see next section). Not surprisingly, these patients have fairly poor prognosis for psychotherapy and are unlikely to attend on a regular basis.

A low score on Scale Ma (especially below 40) indicates an individual with a low energy level. The person may be lethargic and listless, and may report chronic fatigue. If not severely depressed, however, these individuals are described as reliable, sincere, modest, and overcontrolled. They may also be withdrawn (often showing high Social Introversion and Depression scores) and unpopular with others.

Scale Zero (Si)

The Social Introversion scale attempts to measure the tendency of the individual to withdraw from others. The scale correlates both with the tendency to withdraw and with symptoms of depression: psychomotor retardation and low levels of activity. There is also a strong relationship to anxiety and phobia, as well as preoccupation with bodily concerns. Thus, the scale has more significant diagnostic implications than simple withdrawal.

Individuals with high scores on Scale 0 are generally found to be socially introverted, although they may enjoy being with a single friend or a small group. Such individuals are not usually antisocial, but in more extreme forms, especially with a high Schizophrenia score, may show distinct schizoid qualities. High scorers are generally uncomfortable around members of the opposite sex and lack self-confidence. They are hard to get to know and troubled by involvement with others, although they may be very sensitive to what others are thinking or doing. They are accepting of authority. They hide their feelings and have great difficulty expressing them to others. These individuals are serious, reliable, and dependable, although they tend to be slow in personal tempo (associated with a low Mania score). They tend to be cautious and conservative, rarely finding original ways to do things. They enjoy work and personal achievement. They can experience periods of depression (with elevated Depression score) and irritability and may appear moody.

A low score on this scale generally has more meaning than do low scores on many of the other scales which simply reflect the absence of a pathological condition. Individuals with low 0s are sociable, extroverted, active, intelligent, confident, and interested in leadership. If the score is less than 40, they usually get along well with the opposite sex. Such individuals may also be childish, impulsive, and self-indulgent, and many show a strong tendency to form only superficial relationships, especially if there is a high score on Scale 4. These latter individuals may also be manipulative and opportunistic, and may arouse resentment in others.

TWO-POINT CODES

Extensive MMPI research has examined the behavioral and diagnostic correlates of two-point high codes in MMPI profiles.

This research examines the relationship of the two highest scales on a given profile, excluding the validity scales, to MMPI interpretation. These codes have been found to be highly useful in the interpretation of the MMPI and are usually the starting point for an MMPI interpretation. As a rule, this research has ignored which of the two points is higher; profiles with Scales 3 and 4 highest are regarded the same as profiles with Scales 4 and 3 highest. In most cases, it has not been found to matter which is highest. As a simple rule of thumb, however, if the difference between the two highest scales is greater than 10, the behavior of the individual tends to reflect the characteristics of the higher scale much more strongly than in profiles in which the difference is less than 10.

Most profiles have one clear set of high points. There are, however, numerous profiles that do not. These include profiles in which two or three scales have the same T score. Thus, a profile may have a Scale 4 score of 70, a Scale 3 score of 68, and a Scale 6 score of 68. It is not possible to tell in this profile if there is a 43 or 46 high point. In these cases, both can be examined and used in the interpretation. A second important case occurs when several scales are quite close to one another. Thus, a profile may have scores of 75, 76, and 77 on Scales 1, 2, and 3, respectively. While this profile has a clear high point pair (32), the difference between the scales is slight. Thus, one would also look at the meaning of the 31 and 21 profiles in interpreting this individual's scores. Finally, a profile may have a clear high point pair but may also have outstanding peaks in other parts of the profile. For example, a profile may have a clear 87 high point pair but also a secondary pair of high points on Scales 1 and 3. In this case, the interpretation of both the 87 and 31 high points considerably extends our understanding of the profile. It is important, in this regard, to be observant and recognize certain high point pairs (to be discussed) that have important characterological or personality implications. In this manner, an acute condition (e.g., represented by the 87 high point), as well as an underlying personality disorder (e.g., represented by the 31 high point), can be interpreted.

When multiple high point codes are interpreted in a single profile, the process is much the same as when the 10 clinical scales are interpreted. The highest two-point pair is given more weight than lower pairs if there are contradictions, and the overall descriptions are merged to form a psychologically meaningful constellation of behaviors and dynamics. This, of course, presupposes a knowledge of personality functions and of psychopathology by the interpreter. The following pages describe the more common and more heavily researched two-point codes. The reader should note that only one code is presented involving Scale 5 or Scale 0 because many researchers do not regard these as clinical scales. Profiles with high points on these scales should also be examined for high point pairs when these scales are excluded, as well as for the meaning of high scores on Scales 0 and 5.

12/21

The individual with this profile is reporting significant somatic concerns along with depression. The somatic problems in this code can be the result of either organic or functional problems. Individuals with a 123 triple high point are generally hypochondriacal and have little basis for their pain. The raised 2 score is often related to a significant collapse of their defenses, causing the onset of depression and anxiety along with more acute and severe somatic complaints. This profile, however, may also be seen in chronic pain patients who have an organic basis, but who have essentially given in to their pain and are exaggerating it considerably at the present time. This high point pair may also be seen in individuals who have undergone recent severe accidents, whose depression is acute and in whom a reaction to the serious injuries has occurred. In distinguishing these possibilities, it is necessary to know to what extent the patient's physical injuries can be objectively discerned, as well as the history about the onset of the pain. In a recent study we completed on pain, we found the 12 pattern to be the average profile in an organically injured group; other research, however, has also reported the profile in psychosomatic groups.

Individuals with this profile do tend to exaggerate their physical problems beyond what is physically confirmable and often misinterpret normal pains or bodily functions. When the pain is functional, these individuals tend to be shy and withdrawn. When the pain is organic, they may be loud complainers and generally uninterested in others. Psychiatric patients with this profile may have histories of drug or alcohol abuse (usually justified as pain therapy), and are suspicious of any attempts to suggest otherwise. This is especially true in men with this profile who may see themselves as macho (low Scale 5).

The most common diagnoses for these groups are hypochondriasis, anxiety, and depressive neurosis. The latter is most likely when the depressive symptoms are predominant, whereas anxiety neurosis is most likely when there is a 127 profile. These are rarely diagnosed as personality disorders, except when there is a 124, 126, or 1264 pattern suggesting passive-aggressive personality, dependent type with acute depression. Patients with 128 profiles and high F's may be diagnosed as schizophrenic (usually chronic undifferentiated type).

13/31

This profile is associated with the classical "conversion V" in which a 13 high point pair is accompanied by a lower Scale 2 score. These individuals generally show a great deal of somatic complaining, and may be showing classical conversion hysteria, although that is rare in this profile type. The pattern has also been found in numerous groups of chronic pain patients with known organic causes such as ruptured disks. These individuals generally do not show severe anxiety, the level varying with the height of the Scale 2 score. The higher the 2 score, the more likely the patient is experiencing the stress and anxiety that he or she identifies. In patients in whom the 2 score is considerably lower, especially where it is the profile low point, the likelihood of conversion hysteria becomes significantly stronger. This may also be associated with an elevated 4 score and a low 5 score in women or high 5 in men.

All 13/31 profile types, whether the pain is initially organic or functional, suffer from gross exaggeration of pain and a strong psychogenic factor. These patients tend to be superficial in relationships with others, and may lack skills with the opposite sex (Scale 5 is often a clue in this direction, as is Scale 0). These individuals generally have considerable repressed hostility, often seen in a very low or relatively high 6. The very low 6 suggests a strong active repressive tendency that can cause extremely difficult problems with these patients, as overcontrolled individuals can release their hostility all at once in temper tantrums (especially if there is a high 4) or in suicide threats or attempts.

These patients are given a diagnosis of neurosis, usually hypochondriacal or hysterical, psychophysiological reaction, or are described as chronic pain patients when there is a 132 pattern combined with a history of definitive organic injury.

14/41

Fourteen/forty-one patients, who tend to be rarely seen, present themselves as severely hypochondriacal. These patients may be highly manipulative in nature (reflecting the 4), but there are few if any signs of asocial behavior. These individuals may be extroverted (low 0), but are rarely skillful with the opposite sex (see Scale 5). As with other individuals with peak 4s, there may be a history of alcoholism, poor work history, drug abuse, and poor marital history. These individuals are complainers and may be difficult to get along with. As are people coded 12 and 13, they are highly resistant to psychotherapy. Diagnosis is generally hypochondriacal neurosis, occasionally with additional diagnosis of a personality disorder, depending on the constellation of the remaining scales.

18/81

When there is a high F score with this profile, these individuals are often diagnosed as schizophrenic. They have great trouble handling stress and anxiety, and may show clearly delusional thinking about bodily functions and bodily illness. They do not trust others and may appear paranoid, irrespective of the height of Scale 6. These individuals may be confused and unable to concentrate. When the symptoms are less severe and the F score is in the normal range, the likely diagnosis is hypochondriacal or anxiety neurosis. The latter is more likely as Scale 7 approaches the height of Scales 1 and 8.

19/91

These individuals show a great deal of somatic complaining, combined with an extroverted, verbal, and socially outgoing personality. The rise on Scale 9 in these individuals tends to be a reaction to their basic personality. Rather than give in to their dependent needs, these patients attempt to establish that they are independent and strong. This profile may have several other scores suggestive of a basically passive underlying personality. These individuals expect a great deal from themselves, but their goals are unclear and often unrealistic. This profile can be seen in reaction to physical injury, which limits an individual's capacity to cope and to achieve goals that were formerly possible. These patients can be diagnosed as hypochondriacal, manic, or a combination of both. They may also be seen as passive-aggressive, especially with high 4 and low 6 scores.

23/32

These individuals report that they are fatigued, tired, weak, depressed, and anxious. They often have inadequate personalities and are unable to do things for themselves, relying instead on others to take care of them. Somatic symptoms are usually present but are often inconsistent and changing. The patients are generally found to be immature and childish and to have difficulty expressing their feelings. They may be insecure, socially inadequate, and unable to deal with the opposite sex. It is important to observe the relative heights of the 5, 6, and 0 scales, as these may reveal information about the patient's adjustment. A diagnosis of depressive neurosis is common, unless there are rises on both Scales F and 8, suggesting psychotic depression. In cases of psychotic depression, one must also examine the patient's personal history for the possibility of manic-depressive psychosis. Response to psychotherapy in these patients is poor.

24/42

Some have suggested that this profile represents the psychopath in trouble: the antisocial individual (Scale 4) who is caught, usually by the law, and thus becomes depressed (Scale 2). In other cases, these are chronically depressed people whose high 4s are associated with extreme hostility, either overt (high 6) or suppressed (low 6). These individuals generally have little regard for the rules of society or for working with a mental health professional. Their acting out behavior is deeply ingrained and may be expressed in crime, drug or alcohol abuse, and promiscuous sexual activity. When associated with high energy levels (9) and high overt hostility (6), these individuals may be extremely dangerous to others. When this profile is extremely elevated (near 90), the behavior may be overtly psychotic or prepsychotic, depending on the levels of the F and 8 scales. There is also a strong chance of manipulative suicide attempts in the elevated profile. The interpreter must be careful at this point, however, as a 2468 pattern is also characteristic of malingering profiles.

While these individuals may express (and sometimes feel) guilt, their sincerity is limited. They work to get themselves out of current difficulties, but return to their old patterns as soon as they are free. Consequently, they are poor risks in therapy. The clinician should especially beware of quick, overnight cures and promises to reform. In an acute hospital setting, these individuals may come across as friendly and sincere and can often manipulate staff into helping them out with their problems (which are often with the law). These individuals also tend to have poor marital and work histories and do not do well in school.

The 246 pattern may be associated with strong personality disorders (passive-aggressive or mixed antisocial and passive-aggressive), accompanied by acute depression. In these cases, Scale 2 is often greatly elevated over Scales 1 and 3. There are generally higher scores on 1 and 3 when the 2 component is more chronic. In addition, the integration and evaluation of the patient's history is important in making the chronic/acute distinction. The history is best trusted when corroborated by a reliable source.

26/62

Patients with this profile show strong evidence of paranoid trends, sometimes to the point that the paranoid ideation is psychotic or prepsychotic. Psychotic profiles may be associated with raised scores on F and 8 as well as on 9 (see 69 patterns). Encapsulated paranoia, however, may show only an elevation in the 60s on the F or 6 scale. These individuals are often aggressive and sensitive to others as well as depressed. The depression is usually related to physical disorders (often real) whose causes are blamed on others. These individuals have difficulty with interpersonal relationships. Diagnosis can include depressive neurosis, passive-aggressive personality (especially in 624 combinations), paranoid state, or (incipient) paranoid schizophrenia. In rare instances, this can be associated with an involutional paranoid state.

27/72

This is one of the most common codes in psychiatric populations. These individuals are generally seen as depressed with additional symptoms of agitation, restlessness, and nervousness. The patients may show symptoms of neurasthenia (especially if combined with a 123 pattern) and report generalized weakness and fatigue. These individuals have a great need for recognition and are often depressed over their failures. They are rigid, compulsive, and perfectionistic. They often have a great deal of trouble handling hostility (which can be reflected in the Scale 6 score) and appear to be passive-dependent (reflected in Scales 3, 4, and 6). These patients are most likely to be diagnosed as suffering from depressive neurosis or anxiety neurosis, although a diagnosis of psychotic depression (with a rise on F) is possible, as is manic-depressive psychosis (but only with a confirming history).

28/82

This code profile is common in psychiatric populations. Most of these patients complain of depression or anxiety, as well as sleep disturbance, confused thinking, and memory problems. They may present as physically ill or simply as seriously depressed. These are generally dependent and ineffective individuals who have difficulty expressing emotions openly. They do not get along with people as a result, and tend to be suspicious and wary of them. If both scales as well as F are above 70, the most likely diagnoses are psychotic depression, manic-depressive psychosis, involutional depression, or schizoaffective disorder. The latter diagnosis is most likely when the 8 peak predominates over the 2 by a significant amount. If this profile does not suggest psychosis, the diagnosis of schizoid personality with depression is possible, as is depressive neurosis (287). These individuals are suicide risks and must be watched carefully.

29/92

In the 29 patient, the most predominant behaviors are usually manic, although these may alternate with depressive episodes. The manic behavior serves to disguise the depression, making these individuals appear more intact than they actually are. If not overtly manic, these individuals appear to be tense and restless. In younger individuals, this pattern may indicate someone who is unsure of his or her social role. In older individuals, this may be a reaction to physical disability or involutional depression. The high 9 serves as a denial mechanism in that the person avoids recognizing his or her limitations. This profile is reported by some in brain injured patients; however, in our own samples, it did not appear to be particularly more prevalent than numerous other profile codes. The most common diagnosis in these cases is manic-depressive psychosis if both scales are elevated. Cyclothymic personality is occasionally diagnosed as well.

34/43

These patients are characterized by chronic and severe anger that they have great trouble expressing. Depending on the level of Scale 6, they may or may not be able to clearly recognize this hostility and its source. If Scale 4 is higher than Scale

3, or the scales are essentially equal (within five points), the individual is likely to have an explosive personality that erupts in periodic temper tantrums. Individuals with this code are likely to develop a wide variety of medical disorders, including headaches, menstrual problems, and other conversion or psychosomatic disorders. It is not unusual for explosive periods to alternate with somatic periods, during which the patient is sociable, cooperative, and friendly. These individuals are usually hostile toward their families, and have histories of chronic marital problems. Antisocial acts, including savage crimes of violence, are not uncommon. Women with a 43 profile and a low 5 may be very seductive toward male therapists and are often sexually promiscuous. Suicide is a possibility as the result of an inwardly directed outburst or alcohol or drug intoxication. Diagnosis can include hysterical personality, passive-aggressive personality, explosive personality, or mixed personality disorder. Parents of these patients are often found to be alcoholic.

36/63

Individuals with this code may report somatic symptoms, such as gastrointestinal difficulties, as well as anxiety and nervousness. As in the 34 group, the problems arise from chronic and intense hostility toward family. These feelings are rarely recognized openly, however. These patients are rigid and reject suggestions that their problems may be psychogenic. These individuals are self-centered and blame any conscious feelings of hostility on the behavior of others. They prefer to deny problems, however, than directly blame them on someone else. This pattern can lead to significant marital disharmony.

38/83

These individuals may report anxiety as well as feelings of depression. A large number of somatic complaints are possible. These individuals show unusual thought patterns and strong repressive defenses. They often have delusions, have poor concentration, and show significant social withdrawal. Delusions and other more bizarre behavior may not be readily apparent because of severe withdrawal and lack of cooperation, as well as extreme loss of insight. These individuals are immature, dependent, and unable to plan rationally for themselves. They are frequently diagnosed as schizophrenic, but occasionally are seen as suffering from hysterical neurosis (especially if 8 and F are not above 70).

39/93

Patients with this profile are subject to considerable hostility, episodic attacks of acute anxiety, and medical complaints that appear overtly hysterical. The high 9 may indicate an attempt to cover up a basically dependent personality with an aggressive, arrogant, egocentric facade. The patient's lack of insight is reflected in their belief that they are liked and admired by others, when in fact they may be seen quite critically. Periodic depressions are possible in these patients. Diagnoses include hysterical neurosis, anxiety neurosis, and passive-aggressive personality, aggressive type.

45/54

Individuals with this code type are likely to have significant troubles with sex role identification. Overt homosexuality or other sexual dysfunction is a strong possibility if both scales are above 70. Females with this code type are unusually aggressive, whereas males tend to be passive, dependent, and self-centered. These individuals are often nonconforming but rarely delinquent, although acting out is a possibility under stress or alcohol. Feelings of guilt or remorse are generally transient and rarely affect future behavior.

46/64

These individuals are generally passive-dependent, demanding a great deal from others but resenting any requests made of them. They are often depressed, irritable, withdrawn, and nervous. Significant repressed hostility is common, but acting out is possible if there is a high 9. Patients with 46 high points are generally self-centered, immature, and unable to form deep emotional involvements. Their need for support and their extensive demands are insatiable. Consequently, little can be done to make them happy. As a result, marriage problems are common, as are work problems. They deny problems in themselves, projecting them upon others. Likely diagnoses are paranoid schizophrenia, involutional paranoia (with 6 higher than 4 and both over 70), or passive-aggressive personality.

47/74

These individuals are insensitive to others (4) and have a high tendency toward guilt over their behavior (7). They frequently show cyclic behavior as a result, with periods of acting out alternating with periods of guilt and self-condemnation. During acting out periods, symptoms such as promiscuity and alcoholism are possible. Although the subsequent guilt may be real, it does not prevent future episodes. During the guilt phase, there may be vague somatic complaints besides overt guilt and anxiety. This is a chronic pattern that does not change easily with any type of therapy. Antianxiety agents often act to intensify the antisocial episodes. Diagnosis can be a combination of anxiety neurosis and psychopathic personality, despite the seeming contradiction in joining these disorders.

48/84

Patients with this profile are seen as odd and peculiar, often belonging to unusual religious or political movements. Their behavior can be erratic and unpredictable, and they may act out in antisocial ways. Such acts, however, are generally poorly planned and impulsive, and may be vicious. These individuals can be insecure, sexually perverse, obsessive, socially withdrawn, and isolated. When Scale 8 is elevated, disorders of thinking, memory problems, confusion, and other schizophrenic symptoms may be prominent. These individuals generally are diagnosed as schizophrenic and show strong paranoid delusions. If there are no signs of psychosis, the most likely diagnoses are schizoid personality, paranoid personality, or sociopathic personality. Borderline elevated profiles may indicate a prepsychotic pattern.

49/94

This profile is associated with a variety of antisocial behaviors. These patients are often manic, irritable, violent, extroverted, manipulative, and energetic. They possess a marked disregard for social rules and conventions, and may commit any number of antisocial acts, including confidence games, promiscuity, alcoholism, sexual perversion, rape, child abuse, assault, drug addiction, arson, frequent traffic violations, extortion, and a variety of white collar crimes. Patients with this profile are often impulsive, doing things with little or no forethought, unable to postpone desires, self-centered, unable to form close relationships except for manipulative purposes, immature, irresponsible, moody, resentful, and ambitious. They possess deep seated feelings of hostility and act them out whenever it is possible. They may profess the desire to "go straight" when caught, but invariably return to earlier behavior patterns if given the opportunity. The most common diagnosis with this pattern is antisocial (or asocial) personality.

Among high school and college students, an elevated score needs to be in the 80s or 90s (rather than the 70s) for there to be significant concern. The rise in these individuals appears to be more related to a questioning of authority and general rebellion against the establishment than to specific antisocial acts. In diagnosis, it should be recognized that antisocial personality can be diagnosed only when there is a significant history of onset before age 15.

68/86

Individuals with this code are distrustful and lack self-confidence and self-esteem. They may withdraw from everyday life, show a flat affect, become apathetic, and show disorders of thinking and marked confusion. Hallucinations and delusions of a paranoid type are often present, and the individual is unable to maintain emotional ties with others. These people can lose contact with reality and withdraw into a fantasy world. Cognitive deterioration may be present, but it does not necessarily occur, especially in individuals younger than 30. When Scales 6, 8, and F are elevated over 70, the diagnosis is almost invariably paranoid schizophrenia. Occasionally, in less elevated profiles, the diagnosis is paranoid state or schizoid personality. In individuals in which the delusional material is encapsulated into specific, limited areas of the patient's life, paranoid schizophrenia may exist without a significantly elevated profile. Chronic drug abuse (e.g., amphetamines) or use of drugs such as PCP may show this pattern until the drug effects wear off. Such profiles are usually markedly elevated in drug disorders. The 68 pattern may also be seen in thyroid disorders. Treatment for these individuals generally involves antipsychotic medication.

69/96

Individuals with this code type may show extreme anxiety or nervousness to the point of physiological signs such as trembling. These individuals generally withdraw into fantasy when threatened. They may appear overcontrolled at one time, with manic emotional undercontrol at other times. There are often strong impairments of conscious thought (associated with high 8 and F scales). Obsessional thinking is not uncommon. When combined with a high 8 and F, the diagnosis in these individuals is often paranoid schizophrenia, or schizoaffective disorder if the manic symptoms appear more predominant. In cases in which there is no overt thought confusion (lower 8), a diagnosis of manic-depressive psychosis is possible. These individuals often respond to a combination of lithium and antipsychotic medication.

78/87

Patients with this profile are often highly agitated and upset. They typically lack defenses to handle stress in their environment; the profile sometimes represents a collapse of a previously stable defensive system. These patients are insecure, ambivalent, indecisive, confused, anxious, and socially inept. They are passive and have difficulty with mature heterosexual relationships. Obsessive-compulsive thinking may be present, as may psychotic symptoms such as confusion, hallucinations, or delusions. Guilt may be present, as may depression and excessive fear. If these individuals drink or abuse drugs, it is often an attempt to cure their own disorders. A number of diagnostic possibilities are present, depending on the complete configuration. Generally, the diagnosis for 78 profiles is anxiety neurosis, although this profile may be the aftermath of an acute psychotic disorder, which would be the primary diagnosis. (Often such individuals are not testable, because of their agitation, until the acute psychotic symptoms have passed.) In 87 profiles, the greater the distance between 8 and 7 and the higher the relative height of 8, the more likely the diagnosis is schizophrenia. The height of the 87 pattern compared with the rest of the profile is important in these cases. If the 87 pair is significantly elevated over the other scales, an acute psychotic disorder is probably present. If the entire profile is elevated, a chronic profile is suggested. In this profile and the 86 profile, one must be aware of the possibility of random or faking bad profiles, however. In cases diagnosed as acute neurotic or acute psychotic, there is also the possibility of schizoid or borderline personality, which can be determined on a retesting after the acute symptoms have dissipated.

89/98

Individuals with this profile tend to be hyperactive, energetic, and emotionally labile. They are unrealistic, often having delusions of grandeur (with a rise in 6) about their role in life, contacts, importance, and so on. They rarely have insight about their disorder and resent hospitalization. They demand a great deal of attention, and are seen as immature and childish. They cannot form close social relationships, and a thought disorder may also be present. Diagnosis for these cases may include schizophrenia or manic-depressive psychosis, depending on the relative contributions of the thought and affective disorder. Diagnosis of schizoaffective disorder, manic type, is are also possible. Often these individuals must be treated with medication both for the psychosis and for the mania. Antipsychotic medication is necessary when strong delusional or hallucinatory material is present. Severity of the current disorder may be seen in the height of the F scale.

SPECIAL DIAGNOSTIC CONSIDERATIONS

A number of major issues generally arise in the interpretation of an MMPI profile. These issues include the prediction of suicide, the determination of whether a disorder is functional or organic, the chronicity or acuteness of a profile, the presence of a psychotic or neurotic condition, the prognosis for a patient in psychotherapy, the likelihood of acting out behavior, and the likelihood of drug or alcohol addiction.

Chronic versus Acute Profiles

The acuteness of a profile may be inferred in several ways. Profiles that have one scale or a two or three high point combination of scales, such as 687 or 27, significantly above the level of the remaining scales have a greater likelihood of being acute profiles. Although there are no formal cutoffs, differences in the range of 15 to 20 T score points between the raised scales and the rest of the profile are generally indicative of an acute profile, whereas differences of 10 to 15 points are often indicative of an acute disorder. Another major measure is the average level of the profile. In a pathological individual, the higher the average level of the entire profile, assuming it is valid, the greater the degree of chronicity. It is possible, it should be noted, to have a generally elevated profile, suggesting a chronic disorder, with an acute rise on such scales as 6 and 8 that suggests a current, acute exacerbation of the chronic condition.

Another major measure of chronicity is the slope of the profile. The slope is determined by drawing through the profile a single straight line that minimizes the deviation of the individual scales from that line. (Statistically, this is the best fit regression line. In clinical cases, of course, one estimates this by eye rather than by calculating the correlation between scale number and scale elevation.) Any line connecting the scales at the same T value, a horizontal line, has a slope of 0. The more a line deviates from being parallel with this line, the greater the slope. If the line is higher on the left side of the profile, not including the validity scales, then the scale is said to have a neurotic slope. If the line is higher on the right side of the profile, the line is said to have a psychotic slope. Examples are seen in Figure 4-10. The greater the slope, whether neurotic or psychotic, the greater the acuteness of the profile and the higher the degree of current acute disturbance for the patient from his or her baseline levels.

Psychotic or Neurotic Conditions

This differentiation can also be made by several methods. In general, the two-point codes, as discussed before, can be

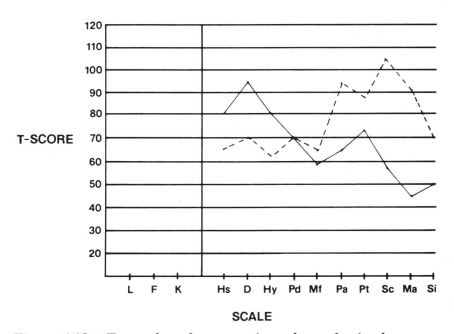

Figure 4-10. Examples of a neurotic and psychotic slope on an MMPI profile. The solid line represents a neurotic slope, and the dotted line represents a psychotic slope.

used to generate likely diagnoses, which in turn determine the psychotic or neurotic question. Neurotic conditions are generally characterized by high scores on Scales 1, 2, 3, and 7, and are generally higher than elevations on Scales 6, 8, and 9. The relative elevations of these scales determine the slope of the profile, as discussed above. Thus, the higher 1, 2, and 3 scales cause a neurotic slope, whereas the higher 6, 8, and 9 scales cause a psychotic slope. In cases in which there are multiple scale elevations, the comparison between Scales 7 and 8 are useful in establishing the presence or absence of psychosis. In general, if Scale 7 is higher than Scale 8, or within 5 T score points of Scale 8, the condition is likely to be neurotic. If Scale 8 is higher than Scale 7 by 10 points or more (and above 70), the condition is likely to be psychotic, especially if there is an elevation on F as well. The relative levels of cutoff points, it should be noted, depend on where one is working and with whom one is working. For example, I have worked in hospitals in which a psychiatric diagnosis of psychosis corresponded to elevation on the MMPI of 75 or more, whereas in another setting the psychiatrist was willing to diagnose as psychotic patients whose F was between 60 and 70. There are also changes with the diagnostic system employed in a particular setting, some psychiatric criteria being more specific and rigorous than others.

A third method of diagnosing psychosis or neurosis is the use of formulas that combine a variety of MMPI scores. For example, Goldberg (1965) suggested that one should use the following formula on the Scale T scores: $L + Pa + Sc - Hy - Pt$. Using a cutoff of 45, Goldberg found that he could correctly classify 70 percent of his cases. This has been one of the more promising formulas, even its success is not at a significantly high level for daily work. (One could probably get 60+ percent accuracy simply by talking to the patient for five minutes. A diagnostic system needs to do significantly better than this.) It must be concluded that the clinician cannot allow a simple formula, no matter how attractive, to decide such major questions. This must be done on the basis of all the information available to the diagnostician.

Functional or Organic Disorder

A major issue is the discrimination of physical disorders due to organic disease from those due to functional disorders. This research has fallen into two main areas: the differentiation of serious psychiatric disorders and organic brain disease, and the discrimination of medical symptoms due to conversion reactions from those due to organic injury or disease.

A number of researchers (e.g., Reitan, 1955a) have demonstrated that brain injured patients have profiles suggestive of psychiatric pathology (significant elevations on F, Pa, R, Sc, and Ma). More recent research (e.g., Osmon & Golden, 1978) has found that these elevations on the MMPI are related to the loss of speech skills rather than factors common to all brain injuries. Brain injured patients with loss of only spatial or nonverbal skills are more likely to show normal profiles or elevations on K and Hy. The presence of the elevations on the more pathological scales in a significant portion of the brain injured population makes it difficult to discriminate the brain injured group from many psychiatric groups, especially chronic schizophrenic patients

In an attempt to deal with this problem, a number of investigators have attempted to design scales or decision keys that discriminate brain injured from psychiatric patients (e.g., Hovey, 1964; Russell, 1975; Shaw & Matthews, 1965; Watson, 1971; Watson & Thomas, 1968). Although each of these scales has been supported in the introductory studies, none has stood up under cross validation at any level of accuracy higher than that of the Sc scale (the higher the Sc score, the more likely the person was schizophrenic rather than brain damaged). Even in carefully chosen populations, however, the Sc scale has not been more than 75 percent successful, a rate much too low for diagnostic purposes when one considers that 50 to 60 percent accuracy is chance level. The Sc scale is also a poor choice, since its use assumes that one cannot be both brain damaged and psychotic, a phenomenon common in many disorders, especially left temporal lobe injuries (Golden, 1978). Overall, this research has not yet been encouraging on the ability of the MMPI to separate the brain damaged from the schizophrenic groups. More reliance should be placed on tests directly measuring neuropsychological effects in investigating such diagnostic questions.

Similar attempts have been made to separate patients with pain and other medical symptoms from patients whose symptoms are due to functional disorders. As can be seen in the review of two-point code types, many profiles associated with conversion reactions are also associated with chronic pain profiles in organically damaged patients. In my own experience, pure functional disorders are more likely to be seen in 13 patterns that have very low 2 values (2 is usually the lowest or next to lowest scale overall). Conversion patterns may occur within higher 2 scores, but they are often indistinguishable from the scores of the true organic patients. Conversion problems are also seen in 43 patterns, especially when there is a low point 5 or 6 in women and a low point 6 in men. Other 43 patients also show conversion reactions but with significantly less consistency. It should be noted that conversion patients may also show numerous other patterns, especially on an acute basis. For example, if the conversion reaction fails to control stress in an individual's life, a 13 pattern may become a 12, 21, or 23 pattern. Consequently, the presence of such patterns in the absence of medical evidence supporting a physical diagnosis should be taken as suggesting the possibility of conversion reaction.

Hanvik (1949, 1951) attempted to devise a scale for the identification of functional low back pain. Unfortunately, the additional research on this scale has been limited (Dahlstrom, 1954; Lewinsohn, 1965) and has not yet been convincing. In my own practice in a community general hospital, I found Hanvik's scale little better than chance. It is possible that the scale may be useful with some specialized populations, but use of the scale is cautioned unless validated in a specific population.

Suicide

A frequent referral question involves the likelihood of suicide. Although there are no definitive signs, there are a number of patterns and changes in profiles that suggest a higher likelihood of suicide. One obvious indicator is the presence of severe depression. The greater the rise on Scale 2, the greater the likelihood that the person is considering suicide. In individuals with acute depressions, the profile is most likely to be 27 or 72, as discussed in the section on high point codes. Prediction of suicide likelihood is influenced by the rise on other scales as well; for example, high elevations on Scales 4, 8, and 9 reflect high energy levels and impulsiveness. These individuals, as a result, are considered high suicide risks. Suicide is also likely, however, when an individual's depression begins to improve, as this may reflect a decision to finally "end it all" which resolves the individual's ambivalence over what to do. Thus, an individual with repeated MMPI tests who shows a sudden drop in Scale 2 or a person observed to be seriously depressed who shows a subsequent low Scale 2 must be evaluated carefully for suicide ideation.

Particular attention should be paid to individuals with previous suicide attempts. Individuals with 24 or 28 profiles, being impulsive, are always high risks for further suicide attempts. The individual with a high 4 profile or 64 profile who attempts suicide is especially dangerous, as this may be an expression of revenge or an attempt to manipulate others. Once this type of individual finds out that suicide threats allow him or her to control others, frequent attempts may ensue. As a rule, the number of attempts escalates in an attempt to get more information or to manipulate others (e.g., doctors) who, in the mind of the patient, may not be taking their attempts seriously enough. Because of this escalation factor, these manipulative suicides can often lead to death.

Prognosis in Psychotherapy

Barron (1953) attempted to devise the Ego Strength scale (Es) for the prediction of psychotherapy outcome in neurotics. Research on this scale has suggested that it basically measures an individual's fundamental adjustment to the world regardless of current situational difficulties. Thus, an individual with a high Es score is likely to be better adjusted and possess more cognitive resources for dealing with his or her problems. Such individuals are consequently much better risks for therapy, as well as for spontaneous recovery. Lower scores, on the other hand, suggest individuals with low tolerance for stress, low self-concepts, and few resources available to them. These individuals tend to have less insight into their problems than high Es scorers. As a result, these individuals are less likely candidates for brief psychotherapy, although they may be candidates for long-term psychotherapy depending on their motivation and their intellectual resources. In general, the higher the individual's intellectual resources, the better the chance that the person will respond in verbal psychotherapies. The reader should note that these relationships are altered for different populations or different therapies. As a result, such scales as Es need cross validation in the particular population with whom one is working.

Other factors enter into response to psychotherapy. Acute or neurotic disorders respond better, in general, than personality disorders or psychosis, although the latter may respond to proper medication plus appropriate therapy, counseling, and vocational or other training opportunities. Acute disorders, especially transient situational disorders, are by definition generally responsive to therapy and most likely to spontaneously recover. Extremely low or high 6 scores, even in nonpsychotic individuals, are often indicative of chronic hostilities, which respond, if at all, only to long-term therapy.

Acting Out Behavior

As discussed earlier, elevations on Scales 4, 6, 8, and 9 are highly characteristic of individuals with poor impulse controls. Thus, elevations on these profiles are often associated with a variety of assaultive behaviors. Such profiles as 49, 469, 694, 468, 84, and so on, have often been associated with periodic or continual antisocial behavior that includes assaults on other individuals. As noted in the discussion of two-point codes, the 43 profile may be associated with alternate hysterical and assaultive periods in both men and women. Although the relative elevation on Scales 4 and 3 have been said to be related to the likelihood of such behavior, the probability of assault appears to be about the same for all 34 and 43 codes until 4 exceeds 3 by 10 or more points. If 3 exceeds 4 by 10 or more points, especially if 4 is at normal levels, the patient is much more likely to show hysterical behavior. Patients with 34/43 codes who do not show assaultive behavior, whether verbal or physical, should be considered potential risks for suicidal ("self-assaultive") behavior.

Alcohol and Drug Addiction

Alcohol and drug addiction are frequently encountered in all two-point codes including scale 4. This addictive potential has been reported in numerous studies from a wide range of hospitals. Individuals with these scale profiles who are not currently using alcohol or drugs generally have a higher chance of showing such behavior later if placed under sufficient stress. In addition, individuals with psychotic profiles (84, 86, 89, 82, and 87) may turn to alcoholism in attempts to medicate their own psychoses. Some drink to suppress strong feelings of anxiety, and others to stop "voices" or other hallucinations and delusions. Alcoholism may be the presenting complaint in these individuals, but it is in fact secondary to the more serious psychotic disorders.

In addition to observations from the profile, a large number of studies have attempted to develop alcoholism scales. Most of these scales are not in general use, although one has received some widespread acceptance despite contradictory research data. The scale was developed by McAndrews (1965) as an attempt to develop an instrument that could differentiate alcoholics from other psychiatric populations. McAndrews's original study reports an accuracy of about 84 percent using a raw score cutoff of 24. Subsequent studies have varied from those finding strong support for the scale to those finding it essentially useless. The effects of the scale seem to differ depending on the definition of alcoholism used, the base rate of alcoholism in the population studies, the relative proportion of primary alcoholics (with high 4 profiles) and secondary alcoholics (who initially drink as a psychiatric "treatment"), and the type of population (including such parameters as sources of referral, age, sex, and psychiatric diagnoses).

ADVANTAGES AND DISADVANTAGES

As the preceding discussion has outlined, the MMPI has a number of major advantages as a test of personality: it can be given as a screening device with little of the psychologist's time involved and can be scored easily and objectively; it is based on extensive research studies on numerous populations and for numerous problems, both major and minor, and can be repeated when necessary without difficulty; and, most importantly, it has been shown to identify significant personality characteristics in psychiatric populations, to be useful in establishing psychiatric diagnoses, to be useful in identifying the underlying characteristics and dynamics in an individual, and to be useful in providing the information necessary to initiate and choose appropriate treatment strategies for a patient.

With this variety of advantages, one can often overlook the disadvantages of the test. The test requires certain levels of reading ability and individual cooperation that are not present in all patients. In these populations, projective tests are generally more appropriate than the MMPI or other similar tests. Another positive feature of the MMPI leads to a significant problem. The objective format of the MMPI and the objective scoring have led to a proliferation of computer systems for scoring and interpreting the tests. These systems have led many clinicians to abandon their own interpretations of the test in favor of the computers' interpretations. More importantly, many individuals with little or no training with the MMPI have used these computer systems' analyses as the "absolute truth," developing the attitude that a psychologist is not necessary to interpret the test. This has resulted in misuse of the MMPI to a serious degree which cannot be ignored. As stated before, the clinician is necessary to interpret all of the factors and to integrate the interpretations. While one may choose to use a computer interpretation system, this approach is best used only as an adjunct to an individual interpretation system.

There is also a tendency for MMPI users to divorce the clinician from the patient. As stated before, interpretation of the MMPI may be done blind initially, but it is necessary to eventually integrate the test findings with the actual patient as he or she presents, as well as with the patient's history and other psychological characteristics. There is a strong need to avoid separating the clinician from the patient if maximum usefulness of the MMPI is to be achieved. Alternatively, it is important to recognize that the combination of the clinical interview, the judgment of the experienced clinician, and the MMPI results offers a powerful and valuable approach to the psychological assessment of the individual.

Before turning to the case examples, one additional note should be added. At the time of the revision of the current edition, the authors of the MMPI were engaged in a new normative study to examine the norms used with the test. Although the final results were not available when this book went to press, the preliminary data suggest that the new norms will not affect the interpretation of the MMPI as presented here, although some specific cutoff points may be changed, resulting in more accuracy in interpretations.

CASE EXAMPLES

Case 1.   Case 1, a 28-year-old female whose MMPI profile is presented in Figure 4-11, is an example of a chronic paranoid schizophrenic as indicated by the elevations on Scales 8, 6, and F. The profile also suggests a high score on hysteria, suggesting strong repressive defenses. Thus, although the patient has considerable hostility, she has little awareness of the problem, and projects the hostility onto auditory hallucinations and/or other individuals. The high 4 suggests impulsiveness in the patient, as well as a tendency toward manipulativeness. The patient is complaining of some fatigue and general physical disability (1), as well as indicating a strong tendency toward social withdrawal, isolationism, and depression (9, 2, 8). This description was confirmed by interview.

Case 2.   Case 2, a 65-year-old male whose MMPI profile is presented in Figure 4-12, suggests at first glance a normal profile as no score is elevated above 70. The elevation of the F scale into the 60s, however, is suggestive of a possible intact paranoid, an individual with a well-encapsulated delusional system.

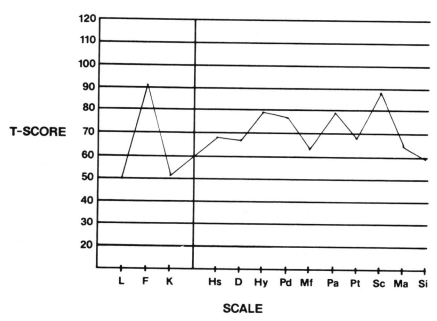

Figure 4.11. Results for Case 1.

In addition, the 46, 43, and 47 high point pairs are suggestive of impulsiveness, extensive anxiety, extensive hostility, and a possible passive-aggressive or paranoid personality. Such a person may represent a paranoid psychosis with a limited but significant delusional system, or a passive-aggressive personality that is seriously disturbed at the time of the testing. Interviews with the patient revealed an intelligent, 65-year-old man with an onset of an involutional paranoia. The patient believed he was in contact with space creatures who offered to take care of him, making it unnecessary for him to ever leave his apartment. No obvious signs of other thought disorder were present in the patient.

Case 3. Case 3, whose MMPI profile is presented in Figure 4-13, shows a markedly elevated 2 score (a T score over 110) with extremely high scores on 1 and 3. In addition, there is a clear elevation of the 78 high point pair. The high 2 combined with the 78 elevation is highly suggestive of a reactive depres-

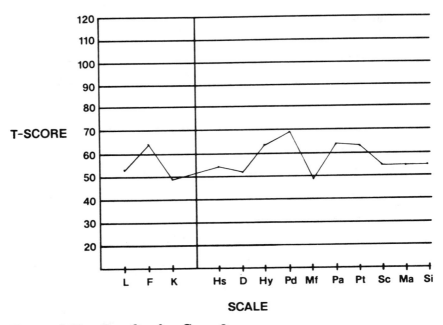

Figure 4.12. Results for Case 2.

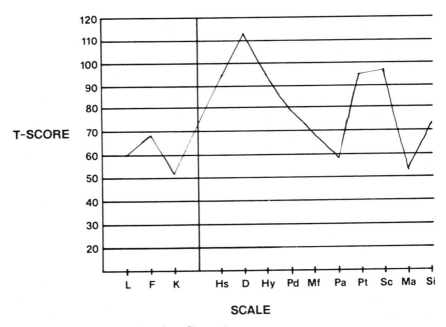

Figure 4.13. Results for Case 3.

138

sion. In addition, the patient shows strong tendencies toward developing somatic complaints in the face of anxiety. The current situation, while acute, is probably an exacerbation of a previously unstable personality (anxiety neurosis, passive-aggressive personality), as normal individuals rarely decompensate to this degree. The patient shows a strong tendency to withdraw from people, passivity, a denial of hostility, and an extensive inability to deal with anger and hostility (common in individuals with a 6 as a low point or near low point).

Interviews with the patient revealed a passive, dependent individual who was in the hospital because of the death of his father. He was extremely depressed. His premorbid adjustment was characterized by efforts to allow others to take care of him because of diffuse and generally unreal physical problems.

Case 4. Case 4, a 35-year-old male whose profile is presented in Figure 4-14, has a clear 98 profile, along with an F score of 70 and elevations on Scales 1, 2, 3, and 4, all of which

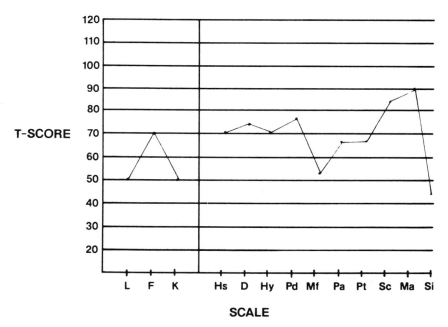

Figure 4.14. Results for Case 4.

were between T scores of 70 and 80. Individuals with the 98 profile tend to be hyperactive, to be emotionally labile, and often to show delusions of grandeur. While the manic behavior is often accompanied by depression, the mania serving as a cover, the depression is rarely seen in the patient's behavior during manic episodes. Thus, the 1234 elevation on the MMPI is not accompanied by clear depressive or hypochondriacal symptoms, although asocial behavior (as represented by Scale 4) of an impulsive nature is quite likely. The patient is extremely extroverted and friendly, as is typical of this disorder, but likely has difficulty in forming meaningful close relationships. The F score and 8 score suggest some bizarre behavior, but this is limited and partially under control. In these patients, as noted previously, the bizarre behavior generally takes the form of delusions of grandeur and extremely elevated moods no matter what the situation. These individuals are prone to cyclic periods of depression when the more somatic and hysterical tendencies are clearer. Interviews with the patient confirm the impression gained from the MMPI. The patient carried a diagnosis of manic-depressive psychosis.

CHAPTER FIVE

The Sixteen Personality Factors Questionnaire

The Sixteen Personality Factors Questionnaire (16PF) is the end result of extensive factor analytic work by Cattell and his associates. Unlike the MMPI, the 16PF was designed to be a factorially pure test, in which each scale reflects a basic aspect of personality structure. In addition, the 16PF was largely designed by working with normal rather than pathological populations. As a result, the 16PF places a much greater emphasis on day-to-day personality traits rather than containing the pathological focus seen in the MMPI.

The 16PF was not originally designed as a clinical instrument, and has seen little clinical use and research compared with the MMPI. There is an impressive amount of research literature on the 16PF, but it does not generally address the medical and psychiatric problems seen by many clinical psychologists. This state of affairs has begun to change in recent years, however. Several books have been published on the clinical or medical use of the MMPI, and increasing clinical research with the 16PF is appearing in such journals as the *Journal of Consulting and Clinical Psychology* and the *Journal of Personality Assessment*. This growing literature, aimed at the clinician rather than the experimental personality theorist, indicates a valid and growing use for the 16PF in clinical practice.

PURPOSE

The purpose of the 16PF is to delineate the major personality factors in such a way as to allow the clinician to form a broad picture of the individual's personality functioning. It does not seek to recognize severe pathology or specific diagnostic entities, but rather concentrates on deviations in the personality characteristic of the normal individual. It also allows for a more extensive evaluation of the tendencies in an individual classified as "normal," enabling the clinician to gain a more effective picture of the client's weaknesses and strengths, even in the absence of pathology of any kind.

ADMINISTRATION

The 16PF is relatively simple to administer. There are five forms of the test, each presented in a paper booklet. Forms A and B have 187 items and are used with adult patients and are most frequently given in clinical practice. Forms C and D represent shorter forms of A and B, but are not recommended for clinical use. Form E is used with individuals having low reading levels, usually below the sixth grade level. Each question on the test is multiple choice and has three possible answers (a, b, or c).

The test may be taken individually or in a group. The patient answers each question on a computer answer sheet. The answer sheets can be scored by computer (if the proper pencil is used) or by hand. Although many prefer computer scoring services because of the convenience, our own tests are scored by hand since this takes little time and provides instant feedback rather than the delay of using an outside scoring service. Hand scoring employs templates that can be bought for each form of the 16PF.

After the raw scores for each scale have been determined, these are translated into sten scores. Sten scores have a mean of 5.5 and a standard deviation of 2. The highest score possible is 10 and the lowest score possible is 1. As a result of this scoring system, scores may vary only 2.25 standard deviations in either direction, for a total variation of only 4.5 standard deviations. Some of the MMPI scales, on the other hand, can vary over 8 standard deviations.

Overall scoring is available for 16 standard scales (discussed below). Karson and O'Dell (1976) reported the development of several scales that serve the same purpose as the MMPI validity scales. Two of these scales are the Faking Bad and Motivational Distortion (faking good) scales. The items on the faking bad scale (and answers indicating a scorable response) are 14(a), 38(a), 42(c), 51(b), 52(c), 55(c), 68(c), 80(a), 89(c), 117(a), 119(a), 123(a), 143(a), 176(c), and 182(c). For the motivational distortion (faking good) scale, the scorable answers are 7(c), 24(c), 61(c), 62(a), 81(a), 97(a), 111(a), 114(c), 123(c), 130(a), 133(c), 149(c), 173(a), 174(c), and 184(a). These items are taken from Winder, O'Dell, and Karson (1975).

A third supplementary scale is the Random scale (O'Dell, 1971). This scale includes answers that very rarely occur in normal protocols or answers that are very rarely omitted. One point is given for each answer of A to Items 38, 54, 77, 78, 80, 93, 102, 118, 119, 121, and 143; B to Items 12, 20, 23, 51, 52, 66, 87, 91, 109, and 127; and C to Items 4 and 73. One point is also scored if any of the following answers are omitted: 1(a), 2(a), 28(b), 29(a) 53(b), 112(a), 116(c) and 128(b). For each of these supplementary scales, there is no key provided with the 16PF. Keys must be made by the user. These validity scores are not translated into sten scores.

After the basic scale scores have been calculated, second order factor scores can be calculated. These scores represent more basic tendencies that underlie two or more of the basic scales. These scores are calculated automatically by the computer, or can be done by hand employing formulas in the 16PF handbook (Cattell, Eber, & Taltsuoka, 1970).

INTERPRETATION

Validity Scales

The Motivational Distortion scale (MD) and the Faking Bad scale (FB) both use cutoffs of six. Any score above this point indicates faking good in the case of the Motivational Distortion scale, while a score above six on Faking Bad suggests that the patient has been faking bad. Winder et al. (1975) reported a high rate of accuracy for these scales: MD picks up 85 percent of the faking good profiles while misidentifying only 10 percent of the normal profiles. FB identifies 94 percent of the faking bad profiles while misidentifying none of the honestly answered profiles. For the Random scale, a score of five or greater suggests randomness. This scale is able to identify about 90 percent of the random files while misclassifying only about 6 percent of the nonrandom records.

As was the case with the MMPI, there is no need to throw out a protocol with a high score on any of the validity scales (except Random). Tendencies to answer in a faking good or faking bad direction can be used to modify interpretations of profiles presented by patients, and they have clinical significance. For example, as we saw in the MMPI chapter, faking good can be associated with strong repressive and hysterical tendencies, whereas faking bad may indicate a person crying for help or a person strongly divorced from reality.

Clinical Scales

Several important factors must be recognized when interpreting the 16PF scores. Although standard interpretations are provided for scores, one must be careful not to simply string together the appropriate adjectives for an individual. Otherwise, one ends up with a diagnosis that describes the same person as hostile and friendly, tense and calm, and other equally unusual combinations. These cases require careful integration of the full profile to account for possible contradictions. Although such blatant cases of contradiction are rare, more subtle cases, such as one anxiety indicator being up and another down, are more common. These cases also require careful evaluation to determine the aspects of anxiety or other dimensions important to the case.

The 16 scales of the 16PF are indicated by letters or letter-number combinations: A, B, C, E, F, G, H, I, L, M, N, O, Q1, Q2, Q3, and Q4. The following discussions of each scale are drawn from several primary sources: Cattell (1957, 1973), Cattell et al. (1970), Cattell and Warburton (1967), and Krug (1977). The Karson and O'Dell (1976) book must be regarded, at present, as the single most useful clinical reference on the 16PF, while the Cattell et al. (1970) reference includes the basic material on the 16PF, including references to much of Cattell's earlier work.

Scale A

Scale A is theoretically a measure of warmth. As with the other scales of the 16PF, Cattell attempted to describe the difference between high and low scores in terms of dichotomies such as, in this case, reserved, detached, aloof, stiff, critical, rigid, cold, and prone to sulk (low score) versus good natured, warmhearted, outgoing, soft-hearted, trustful, and attentive to people (high score). Low A scores are generally associated with what are seen as negative traits (e.g., hostility, egotism, and suspiciousness), many of which are traits associated with paranoid schizophrenia (although the scale does not measure such a pathological dimension). Cattell associated the concept of flat affect with low scores, whereas high scores are more emotionally expressive. High scores can be associated with manic-type states in extreme cases.

High A scorers generally like to be around people, especially if other scales are consistent with this interpretation. Their adjustment is likely to be troublesome if forced into a position where they are not allowed contact with others. Low scorers, on the other hand, may find contact with others to be anxiety provoking or even painful. As noted above, frankly schizoid symptoms are possible in these individuals. It is important that extremely low scores on A be considered seriously by the clinician.

Scale B

Scale B is a measure of intelligence. In this respect, it differs considerably from the other scales on the 16PF. Low scores on Scale B are associated with low mental capacity, poor judgment, low morale, low perseverance, and low ability to work with abstract problems. High B scores are associated with high intelligence, ability to work with abstract ideas, good judgment, good morale, and perseverance. Users should note that 16PF norms are available for different populations. Thus, IQ is figured in comparison with IQs of others in the same reference group, rather than with those of the population as a whole. Since this is also a very short scale, the reliability of Scale B is questionable.

Poor scores on Scale B may be associated with anxiety, inability to concentrate, and poor intelligence. Scale B may also be used to modify interpretations on other scales: for example, a person with scores indicating manipulativeness would be looked at considerably differently if the person had a low score on B (suggesting that the attempts at manipulation are likely very concrete and not too subtle) or a high score on B (suggesting that the person is a shrewd, active, subtle manipulator of others).

Scale C

Scale C was described by Cattell as a measure of ego strength. Low scores on the scale are suggestive of an inability to handle frustration, a general emotional lability, an evasion of responsibility, and a tendency to worry and give up. High scores are associated with emotional maturity, general lack of anxiety, and an ability to deal with frustrating or difficult situations. As might be surmised from this description, Scale C plays a prominent role in many psychiatric disorders. Low scores on Scale C suggest a general inability to deal with stress (or faking bad), as well as a poor prognosis in psychotherapy because of a tendency to avoid difficult situations and a lack of resources on an emotional level. Similarly, high scorers on Scale C, if seen for psychiatric problems, are likely experiencing temporary, situational difficulties rather than long-term personality problems.

Scale E

Scale E is suggested as being a measure of dominance. Low scores on the scale are associated with submissiveness, obedience, conventionality, docility, and dependence. High scores are associated with dominance, aggressiveness, hostility, rebelliousness, and independence. Low E scores may be related to excessive passivity, and can be associated with passive-dependent problems. Such individuals may also serve as "door-mats" to others, even to the point of being the scapegoats in pathological family situations. A high E score is not likely to be pathological, but it can be a serious sign in connection with other scale elevations that suggest a sociopathic personality or a tendency toward emotional outbursts.

Scale F

This scale is a measure of impulsivity. Low F scores are associated with seriousness, introspective behavior, the presence of inner values, and a generally slow or cautious approach to problems. High F scores are associated with enthusiasm, cheerfulness, quickness, alertness, impulsiveness, and a tendency to be very talkative and group involved. Low F individuals were described by Cattell as being dull, depressed, anxious, suspicious, and rigid. Although it is not actually an indication of depression, low Fs are frequently seen in association with depressive states. High Fs reflect impulsivity, extraversion (although self-centered, according to Karson & O'Dell, 1976), originality, and adaptability. Karson and O'Dell suggested that in extreme cases, high F scores may be associated with manic phases of emotional disorders. As with other similar measures, F scores tend to decrease with age, reaching a stable level in the person's 30s.

Scale G

Scale G is a measure of group conformity. Low scores suggest a tendency to be fickle, frivolous, self-indulgent, undependable, and generally unconcerned about group standards or morals. High G scores are associated with strong superegos, responsibility, conscientiousness, moral correctness, and a strong sense of duty. The items on Scale G are similar to those of the MMPI L scale. Hence, high scorers either are excessively rigid and moralistic or are answering in a faking good direction.

These scores may also be associated with strong repression and a tendency toward conversion hysteria, an important consideration in a medically referred population.

Low G scores, on the other hand, may suggest a tendency toward admitting faults or faking bad. They may also be associated with lack of superego, the classic definition of the sociopathic or antisocial personality. If combined with indications suggesting acting out, this scale could indicate a tendency toward crime, drug abuse, and other disorders associated with the MMPI 49 profile.

Scale H

Scale H represents the concept of boldness. Low H scores are associated with shyness, restraint, sensitivity to threat, emotional cautiousness, and unfriendliness. High H scores are associated with adventurousness, extroversion, social boldness, interest in the opposite sex, responsiveness, impulsivity, and a general insensitivity to danger signs.

Cattell associated low H scores with tendencies toward schizoid personality (like Scale A scores). Combined with other traits indicative of schizophrenia, low scores on this scale can be a significant warning sign. Cattell described the low H as shy, hostile, withdrawn, and cold – all qualities of the schizoid or frankly schizophrenic individual. High H scores do not have the significance of low H scores, but can be a problem in a patient whose adventurousness is not matched by socially appropriate skills and intelligence.

Scale I

Scale I is a measure of emotional sensitivity. A low score is associated with tough mindedness, self-reliance, lack of sentimentality, cynicism, logic, practicality, and lack of hypochondriasis. High I scores are associated with emotional sensitivity, insecurity, dependence, imaginativeness (in inner life and conversation), attention-seeking behavior, and hypochondriasis. Karson and Pool (1957) found a close relationship between this scale and the Mf scale of the MMPI, reflecting the kind of cultural interests people have and their reactions to hostility.

This factor is not closely associated with pathology, as is the MMPI Mf scale. Low scores involve some repression of emotionality, but this is not pathological unless one is in situations that demand emotional sensitivity. The high I persons may be somewhat more sensitive to stress because of their emotional sensitivity, which can be a problem in some situations demanding logical, rational decisions no matter what the human factors in the situation are.

Scale L

Scale L is a measure of suspiciousness. Low scorers on L may be characterized as trusting, nonhostile, permissive, tolerant, and generally uncritical. High L scorers are likely to be jealous, dogmatic, suspicious, frustrated, domineering, and irritable. At the extreme, high L scorers may show distinct signs of paranoia. Thus, high scores on this scale combined with high scores suggesting schizoid behavior should be indications for more extensive evaluation.

Low L people are trusting and nonsuspicious, according to their self-description. In general, this score is looked upon as an indication of health. As we saw in the MMPI, however, extremely low Paranoia scores may be associated with intense suspiciousness and denial. Similarly, extremely low scores on L, if found in profiles with strong indicators of pathology, must not always be taken at face value.

A high L score, at the very least, suggests an individual who is probably very difficult to get along with in everyday situations. These patients typically project their negative feelings onto others, and appear hostile and sullen themselves. One should be careful to remember, however, that this scale does not get into the more delusional, hostile material that characterizes MMPI Paranoia scores over 70. Thus, high scorers may be normal people who are simply high on suspiciousness and who may be functioning quite well otherwise, or they may be overt paranoid schizophrenics. Hence, the lack of items at more pathological ranges makes it impossible to discriminate on the basis of this test result alone.

Scale M

This scale is a measure of imagination. Low scorers are generally described as conventional, practical, objective, conservative, and not overly imaginative or farseeing. High scorers, on the other hand, are imaginative, interested in art and philosophy, fanciful, subjective, and unconventional. This scale is not a major measure of psychopathology.

Individuals with low scores are generally suited to jobs with many practical, realistic demands and generally perform better in these situations than do high M individuals. Low scorers are generally seen as tough minded, especially with a high score on I as well. High scorers do better in jobs requiring imagination and artistic skills. Karson (1959) found that anxiety neurotics tend to score higher on M (reflecting general worry over basic, philosophical ideas) than do psychosomatic individuals, whose concerns and worries are more practical and concrete.

Scale N

Scale N is a measure of shrewdness. Low scores on Scale N are suggestive of genuineness, spontaneity, vagueness, a lack of self-insight, simple tastes, passivity, and a blind trust in human nature. High scores on Scale N suggest social awareness, a calculating mind, emotional detachment, worldliness, ambition, and alertness to cutting corners and taking advantage of situations. Scale N significantly correlates with the Hysteria scale of the MMPI.

Karson and O'Dell (1976) classified this scale as one of the least useful on the 16PF. They noted that it can be important in the right context. Indications of high N along with rebelliousness and intelligence, for example, suggest an individual for whom a superior would do well to watch. In addition, it would not be rare for sociopaths to show high N scores, but rare for them to show low N scores.

Scale O

Scale O is a measure of guilt proneness. Low O scores are suggestive of an untroubled, adequate individual, who is likely to be self-confident, cheerful, and internally controlled, and who is likely to act when it is necessary. The high O scorer, however, is an apprehensive, insecure, and troubled individual who is likely to be anxious, depressed, sensitive to the disapproval and approval of others, hypochondriacal, phobic, and lonely. Clearly, this scale is of immense importance in the clinical analysis of the 16PF, although it is generally considered only a minor scale in Cattell's theoretical system. Low scores on O may be associated with weak superego controls, whereas high scores on O suggest overly dominating superego controls. Thus, deviations in both directions can suggest psychopathology.

High O scores may be a measure of both anxiety and depression. As would be expected from this description of symptoms, high O scores can be either chronic or reactive to environmental events. Chronic high O scorers do not respond well to psychotherapy, as a rule, and are better off with directive counseling aimed at eliminating the behaviors that cause their guilt and depression. Low O scores may be associated with sociopathic personalities, or with intense denial patterns in which the person is unable to face his or her guilt and anxiety.

Scale Q1

Scale Q1 is a measure of rebelliousness. Low scores are associated with conservatism, whereas high scores are associated with radicalism, a tendency to be experimenting, liberal, analytical, and free thinking. Extreme Q1 scores may be associated with radicalism and an inability to accept authority, a trait commonly seen in the sociopathic patient. Such individuals are difficult to have as subordinates. Low Q1 individuals tend to be respecting of tradition and unwilling to change the way things are done. This is pathological only in situations in which nontraditional change is needed to work out serious life problems.

Scale Q2

Scale Q2 is a measure of self-sufficiency. Low scorers are apt to be group dependent, frequent joiners, and good followers. High scorers are likely to be self-sufficient individuals, who prefer depending on their own resources and their own judgments. Clearly, this is also an alternate measure of introversion-extroversion, with the introversion being a healthier, more creative type of trait. The scale does not indicate pathology by itself, although it can be part of a general extroverted or introverted style (see the section entitled Second Order Factors).

Scale Q3

Scale Q3 has been characterized as a measure of the ability to bind anxiety. Low scorers are characterized by a lack of control, a carelessness with respect to social rules, and a tendency to follow one's own urges. High scorers are controlled, socially precise, and compulsive, and they possess strong will power. The high Q3 individual thinks before acting and does not let emotional upset disturb routine. Such individuals are dependable, well controlled, and good workers. High Q3 scores are associated with good mental health, although taken to extremes they can indicate extreme obsessive-compulsive behavior.

Low Q3 scores are associated with overreactivity. These individuals are not able to handle stress productively, and have difficulty in large organizations in which responsibility is an important factor. If a low Q3 is found in the presence of other anxiety indicators, there is strong reason to suspect that the person is currently in emotional trouble, often of a serious nature.

Scale Q4

Scale Q4 is a measure of free-floating anxiety and tension. Low scores are associated with low tension, low anxiety, a relaxed and tranquil approach to life, and a general lack of frustration. High scorers on Q4 are characterized by tension, frustration, and a generally highly anxious approach to problems. This scale is the single best indicator on the 16PF of neurotic anxiety. High scores can indicate a person with extreme problems, a cry for help, or a faking bad profile. One should also recognize that this scale is subject to daily fluctuations depending on the current status of the individual. The score may also be low in individuals who have bound their anxiety into medical symptoms or into obsessive or compulsive behavior. Q4 has a .75 correlation with the MMPI Psychasthenia scale, and consequently should be taken very seriously whenever it is elevated. When the scale does not flat in with the rest of the profile, it is better to discuss the scale with the patients rather than ignore it (Karson & O'Dell, 1976).

SECOND ORDER FACTORS

Second order factors attempt to identify basic symptoms underlying the 16 primary scales on the 16PF; they represent broader and more basic trends in personality than do individual scale scores. As a result, they can be very important in a more generalized clinical impression of the patient. A number of second order factors can be identified on the 16PF, but Karson and O'Dell (1976) suggested that five factors have basic relevance to the clinician. The order of the factors represents their sizes in the factor analytic studies that derived them. As a consequence, the first factors are more significant to behavior than are the later factors.

Factor I

Factor I is the measure of extroversion-introversion, a finding consistent with other theories of personality. A person who scores high on this factor is typically high on Scales A (warmth), F (impulsivity), and H (boldness), and low on Scale Q2 (self-sufficiency). The opposite profile is characteristic of the patient with low extroversion (introversion). Intermediate scores, as well as moderate deviations from the mean in either direction, can be achieved by manipulating the scores of these four scales. In some of these cases, one or more of the scales may be in the wrong direction.

Profiles suggesting a high level of introversion should be evaluated carefully, as introversion is associated with depression, neurotic disorders, and schizophrenia. This is especially serious when sten scores are greater than eight or less than three (this is true of all the 16PF factors). High extroversion scores are not considered as pathological, as our society tends to reward such behavior. Extreme extroversion scales, however, may be seen in manic-depressive disorders (manic phase), in sociopathic disorders, in normal people who are successful salesmen, and in psychologists and physicians.

Factor II

Factor II is the second-order measure of anxiety. The major scales that contribute to this factor are Q4 (free-floating anxiety), O (guilt proneness), C (ego strength), L (suspiciousness), and Q3 (ability to bind anxiety). High anxiety scores are associated with low scores on C and Q3, and with high scores on L, O, and Q4. Each of the scales contributing to the anxiety factor are easily faked; as a consequence, it is necessary to interpret this scale only after consideration of the validity scales.

High scores on this scale are associated with significant psychological problems (unless the profile is the result of faking bad, which can be a call for help or a deliberate malingering or falsification for some external gain). In general, the level of scores on Scale C (ego strength) is important in determining chronicity: high scores (good ego strength) are associated with acute disorders that respond well to treatment, while low scores suggest chronic anxiety and anxiety related problems that are less responsive to treatment.

In profiles with general anxiety indicators up and ego strength down, therapy leading to a reduction of environmental stress (by changing the patient's environment), as well as appropriate medication, is more effective than traditional psychotherapy. Attempting to force such individuals to be more self-sufficient generally causes the patient to stagnate or even to get worse, as the requisite psychological skills are not there. In one of our patients (with a high intelligence score), we were able to reduce stress by transferring the patient into an academic/research setting with little pressure (except intellectual pressure, which was all the patient could handle). In this environment, the patient was able to make positive contributions, though still requiring frequent directive therapy and close follow-up.

Factor III

Cattell named this factor "tough poise." An individual high on this factor is low on A (warmth), I (emotional sensitivity), and M (imagination). These are people who are not easily swayed by feelings. Low scorers are more likely to be swayed by their emotions and reactions to personal factors in a situation. While this has some relevance to job selection (where this trait may act as a hindrance or advantage, depending on the setting), the factor does not appear to be important in most clinical situations. Extremely low scores in a person with emotional problems, however, may suggest an unusual degree of repression or an avoidance of people to reduce interpersonal stress.

Factor IV

This factor is a measure of independence. High scores on the factor are associated with high scores on Scales E (dominance), L (suspiciousness), M (imagination), Q1 (rebelliousness), and Q2 (self-sufficiency). Cattell suggested that individuals high on this scale are a law unto themselves. This does not necessarily indicate hostility toward others, although this is possible when seen in a patient with other pathological signs.

Factor V

Sociopathy is the title of this final factor. High scores on G (group conformity) and Q3 (ability to bind anxiety) suggest conformity, rigidity, and lack of spontaneity, whereas low scores are associated with freedom and lack of restraint. Extremely low scores are associated with sociopathic tendencies, an important consideration in many clinical examinations.

GENERAL INTERPRETIVE STRATEGIES

In interpreting a 16PF profile, the clinician should be alert to those patterns that signal high anxiety, sociopathy, or extroversion/introversion. Beyond this, interpretation begins with scales whose scores deviate most significantly from 5.5, especially scores of 9, 10, 1, and 2, which are indicative of extreme tendencies in one direction or the other. From this, one works to those scores significantly different from 5.5 but not as extreme (7, 8, 3, and 4). Scores of 5 or 6 are normal and rarely need comment (unless pathology in the area has been suggested by another scale or by the referred source).

In this way, an initial description may be generated. For the inexperienced user, some points of the interpretation may conflict or be vague. Thus, one must review the profile and interpretations to correct for these tendencies based on the profile as a whole. One should be especially attentive to scales that disagree with the major profile interpretation as these can offer valuable modifications.

The validity scales should also be closely considered in making interpretations. This takes some clinical experience with known cases in an individual population, because the general validity of these scales has not been fully validated. Indeed, the validity scales and the effects of distortion by patients are the weakest parts of the 16PF. While some users have suggested that such scales are not necessary as patients rarely distort on the 16PF (see Krug, 1977), I have found that such manipulation is common in medical populations suspected of psychiatric disorders.

A final caution on the 16PF is not to confuse extreme scores on this test with extreme scores on the MMPI. Extreme scores on the 16PF between and including scores two and nine are all within the normal two standard deviations from the population mean. Variant normal people and extremely pathological individuals may thus get similar scores on a single scale, although it would be rare for a normal individual to come up with extremely pathological patterns (except when in acute distress).

As a result, the 16PF is generally inadequate to fully diagnose a pathological condition. In those cases in which such a condition is suggested, follow-up testing with the MMPI and other instruments described in this book is advised. We rarely use the 16PF to give a definitive diagnosis, but rather use it to develop a description of the individual's personality processes.

CASE EXAMPLES

Case 1. The most outstanding scores in case 1 (Table 5-1), a 37-year-old male, are scores of 9 on L, 10 on O, 10 on Q4, 1 on C, and 2 on Q3. Overall, this is a pattern consistent with a very high level of anxiety in a fairly intelligent (B) individual. The anxiety seems to be the basic and only problem in the profile.

TABLE 5.1   Case Profiles

Scale	Case 1	Case 2	Case 3	Case 4
A (Warmth)	5	2	10	2
B (Intelligence)	8	10	8	3
C (Ego Strength)	1	7	7	4
E (Dominance)	4	10	6	4
F (Impulsivity)	4	8	9	1
G (Group Conformity)	6	3	4	3
H (Boldness)	4	7	9	2
I (Tender-mindedness)	7	3	4	5
L (Suspiciousness)	9	10	6	8
M (Imagination)	5	7	5	6
N (Shrewdness)	6	8	7	4
O (Guilt)	10	3	5	7
Q1 (Rebelliousness)	5	8	6	7
Q2 (Self-sufficiency)	6	9	1	10
Q3 (Compulsiveness)	2	6	6	5
Q4 (Anxiety)	10	2	5	8

This individual is probably neurotic, as there are no clear signs of a more psychotic disorder based on the patient's scores on A, G, I, and Q2. Further testing would be in order to determine the exact nature of the disorder and whether it was acute or chronic. (The individual was suffering from an acute anxiety disorder because of recently losing a job held for 15 years.)

Case 2. Case 2 (see Table 5-1) is a highly intelligent (B), dominant (E), suspicious (L), self-sufficient (Q2), calm (Q4), and aloof (A) individual. This profile is characteristic of individuals who are sociopathic. They are often able to manipulate people, because of their high intelligence and their general disregard for the feelings of others. These individuals do not respond well to psychotherapy and are prone to involvement in confidence games, violence (of a well planned type), and other antisocial behavior. On the other hand, this type of individual could be a highly successful professional with a reputation for competence, organization, and intelligence. It is important in these profiles to get a good history to allow one to discriminate between these possibilities.

Cases 3 and 4. These cases, the first a 28-year-old male and the second a 31-year-old male, are included to show the differential profiles of an extrovert and an introvert. The first profile is of an individual who is warm, intelligent, outgoing, and impulsive, and who prefers group situations to being alone. Such an individual may be at one extreme of normal, although the present case was taken from an individual with a diagnosis of manic-depressive disorder. The second profile represents an individual of low intelligence, who is aloof, shows schizoid tendencies, is very controlled, lacks boldness, and is very self-sufficient and quite anxious. Again, this can represent one normal extreme in some cases, but was taken from the case of an individual with a schizoid personality disorder who was not actively psychotic.

These latter two cases emphasize the importance of carefully evaluating extreme profiles for possible signs that must be investigated through history or other diagnostic instruments.

CHAPTER SIX

Wechsler Memory Scale

Clinical psychologists and physicians alike have long recognized the need for the evaluation of memory functions, which are found to be impaired in many neuropsychological and psychiatric conditions. Despite this, there have been few memory tests that have gained any real acceptance.

The first major test in this area, the Wechsler Memory Scale (WMS), developed in 1945 by David Wechsler (the same man who devised the Wechsler intelligence scales), was an attempt to measure both verbal and nonverbal components of memory. Although many criticisms were made of the test, its importance lies in that it quickly became the dominant test in the field, used in countless clinics across the country.

In recent years, in response to these criticisms, the test was given a detailed "overhaul" with nothing except the name remaining the same. New norms, new procedures, new approaches, and new administration guidelines were presented in the WMS-R. Work on the WMS-R was begun by Wechsler before his death in 1981, but was subsequently completed by a team of psychologists and others under the guidance of the publisher, The Psychological Corporation.

There is little doubt that, despite the newness of the WMS-R, it is vastly superior to the initial form. Unlike the other revisions we have discussed in this book, it actually represents a new test rather than a modification. It is my conviction that the WMS-R should be used in lieu of the earlier WMS (Form I or Form II) in all circumstances, with the possible exception of when one wishes to compare earlier performance on the WMS to current performance on the WMS.

Despite the improvements evident in the WMS-R, however, the WMS remains a major instrument that is still used by numerous clinicians. In light of this, this chapter presents both forms of the test: first, the newer WMS-R, and, at the end, the original text on the WMS from the earlier version of this book.

WECHSLER MEMORY SCALE-REVISED

The WMS-R is an individually administered test of short- and intermediate-term memory designed to evaluate a wide range of both verbal and nonverbal memory functions. It represents, at present, the most ambitious generally available memory battery for the practicing clinician. It clearly recognizes that memory is not a unitary function, but rather is made up of many skills that can be lumped together under the general heading of memory. The scale consists of 13 subscales designed to measure different aspects of memory. In addition, it provides norms at nine age levels (but is not applicable to children under 16).

Content, Administration, and Scoring of the WMS-R

The 13 subtests are arranged in a specific order (as presented here) and should be administered to each patient in that order. In cases in which the patient is unable or unwilling to cooperate with a given subtest, it can be skipped and finished at the end of the session, although delayed versions of immediate memory tests must be given about 30 minutes after the immediate memory version. Thus, if one is forced to skip Logical Memory I (the immediate memory test), one must also wait until about 30 minutes after later completing Logical Memory I until giving Logical Memory II (the delayed version). This may interfere with the accuracy of the norms, however, and should be avoided whenever possible. Similarly, for those tests with immediate and delayed versions, both versions must be given within the same testing session.

As with other tests, the session is started by gathering identifying information, such as name, age, birthdate, and so on. (This can be omitted, of course, if one already knows this information.) The test manual (Wechsler, 1987) suggests the need to resolve any conflicts between the patient's stated age and calculated age (from birthdate) at this point while the patient is present.

Information and Orientation Questions. The test is begun with information and orientation questions, which are used to make sure the patient is oriented and alert and to alert the tester to any problems likely to interfere with the testing. There are 16 questions, the last 2 of which are not scored. All the questions are read directly from the test manual or test form exactly as presented.

The first 14 questions are scored one (correct) or zero (incorrect). The items include name, age, place of birth, date of birth, mother's first name, current president, previous president, current year, current month, current date, place where the testing is taking place, city where the testing is taking place, current day of the week, and current time (without using a watch and within 30 minutes). The last two questions, which are unscored, are whether the patient is right- or left-handed and whether the patient has hearing problems, the need for eyeglasses, or problems with color blindness.

The score for the subtest is simply the total of the points earned on the first 14 questions.

Mental Control. The Mental Control subtest is a measure of concentration on relatively simple tasks (and is identical to the same subtest on the WMS). It consists of three items: counting backward from 20 to 1, saying the alphabet, and counting forward by 3s from 1 to 40. Each item is timed, and errors are counted. A perfect performance within the time limit is scored as two, a performance with only one error within the time limit is scored as one, and a performance with multiple errors is scored as zero. On the last item, errors are counted only when there is an error of addition. Thus, if the person counts 1, 5, 8, 11, 14 and so on, one error is counted for misadding 3 to 1, but no errors are counted after that since each number is 3 higher than the previous number. The manual does not describe what to do if the person counts 1, 37, 40 (which is technically one error), but I score any sequence as a zero if there are not at least 12 additions (allowing the patient to continue beyond 40 as necessary in a case such as this). Total score is simply the sum of the scores on the three items.

Figural Memory. This is the first of the new WMS-R subtests. It requires the Figural Memory stimulus booklet, which is supplied along with the WMS-R kit. The tasks consist of the client's being shown a figure, and then having to select that figure from among a larger group of designs. This is a test of nonverbal recognition memory, which does not have the disadvantage of requiring a complex motor response, as do many nonverbal memory tests.

For the first item, the patient is shown a single design for 5 seconds and then asked to select it. If the examinee does not respond within 5 seconds, he or she is prompted by being asked "Which one is it?" If the client errs on this initial item, the item is repeated but not scored. On the second item, the examinee is shown three figures and given 15 seconds to examine them. The examinee is then shown a page with nine designs from which he or must identify the original three designs. On this and subsequent items, the examinee is given 30 seconds to respond. If there is no response after 10 seconds, prompting is required. If patients are wavering between two possible responses or are unclear as to what figures they are choosing, they may be prompted to select one within the 30-second time period. Items three and four are identical to the second item.

Scoring is one point for each correct design selected, with a maximum of 10 points for the four items. When a patient selects more items than were initially presented, he or she should be urged to clarify his or her choices. The manual does not address this issue, but when all correct choices have not been made within the 20-second period, the client's score must be penalized (lose one point for one extra point, two points for two, and so on) up to the maximum possible points on the item.

Logical Memory I. This is similar to the traditional task of retelling a story. The Roman numeral I after the subtest title indicates that this is the immediate memory version of a test with a delayed memory version. The delayed memory version in this case is titled Logical Memory II. In all cases such as this, the Roman numeral I subtest must be given before the Roman numeral II subtest, with an intertest interval of about 30 minutes. As with Logical Memory in the original WMS, scoring is for the number of units remembered. Unlike the WMS, the manual gives detailed instructions on the material that needs to be remembered to get credit for a given unit. The client's response should be taken down verbatim, and the answers analyzed using the manual criteria rather than using clinical judgment as in the WMS. There are two stories included in this test. One point is allowed for each acceptable response. The total score is simply the total number of one-point responses for both stories.

After the second story, the subject is told that he or she needs to remember these stories later in the testing session.

Visual Paired Associates I. In this subtest, a line drawing is paired with a color during the presentation phase. In the response phase, the client is shown the line drawing and then must select the color with which it was paired. No verbal response is required. The subtest requires the Verbal Paired Associates folders and stimulus book, which are supplied with the test. The test begins with a demonstration card. The client is shown a figure and a color square, and is told that the figure goes with the color. The client is then shown the reverse of the card, on which a second drawing-color pair is presented. Then the client is shown one of the figures without the color and asked to point to the right color from Folder A. If this is correct, one proceeds. If the client fails to answer or is unsure, he or she may be prompted for an answer. If the answer is wrong, the client is shown the correct answer; then the examiner proceeds to the next demonstration figure without a color and repeats the above process.

After the demonstration, the main test is given from Folder B. Six color-figure pairs are presented for three seconds each. In the response phase, the six figures are shown and the client must point out the correct color. The client is given five seconds to respond to each figure. If he or she responds correctly, the examiner says "That's right" and then pauses for five seconds before showing the next figure. If there is an incorrect or no response, the examiner points to the correct color, says "This is the right color," and then waits five seconds until presenting the next figure.

After the first trial, the pairs are again presented together, followed by a recall phase as above. The presentation-recall procedure is then done a third time for each subject. Additional presentation-recall trials are given if the patient's recall is not perfect. Once a perfect recall is achieved on the third or later trial, the test is discontinued. The test is also discontinued after the sixth presentation-recall phase regardless of performance. After the last trial is given, the subject is told that he or she needs to remember these pairs later in the testing session.

Scoring is one point per correct answer during the first three trials only. The later trials are simply attempts to improve the patient's immediate memory so as to get more meaningful results in the delayed version of this test.

Verbal Paired Associates I.   This task is similar to Paired Associate Memory on the WMS. The test consists of eight pairs of words which are read (as pairs) to the client. Then the client is given one of the words and asked to repeat the second word. During the recall phase, if the client makes an error, he or she is told the correct word. If the response is correct, the examiner indicates this by saying "That's right." Then there is a second presentation phase, identical to the first, followed by a second recall phase, also done in the same manner as the first. Each examinee is given additional presentation and recall trials until the examinee gets all items correct or a total of six trials is reached. Each examinee, however, is given three presentation/recall trials regardless of performance, as the client's score is based on these trials. At the end of the subtest, the examinee is told that he or she will be asked to recall the words again later in the session.

Scoring is simply the number of correct second words given over the first three trials.

Visual Reproduction I. This task requires drawing a design from memory. The subtest requires four cards with designs on them (Cards A through D), the copying/drawing sheet from the record form, and two lead pencils with erasers. Beginning with Card A, the design is shown to the subject for 10 seconds. At the end of the 10 seconds, the client is asked to draw the figure from memory. Reluctant clients who complain either because they do not remember or cannot draw are urged to do the best they can. Similar procedures are used for Cards B and C. Before Card D, the client is warned that the next card is more difficult because two figures are on the card. The client is also instructed that the right and left figures on Card D are to be placed on the right and left, respectively, of the drawing area. The time limit for showing Card D is also 10 seconds. The examinee, for each card, is given all the time he or she needs to draw the figure or all he or she can remember of it. At the end of the task, the client is told that he or she will be asked to do the drawings again from memory later in the test.

Scoring is more complicated for this subtest. For each drawing, there is a set of criteria that the drawing must meet. For each criterion met, the client is given one point. There are 7 criteria for Cards A and B, 9 for Card C, and 18 for Card D. These criteria (and examples illustrating how to use them) are given in Appendix B of the test manual. It is imperative that the examiner score each time by carefully comparing the drawing to each criterion in Appendix B rather than by judging the figures on the basis of his or her own impressions. Failure to adhere to the criteria invalidates the interpretation of the scores.

Digit Span. This is essentially identical to Digit Span in the WAIS-R. The examinee is read numbers (ranging from 3 to 8 digits), which must be repeated either in order (Digits Forward) or in reverse order (Digits Backward). There are two trials at each level (3, 4, 5, 6, 7, and 8 digits). Digits Forward is discontinued after failure at both trials of a given level, as is Digits Backward. The procedure begins with an example, but the test continues whether or not the example is answered correctly. The score is the number of correct trials for Digits Forward and Digits Backward combined.

Visual Memory Span.   This test is the visual equivalent of Digit Span. The test requires two cards (one with eight randomly distributed red squares for the Tapping Forward section and one with eight randomly distributed green squares for Tapping Backward). Tapping Forward consists of two trials at each of seven levels (from two to eight taps) and Tapping Backward consists of two trials at each of six levels (from two to seven taps).

For each forward trial, the examiner taps the appropriate number of squares in a predetermined pattern as indicated in the manual. The examinee must then tap the squares in the same pattern (requiring visual spatial memory). For each backward trial, the procedure is the same, except that the pattern must be reproduced in the reverse order.

The test continues in both conditions until the examinee misses both trials of a given level or completes the highest level. Scoring is the number of correct trials summed for both backward and forward procedures.

Logical Memory II.   This is the first of the delayed recall procedures. In this phase, the examinee is asked to recall the two stories that were read to him or her earlier. If the examinee cannot recall them, hints may be given: one was about a woman who was robbed and one about a man who had trouble on a highway. No further information or hinting is allowed (although general encouragement to guess or to try is acceptable). Scoring is identical to Logical Memory I.

Visual Paired Associates II.   In this delayed recall procedure, the examinee is shown the figures presented in Visual Paired Associates I and asked to indicate the color associated with each of the figures. The score is the correct number of colors indicated to a maximum of six.

Verbal Paired Associates II.   In this procedure, the examinee is read one word of the pairs learned in Verbal Paired Associates I and asked to recall the other pair. The score is the number of the eight pairs correctly recalled.

Visual Reproduction II. In this delayed memory task, the examinee is asked to recreate as much as possible of the four pictures they were shown and had drawn in Visual Reproduction I. The pictures do not need to be reproduced in the same order as before. Scoring is the same as before, using the criteria in Appendix B of the manual.

Summary Indexes

Several summary indexes are generated from the test. The examiner must list the raw total scores, as discussed above, on the appropriate lines of the answer sheet. Next to each of these raw scores is a weighting factor. The raw score is multiplied by the weighting factor to yield a weighted total score (except for the score on the Information and Orientation items). These weighted scores are then added, as indicated on the form, to yield a total score for Verbal Memory, Visual Memory, Attention/Concentration, and Delayed Memory. A fifth index, General Memory, is reached by adding the Visual Memory and the Verbal Memory total scores. Each of these five scores is then converted into a Standard score with a mean of 100 and a standard deviation of 15, as is used with the WAIS and WAIS-R. This conversion is done using tables in the manual, which are presented for each age from 16 to 74. The test is not appropriate for individuals under 16. Individuals over 74 can be scored by using the norms for 74-year-olds at present, but interpretation should be cautious.

Comparing Scores

In comparing indexes, a difference of about 15 points yields a difference significant at about the .15 level, whereas differences of about 20 points between scores yields differences significant at the .05 level. For most clinical work, when the clinician believes the scores to be reliable and accurate, a difference of 15 points is sufficient to reach tentative conclusions.

Differences of 20 points are clearly meaningful. In general, differences between General Memory and Attention/Concentration are more reliable than other comparisons. The manual presents specific values for the significance of differences between General Memory and Attention/Concentration, between Verbal Memory and Visual Memory, and between General Memory and Delayed Memory.

In addition, the manual presents percentiles for several tests (across the 16–74 age range). These include Digit Span, Visual Memory Span, Logical Memory I and II, and Visual Reproduction I and II. By converting these percentiles into T scores (using percentile/T-score conversion tables found in some statistics books), one can compare Logical Memory I to Logical Memory II, Digit Span to Visual Span, and Visual Reproduction I to Visual Reproduction II. A difference of at least 1.3 T-score points is necessary to find the probability of a difference between the scores (which is usually sufficient for clinical work). In cases where one wishes to be more certain that there is a difference, a criteria of at least a T-score difference of 1.8 can be employed.

For the more adventurous and curious clinicians, the manual also presents the means and standard deviations of the normative groups at each age level for each subtest (Wechsler, 1987, p. 52). This information can be used to compare scores on Digits Forward and Digits Backward, for example, or on Visual Paired Associates I and II, or on Verbal Paired Associates I and II. The latter comparisons are probably most useful when there is a significant difference between the Delayed Memory and General Memory indexes.

These comparisons are made by finding the appropriate mean and standard deviation for each test in the comparison for the client's age. For example, if one wishes to compare Verbal Paired Associates I with Verbal Paired Associates II for a 35-year-old subject, one would find that the mean (and standard deviation) for Part I is 20.6 (SD=3.0) and for Part II is 7.6 (SD=0.7). We would then take the subject's scores for Parts I and II and convert them to z scores. Thus, if the subject's scores had been 24 and 5, respectively, one would convert them to z scores using the following formula:

$$z = (\text{Score} - \text{Mean})/(\text{Standard Deviation}).$$

For the first score, this would become

$$z = (24 - 20.6) / 3.0 = 3.4 / 3.0 = 1.33.$$

For the second score, this would become

$$z = (5 - 7.6) / 0.7 = -2.6 / 0.7 = 3.7.$$

From these numbers, we would then calculate the difference of the z scores. In this case, the difference would be 1.3 − (−3.7), or 5.0.

For conservative purposes, a difference of at least 2 z score points is required for a significant difference. The higher the difference, the more meaningful the finding. A difference of 5, as in this example, is considered significant.

Note that this procedure does not apply to comparing unrelated subtests, such as Digit Span and Logical Memory I. It should be applied only to the immediate and delayed versions of the same test, and more cautiously, to the verbal and nonverbal versions of the same test (e.g., Digit Span and Visual Memory Span).

Interpretation of WMS-R Scores

Like intelligence, memory function is not a unitary process, but represents the sum performance of many specific skills that are normally highly interrelated. In evaluating memory, one looks at several factors: the general level at which the individual functions, a comparison of that level with other general skills such as intelligence, and a comparison among memory skills to see if any specific skills are statistically stronger or weaker than would be expected from the person's general level of performance.

In interpreting these comparisons, several factors must be taken into account. First, since there are many potential comparisons that can be made, great credence should not be given to single isolated differences, but rather to an overall pattern of differences. Thus, in cases in which several signs suggest non-verbal memory dysfunction, this is much more likely to be accurate than in cases in which there is only one such sign. Caution must be employed and other tests, when available, considered as well.

Second, there are influences from outside factors. Overall memory levels are rarely significantly better than overall intellectual levels, as intelligence acts as a limiting factor to memory performance. As a consequence, a poor memory score that is consistent with a poor IQ score may not reflect a specific memory deficit per se, but rather may reflect an overall low level of performance. In addition, probably because of its correlation with IQ, memory is related to educational level, which itself is highly correlated with IQ. Education accounts for some 20 to 25 percent of the variance in the memory indexes. Overall, the manual reports that individuals with less than a 12th grade education will have an average General Memory score 15 points (one standard deviation) below that seen in a group of people who have had more than 12 years of education (with a 12th-grade group scoring almost exactly at 100). This spread holds for all of the memory scores. This difference is also much as we would expect for IQ scores.

There are also age differences that are used to adjust the scores in the WMS-R tables. As a result, the user should be aware that the average performance on a task by a 70-year-old is not comparable to the absolute performance level of a 20-year-old also judged (by the age norms) to be average. This can be important when one interprets how an older person may actually perform on a specific task compared with a younger person. In such cases, using raw scores for comparison may be more appropriate.

Memory scores also differ, of course, by diagnostic group. The manual gives an overview of mean scores for a wide variety of clinical groups, including patients with alcoholism, Alzheimers disease, seizures, dementia, depression, schizophrenia, multiple sclerosis, head trauma, stroke, and so on. While the numbers of patients that some of these means are based on may be small, they do give the clinician some means for comparing a specific patient to a broad group. In general, of course, impaired patients do much worse on the test than normal controls. The exact pattern and meaning of these differences remain as yet undetermined.

Another factor is the results on the Information and Orientation Questions. In general, missing more than two questions may indicate confusion or disorientation, which may suggest that the results as a whole may be compromised. In scoring this, however, common sense must be used to decide if the impairment is a deterrent to interpreting the test results.

With these factors in mind, we can turn to examining the meaning of different comparisons. One should keep in mind, however, that since this is a very new test, all interpretations are subject to change through future research.

The Attention/Concentration index is not a measure of memory and should not be interpreted as such. Rather, it helps (as do the Information and Orientation Questions) tell us whether the person is functioning at a level adequate to allow interpretation of the memory scores. Like IQ, this level acts to limit what the person can achieve. In cases where the score is depressed, caution must be taken to not misinterpret attentional factors as memory factors.

The General Memory score (called the Memory Quotient or MQ on the WMS) is an overall summary of immediate memory skills covering both verbal and nonverbal skills. As such, it is comparable with full scale IQ, and the two scores should be within 15 points of one another if the WAIS-R is employed as the measure of IQ. Discrepancies in which the overall memory score is more than 15 points below IQ suggests memory deficiencies. It is unclear what, if anything, a memory score more than 15 points above the IQ means (other than a relatively good memory).

Both the Verbal and Nonverbal Memory scores can be compared in a similar manner with the full scale IQ. In addition, the Verbal Memory score may be compared with the WAIS Verbal IQ, and the Nonverbal Memory score with the WAIS Performance IQ. Again, memory scores reduced more than 15 points below the corresponding IQ score are suggestive of memory problems worse than any corresponding loss in intelligence. In all cases, however, the absence of a difference does not mean that there are no memory problems.

It is likely that individuals with motor problems, but not

visual-spatial or nonverbal memory problems, will do poorly on the Performance IQ but not on Nonverbal Memory. While this area has not been adequately researched, a significant difference in favor of the Nonverbal Memory quotient may suggest the need to investigate such a possibility.

Deficits in Verbal Memory (as compared with Verbal IQ) or Nonverbal Memory (as compared with Performance IQ) are suggestive of specific problems associated with memory functions of the brain. Traditionally, verbal memory problems are seen as reflecting left hemisphere dysfunction, whereas deficits in nonverbal memory are seen as reflecting right hemisphere dysfunction. Since the deficits here are on immediate memory tasks, they reflect dysfunction in cortical more than in subcortical areas.

The verbal and Nonverbal Memory scores may also be compared with one another. In general, significant deficits in Verbal Memory suggest left hemisphere dysfunction, whereas deficits in Nonverbal Memory suggest right hemisphere dysfunction.

The Delayed Memory score is also a composite of verbal and nonverbal tests. This score cannot be compared directly with IQ because immediate memory is a necessary condition for delayed memory: in few cases can delayed memory be better than immediate memory. Thus, a specific deficit in delayed memory, as opposed to general immediate memory, can be diagnosed only when the delayed memory score is significantly below the General Memory score. When this occurs, it suggests that immediate memory is more intact than delayed, pointing to the possibility of subcortical brain involvement either through injury, disease, drugs, or alcohol. Situations in which delayed memory is better than General Memory are not at present interpretable.

Further comparisons can be made between the delayed and immediate versions of the four tests that make up the Delayed Memory index. Such comparisons may allow one to identify whether the source of the delayed memory problem is due to verbal (Logical Memory, Verbal Paired Associates) or nonverbal (Visual Paired Associates, Visual Reproduction) tests or both. Problems limited to the verbal tests may suggest subcortical left hemisphere dysfunction, whereas problems limited to the nonverbal tests may suggest subcortical right hemisphere dysfunction.

The final level of comparison is between verbal and nonverbal versions of the same procedure. The paired verbal-nonverbal tests include Visual Paired Associates and Verbal Paired Associates, Digit Span and Visual Memory Span, and Visual Reproduction and Logical Memory. Each of these pairs represents a different type of memory process: paired learning recall, rote memory, and memory for logical wholes. Specific deficits may be discovered on these tasks for either the verbal or the nonverbal variant, suggesting as before specific left or right hemisphere deficits.

Advantages and Disadvantages

The primary advantages of the WMS-R lie in its excellent standardization and its recognition of some of the many factors that go into memory. Unlike its predecessor, the WMS, it recognizes the multifactorial nature of memory functions and provides a clinical and research tool that will be a substantial aid to the field.

The primary disadvantage to this test is that it is new. As a result, there is little research available and little clinical experience. While the lack of research is a boon to those looking for a dissertation or thesis topic, it remains a problem for users who must keep up with the new literature as it becomes available in the next few years.

A second disadvantage is the lack of a 24-hour delayed memory test. Although the 30-minute wait imposed by the WMS-R does indeed measure delayed memory, there are cases in which 30-minute memory will be intact while 24-hour memory can be impaired. Such a finding can have great implications for the function of an individual, and clinicians should not assume that intact 30-minute memory means intact delayed memory in general. It is unfortunate that while collecting this excellent sample, the authors failed to collect a 24-hour delayed memory sample. This will unfortunately be left up to others to add.

Despite these disadvantages, this test is vastly superior to most memory tests that are available. It is clearly superior to the WMS and should, under most conditions, be substituted for that test.

WECHSLER MEMORY SCALE

This is the older sibling of the WMS-R. It was created at a time when the emphasis was on yielding an overall memory index rather than on recognizing the varied role of different types of memory. It does not include a delayed memory test of any length. A discussion is included here primarily because the WMS still enjoys widespread use, although this should decline with the introduction of the WMS-R. As noted above, I recommend the use of the WMS-R in almost all situations.

Administration

The Wechsler Memory Test consists of six subtests. The first two subtests, Orientation and Memory, are measures of basic memory for such things as date (year, month, day), current president, governor, mayor, and where the patient is. There are some problems with these measures: mass transportation is currently so available that patients travel extensively on their own, often moving from state to state. Consequently, they may not know who the state's governor is or who the city's mayor is. This is also difficult for the rural patient transferred to the big city hospital. For example, I have worked in hospitals that received patients from four different states. One can substitute and ask for the mayor of the patient's city or governor of the patient's state (if the psychologist knows the correct answer). One can also simply give credit for these questions without using them. One point is given for each correct answer.

The third subtest, Mental Control, asks the subject to count, to add, and to repeat the alphabet within specific time limits. Scoring is based on time and accuracy. Logical Memory, the fourth subtest, requires the subject to listen to two paragraphs individually and repeat from each the details he or she can remember. One point is given for each detail remembered. The total correct for both paragraphs is divided by two.

The fifth subtest is Digit Span, a test basically equivalent to the WAIS Digit Span. This version, however, does not have a three-digit trial for Forward Memory or a two-digit trial for Backward Memory. Scoring is the same as for the WAIS Digit Span. Visual Reproduction, the sixth subtest, is a measure of visual memory. Points are assigned for each detail remembered, as described by Wechsler (1945). The final subtest, Paired Associate Learning, asks the subject to memorize 10 word pairs, 6 of which are defined as easy and 4 of which are defined as hard. The list is read to the subject three times, followed by a recitation of the first word of each pair to which the subject must respond with the other half of the pair. On each recall trial, the examiner notes the number of correct easy pairs and the number of correct hard pairs. At the end of the test, a total easy item and total hard item score is reached. The total score for the test is one-half of the easy item score plus the hard item score.

After all scores are calculated, the scores for each subtest are summed. A factor for age, growing as the individual gets older, is added to this to yield a total score. This score can be turned into a Memory Quotient (MQ) with a mean of 100 and a standard deviation of 15 (equivalent to WAIS IQ) using tables given by Wechsler (1945). Additional normative data is available from Hulicka (1966). This includes normative data for each subtest as well as the overall scores (except for the second subtest).

Discriminative Validity

Despite the importance of memory functions in neuropsychological disorders, the research on the Wechsler Memory Scale has been disappointing. Many researchers have found the test unable to differentiate between organic and psychiatric patients (Cohen, 1950) or between organic and normal patients (Parker, 1957). Bachrach and Mintz (1974) found the Visual Reproduction test alone to be a successful discriminator, whereas Kljajic (1975) found evidence to support the use of Digit Span,

Associate Learning, Information, and Orientation. Holland (1974) and Howard (1950) found the Paired Associate Learning test to be useful.

One problem with the test is that several of the subtests are likely to be insensitive to brain damage. Tests of Orientation and Information and Mental Control, specifically, are rarely affected by brain damage, except in the most severe cases. In addition, although specific left hemisphere injuries may affect some of the verbal tests (although many of the Paired Associates items are so easy that memory is often not required), the design test would not be heavily affected. In right hemisphere injuries, the test would show little overall deficit, as impairment on only the Design subtest would be expected. Thus, some severe to moderate left hemisphere injuries might lower scores on several subtests, whereas patients with right hemisphere injuries would show essentially normal total scores. It is not surprising, then, that the test does poorly in making discriminations when overall scores are considered.

It would appear that the best use of the WMS would not be in calculating MQs, but in comparing subtests with one another. For example, a comparison of Associate Learning, Logical Memory, and Digit Span with Visual Reproduction might be useful in establishing possible differences between a patient's right and left hemispheres, an important aspect of many evaluations (see chapter 9). In addition, specific deficits on any one subtest may be useful in determining the nature of problems that interfere with the patient's social or neurological functioning. However, since no reliable or generally accepted norms exist for subtests or subtest comparisons, this must be done on a qualitative basis.

Advantages and Disadvantages

The major advantage of the Wechsler Memory Scale was its status as the only clinical measure of memory functions in general use. It has been the subject of numerous research investigations. Its use has been continued on this basis despite its limitations, which include its poor reflection of modern memory research, its poor and out-of-date norms, and the difficulty in interpreting its results or in comparing performances across subtests.

Example. TQ was seen after a car accident in which he was briefly unconscious. He was released from the hospital after three days. Because of complaints about difficulties at work, he was given a WAIS-R and achieved a full scale IQ of 120 (Verbal 125, Performance 116). He had a WMS MQ of 118. He was judged to have recovered based on these scores and a normal Bender-Gestalt. It was suggested that he was suffering from a posttraumatic stress syndrome, and he was put into therapy for relaxation and to learn stress tolerance. After several months of therapy with no resolution of his problems, he was referred for another WMS-R.

On the WMS-R, he achieved a General Memory index of 119. His Verbal Memory index was 112, Nonverbal Memory was 123, Delayed Memory was 92, and Attention/Concentration was 112. Comparisons of these scores indicated that although General, Verbal, and Nonverbal Memory scores were within normal limits, there was a 13-point difference between Verbal Memory and the WAIS-R. More importantly, however, Delayed Memory was 27 points lower than General Memory. This pattern indicated that although TQ could understand what he was told and retain it immediately, he had substantial difficulties when he had to recall the information later. Also, although his Delayed Memory performance was within the normal range, the difference in test scores suggested that he was not functioning as he was before the accident. This deficit led to his own complaints about not being able to do things, as well as his boss' observations of his poor performance. Because of inadequate testing initially, however, this deficit was missed, and he was inappropriately told he had fully recovered. The diagnosis of posttraumatic stress syndrome was an error based on misreading of his appropriate concern and complaints about his real problems.

CHAPTER SEVEN

Bender-Gestalt

The Visual-Motor Gestalt test devised by Bender (1938) more commonly known as the Bender-Gestalt or simply the Bender, has been a major instrument used by the clinical psychologist over the past quarter century. It is a test that arouses strong feelings on the part of both supporters and opponents. The former have sometimes seen it as a test that could reflect intellectual skills, organicity, and personality traits, and the latter, who decry the teaching of the test to new graduate students, see it as a prime example of sloppy, unscientific clinical practice (probably second only to the Rorschach). It continues to be used as both an objective and a projective test by many clinicians, although its use has declined with the increasing popularity of such tests as the Halstead-Reitan (for organicity) and the MMPI (for personality interpretations). Despite this, however, the Bender continues to play a significant role in modern clinical assessment.

The test was originally devised as a measure of visual-perceptual skills based on the Gestalt theories of Koffka, Wertheimer, and Kohler, the leaders of the Berlin school of Gestalt psychology. In her original monograph, Bender presented examples of the test's use in diagnosing brain damage, psychiatric disorders, mental retardation, and malingering. Since its inception, the test has inspired extensive research and clinical use. This work has resulted in a wide variety of administration techniques, scoring and interpretation systems (including many that are highly idiosyncratic), and uses in many populations.

179

Extensive research has been both positive and negative, offering support to nearly any position one wishes to adopt in the use of the Bender.

PURPOSE

The major purpose of the Bender as an objective test is the detection of brain dysfunction. This area has been the major source of much of the extensive Bender research. The Bender has also been used as a way to estimate intelligence, but it is less effective in such a role than the WAIS or the other intelligence tests discussed previously. As a projective test, the Bender has been used as a largely nonverbal measure of personality. The way in which the Bender is interpreted projectively is a controversial topic with no one method accepted entirely by most users. The most popular system of projective interpretation is outlined in Hutt (1969).

Administration

Nearly all systems of Bender administration use the nine figures suggested by Bender (1938) as originally presented or as slightly modified by Hutt (1969). The figures on the Bender are reproduced in Figure 7-1, at about 25 percent of the size they are presented to subjects in the testing situation. Each figure is on a card about the size of a large index card.

The wording and actual administration details differ considerably among examiners depending on personal convictions and the systems they were taught. Some general considerations can be stated, however. The patient should have several sharpened pencils available (usually standard no. 2) and at least one sheet of white paper. Examiners differ on the number of pages of paper allowed: Some feel only one (or two) should be allowed so that the subject has to plan ahead and use the space on the page intelligently. Others suggest that a pile of paper should be made available, so that the behavior of the patient in regard to number of pages, number of designs per page, size of figures, and the like, may vary more considerably. This is especially useful when one wishes to test a projective hypothesis, whereas

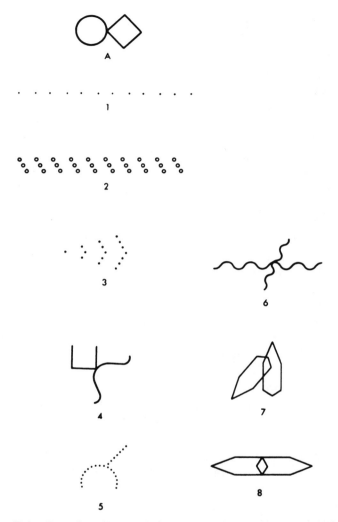

Figure 7.1 Bender figures (reduced to present here). From *The Hutt Adaptation of the Bender-Gestalt* by M. L. Hutt, 1977, New York: Grune and Stratton. Copyright 1977 by Grune and Stratton. Reprinted with permission.

allowing only one sheet is more useful when one is examining for organicity.

For all techniques, the patient is then told something like this: "I have nine cards here, each with a design on it. I want you to copy the design on each card as exactly as you can on the page before you." Then the cards are presented to the subject one at a time with the figures placed directly in front of the patient. (In most systems, the patient is allowed neither to rotate the figure in any way nor to rotate the writing page, except for the minor rotation most individuals use for writing and drawing.) Any additional questions from the patient about any aspect of the task should be answered, "Just draw the figures on the cards as exactly as you can." These instructions can be modified to be more ambiguous if desired. For example, one may say, "I want you to copy what is on each card" rather than mention the word design. On the other hand, they can be made more specific: "I want you to copy the figures exactly as they are on the card: the same size, the same shape, and the same number of figures."

Other administration techniques are available as well. Many clinicians use unstandardized memory techniques, in which the subject is shown the card and then asked to draw the picture after the stimulus is withdrawn. However, I feel that such techniques are best used with tests such as the Benton Visual Retention Test (see chapter 8), that were specifically designed for memory presentations.

A more interesting revision of the Bender has been presented by Canter (1976), who employed what he termed a background interference procedure. This test requires the subject to first draw the Bender figures on a single sheet of clean white paper as described above. Then a second administration is given in which the subject must draw the figures again on a sheet of paper covered by wavy lines. This technique assesses the relative skills of the person to draw the figures both with and without interference from the wavy lines.

SCORING

Scoring systems abound for the Bender-Gestalt. In an informal survey of clinicians, I found that most clinicians do not use any system in its entirety, but rather employ an intuitive combination of several systems. The major problem in such systems is the lack of any evidence establishing validity, as well as the inability to teach the system to others, since the system is more often based on clinical intuition than on hard and fast rules. Hutt (1968) defended a more clinical interpretation of the Bender, suggesting that formal systems may lose much of the major information included in the patient's test performance.

Bender (1938) did not originally propose a system of scoring, but rather relied on qualitative analysis. Pascal and Suttell (1951) presented an early diagnostic system that is still in wide use. The system was intended to measure the amount of disturbance of brain function in the patient, whether the disturbance was due to brain injury or psychiatric disorder. The authors assigned each important deviant response on each card a value. When the deviant response was present, the patient's score was increased by the value of the item. Overall, 106 scorable characteristics were identified in this system, ranging from 10 to 13 for each figure (excluding the first practice figure), as well as seven variables relating to the performance as a whole. The system includes rotations, substituting angles for curves, substituting curves for angles, producing distorted or lopsided drawings, tremor, erasures, drawing over previously completed lines, and other similar errors. This system appears to be generally successful at differentiating normals and neurotics from people with significant brain injuries or psychiatric disorders, although mildly impaired or recovered persons may not be diagnosed accurately.

The scoring system developed by Hain (1964) views the Bender performance as a whole. Hain identified 15 categories, each with a specific weight. Any instance of an error in a category results in the person's being assigned points for that category. Four-point categories include perseveration (repetition), rotation or reversal, and concretism. Three-point errors include added angles, separation of lines, overlap, and distortion. Two-point categories are embellishments and partial rotations. One-point errors include omission of a figure or line abbreviation of designs one or two (involving the rows of dots), separation of figures, erasure, failure to attain closure, and lacking the point of contact between the circle and the square in Figure A. In his original study, Hain reported that 80 percent of his normals scored below six points, while 80 percent of the brain injured patients scored above five points.

Hutt (1969) presented a 26-factor scale to measure the degree of psychopathology in a profile. This system, like Hutt's, evaluates the performance of the figures as a whole. Factor 1, sequence, investigates the placement of the figures. Figures are normally placed either from left to right or from top to bottom. Each time a figure is not placed below or to the right of the previous figure, the patient's sequence score increases by one.

The second factor is the position of the first figure. Any placement within 1 inch of any edge is scored as abnormal. Factor 3 is the use of space. This relates to the closeness of each figure to the succeeding figure. Basically, Hutt outlined normal distances between figures, which relate to the size of each figure. Designs that are placed too close or too far apart are scored as abnormal. Factor 4, use of space II, refers to the size of the designs. Normal limits for the width and height of each design are given by Hutt. A drawing is judged as compressed if either of the dimensions is too small, and expanded if either is too large.

The fifth factor is collision, the running together or overlap between any two figures. Scoring is based on the frequency of such collisions. Factor 6, use of margin, refers to placement of any figure within $1/2$ inch of the margin on seven or more figures. Factor 7 involves 90 degree rotation of the drawing paper for any figures. The score depends on the frequency of such rotations of the paper. Factor 8, shift in the position of the stimulus card, refers to 90 degree rotation of the design card.

Factor 9 is concerned with overall decrease or increase in size of the designs. An overall increase occurs when five figures are expanded; an overall decrease occurs when five figures are compressed. Factor 10, progressive increase or decrease in size, involves a progressively larger expansion over at least six figures or a progressively greater compression oven at least six figures. Factor 11 is an isolated increase or decrease in size. This can refer to a single figure in which one part is one-third larger or smaller than the other parts. Among figures, this refers to a figure that is one-fourth larger or smaller than the other figures.

Factor 12, closure difficulty, involves problems in joining or closing within a figure. This may be reflected in two parts being separated by a gap when they should be touching, or the failure to join or overlap two sides of a figure in a drawing in which the drawn line overshoots the junction point between two lines. Factor 13, crossing difficulty, refers to Figures 6 and 7. It is indicated by redrawing, sketching, erasing, or other problems at the point of contact between the figures. Factor 14, curvature difficulty, involves obvious changes in the curves in Figures 4, 5, and 6. This can occur by replacing a curve with a straight line, exaggerating or decreasing the curve, or increasing the number of curves.

Factor 15, change in angulation, refers to an increase or decrease in the size of an angle by more than 15 degrees. Scoring depends on the frequency of these errors. Factor 16, perceptual rotation, refers to the rotation of any figure when the test card and test paper are in the normal position. Factor 17, retrogression, is the substitution of an immature drawing for a more mature figure. Hutt (1969) suggested that the substitution of loops for well-formed circles, the substitution of dashes for dots, and the substitution of dots for circles are specific examples of this behavior. The error must occur at least twice in a single figure to be scored. The total score is the number of times this criterion is met.

Factor 18, simplification, refers to the substitution of a simpler for a more difficult figure, for example, by reducing the number of curves in Figure 6. Factor 19, fragmentation, involves the essential destruction of the gestalt, such as failure to complete the figure, gross separation of the parts, or failure to draw the figure to resemble the actual design. Factor 20, overlapping, refers to problems in overlapping figures that should not overlap (such as Figure A) or problems in maintaining the overlap when it should be there (Figure 7). Factor 21 involves elaboration or doodling, including additional lines or curves, and extending figures by adding new figures. Factor 22, perseveration, occurs when a subject includes elements from a previous design or repeats a figure beyond the number required in a design.

Factor 23, redrawing of the total figure, refers to a second attempt to reproduce a figure after partially finishing or crossing out an earlier attempt. Factor 24, deviation in direction of movement, involves moving in directions that are unusual while drawing a figure. Except for left-handed individuals, the usual movement directions are left to right, top to bottom, or counterclockwise when drawing circles or other closed figures. Factor 25 is similar to Factor 24 in that it involves inconsistency in movement of direction. This involves a shift in drawing directions from one figure to the next.

Factor 26 is concerned with line quality. Hutt (1969) identified six types of lines: excessively heavy, excessively heavy with poor coordination, excessively faint, excessively faint with poor coordination, poor coordination alone, sketchiness, and irregularities in the line. Sketchiness involves retouching of lines or joinings that result in a poorly reproduced figure. In addition to these factors, Hutt recognized that other scoring dimensions are possible, such as those suggested by other systems.

A final important system was developed by Koppitz (1963, 1975). This system is primarily a developmental system, appropriate for the analysis of children's Bender tests and not usually used with adult subjects. The Koppitz system defines certain possible errors throughout the figures which can be scored. Total scores can be compared with age norms to determine if a child is operating at, below, or above normal age expectations. All adults should show essentially perfect scores within the Koppitz system.

CLINICAL INTERPRETATION

Clinical interpretation of the Bender may be approached at two levels. At the first level, the scoring systems are used to produce total scores, which are used to discriminate between various diagnostic groups: In general, these systems stress differentiation between brain damaged patients and non-brain damaged controls, ranging from psychiatric to normal patients. At the second level, one interprets the research findings on each factor in a system similar to that of Hutt's (1969), using each factor to suggest possible hypotheses that can be integrated with one another and compared with other test data, interview results, and historical data. This information can be further extended by examining each figure for specific signs that may be present.

Discriminative Validity

The results from the different scoring systems are remarkably similar in terms of discriminative validity. Studies supporting the use of the Bender as a diagnostic tool for brain damage have generally reported discriminative rates ranging from 70 to 90 percent (e.g., Brilliant & Gynther, 1963; Bruhn & Reid, 1975; Goldberg, 1974; Hain, 1964; Levine & Feirstein, 1972; McGuire, 1960; Orme, 1962; Tymchuk, 1974). There are, however, a number of problems in interpreting these studies. First, the nature of the organic groups in terms of severity is unclear: In general the more severe the organicity, the better the discrimination. Second, control groups are rarely appropriate. The most meaningful group would be one consisting of possible neurological patients who are eventually found to have no disorder. Unfortunately, such groups have rarely been used. When these factors are taken into account, some general conclusions can be reached. In a general population, the Bender is about 70 to 80 percent accurate in discriminating brain injured from normal or mixed psychiatric patients; the rate increases in more severe brain injured groups and less impaired control groups, irrespective of the system of scoring employed. This rate is consistent with the accuracies of most other single tests attempting to make this discrimination.

The Bender's poorest performance occurs when trying to discriminate chronic schizophrenic patients from those with milder forms of brain injury, a finding common to most tests (Golden & Anderson, 1978). Results are often at chance levels (50 percent) in these populations. The test results suggest that the Bender may be used as a basic screening instrument, but it is not, by itself, an adequate measure for determining the presence or absence of organicity. A common test battery used by clinicians is the combination of the Bender and the WAIS, using both to discriminate brain damage. It is common to find a great deal of redundancy between the Bender and the WAIS Block Design, however, making this combination somewhat inefficient in the analysis of organicity.

Of interest in the most recent literature has been a series of studies on the Canter Background Interference Procedure. After summarizing the literature on the procedure, Canter (1976) found the procedure to add about 15 percent accuracy to that of the Bender, placing it in the 80 to 90 percent range, an excellent result for any single test of brain dysfunction. The accuracy was achieved by scoring the normally given Bender and the interference Bender using a modification of the Pascal-Suttel System. The larger the difference, the greater the likelihood of brain damage. As noted above, the difference score has been able to consistently achieve results in the 80 to 90 percent range. This form has not been studied as extensively as the general Bender, and it is not certain that these results will stand up to extensive cross-validation. If they do, however, this form of the Bender should become a major test in the assessment of organicity.

Factor Interpretation

The extensive work represented in Hutt's (1969) book on the Bender is an excellent example of the organic and personality interpretations that can be made from the Bender. While not exhaustive, the system includes most major categories of errors and surveys most of the dynamic and organic hypotheses that may relate to the patient's performance. As a result, familiarity with the system is useful even if one adopts an alternate approach to the use of the Bender.

Factor 1, sequence, may reflect several dimensions of psychopathology. Compulsive individuals are very precise in how they lay out the figures, whereas highly anxious or impulsive patients show highly irregular sequences. Irregular sequence may generally be seen in any highly confused, disorganized individual. Factor 2, position of the first drawing, is also indicative of abnormal personality, especially if the person selects the lower corners of the page for the first drawing. Factors 3 and 4, use of space, may relate to hostility if there is an excessive amount of space suppressed. Constricted use of space is related to a tendency to withdraw and possibly to schizoid tendencies. If both tendencies are present, a possibility of ambivalence is suggested.

Factor 5, collision, may relate to neurological dysfunction, especially if there is evidence that poor motor control is causing the collisions. This phenomenon does not occur in normals and generally indicates the need for psychotherapy in a non-neurological population. Factor 6, use of the margin, is suggestive of anxiety. Hutt (1969) theorized that excessive use of the margin allows the subject to use an external support (the edge of the paper) to help control anxiety. In organic brain dysfunction, use of margins may indicate a need for supports and reference points, whereas use by paranoids may express considerable fear and suspicion. High Factor 6 scores occur rarely, if ever, in normal populations. Factor 7, shift in paper position, reflects overt or covert oppositional tendencies in the patient.

Factor 8, shift in stimulus card position, is similar in meaning to Factor 7, according to Hutt (1969). Factor 9, overall increase or decrease in size, represents the manifestation of anxiety in the test situation. Increases may be associated with inadequacy and poor self-concepts, and decreases are associated with intense anxiety. In certain subcortical neurological diseases, most notably Parkinson's disease, severe decreases may be associated with attempts to limit the motor functions required for writing. Tremor is often seen in these drawings as well. Factor 10, progressive increase or decrease, may be associated with irritability and impulsiveness if there is a progressive increase. If there is a progressive decrease, there is a tendency to withdraw and be depressed, as well as the possibility of psychosomatic complaints. Hutt noted that this is a weak factor and should not be given excessive weightings in a clinical analysis.

Factor 11, isolated increase or decrease in size, is significant clinically but may have idiosyncratic meanings, usually reflecting disturbed emotional functioning in an area for which the patient has little conscious insight. Idiosyncratic possibilities include the association of circles with females, diamonds with males, or the figures with sexuality in general. A reduction in size for any part would indicate an attempt at regression, whereas an increase may represent a compensatory defense against sexual stimuli. In order to further isolate such data, Hutt (1969) regularly employs two projective stages to his testing. After the drawings are complete, the patient is asked to elaborate on the figures in any way that makes the figures more pleasing. The subject is then asked to give his or her associations to the drawings and the elaborations, much as is done with the Rorschach.

Factor 12, closure difficulty, may represent a difficulty in interpersonal relationships. It may be related to emotional fearfulness, or to a general emotional disturbance in the patient. This can also be related to organic brain dysfunction, especially in the right hemisphere. Factor 13, crossing difficulty, is related to psychological blocking and such symptoms as indecisiveness, compulsive doubting, and phobias. Factor 14, curvature difficulty, is a highly sensitive indicator of emotional disturbance. Increases represent overly active emotions, whereas decreases represent the opposite. Factor 15, change in angulation, reflects affective control. Increases indicate that there is a decreased affective level in the patient, whereas decreased angulation (toward more acute angles) is related to increased affective states. This problem may be related to organic brain dysfunction or mental retardation as well.

Factor 16, perceptual rotation, is frequently found in the records of organic patients or patients who are overtly psychotic. As such, its presence in adults must be taken as an indication of severe dysfunction. Although relatively more frequent in organics and mental retardates, the sign is not exclusively associated with these conditions, since it is also seen in psychiatric conditions in which there are significant disruptions of ego functions. Factor 17, retrogression, is the result of strong and chronic defenses against trauma resulting from a failure in ego functions. This sign is seen in some schizophrenics who have a significantly disorganized personality, as well as in others with severe deterioration of personality, such as significant or highly acute brain disorders.

Factor 18, simplification, may reflect a variety of conditions. This can include deliberate attempts not to work at the task because of oppositional tendencies or an attempt to malinger. Simplification can also be seen in cases of disrupted ego function in which the individual is not able to handle the more complex designs. Factor 19, fragmentation, is associated with inabilities to abstract and categorize, and is almost always indicative of profound disturbance (although this can be either acute or chronic in nature). In organic brain dysfunction, this behavior is seen most often in injuries to the right parietal-occipital areas of the brain. In adults, this factor is always indicative of some kind of serious problem.

Factor 20, overlapping difficulty, is generally associated with brain dysfunction, either of a diffuse nature or of the right hemisphere alone. Factor 21, elaboration or doodling, is indicative of ego dysfunction in all cases where the elaboration or doodling significantly distorts the design. This can reflect a loss of ego control, and can be seen in psychosis, mental retardation, and organic brain damage.

Factor 22, perseveration, can reflect a rigid cognitive set or a motor impairment of the frontal lobe areas of the brain's dominant hemisphere. Both types of perseveration are seen in organic brain dysfunction, with motor repetition (e.g., drawing a circle over and over) indicating a lesion in the middle frontal lobes (the premotor area) and perseveration of a prior figure suggesting damage to the anterior frontal (prefrontal) lobe. If no organic brain damage is present, severe perseveration is usually associated with deteriorated schizophrenia.

Factor 23, redrawing of the entire figure, is related to an overly critical attitude on the part of the patient or the absence of advance planning and consideration of the design. Hutt (1969) cautioned that this should occur at least twice before being seen as significant. Factor 24, deviation in direction of movement, may suggest some oppositional tendencies, especially when clockwise rather than counterclockwise movements are used to draw circles or similar figures. Factor 25, inconsistency in direction of movement, can indicate a psychotic block because of the personal meaning of a given design to the patient. Factor 26, line quality, is significant in a number of conditions. Motor incoordination is associated with brain dysfunction, whereas heavy lines reflect emotional disturbance or anxiety. Tremors are associated with brain damage, usually involving subcortical centers such as the basal ganglia or cerebellum, although intense anxiety or side effects of such drugs as the phenothiazines may also produce tremors. The latter drug effect is especially important for psychologists in hospital settings.

Specific Item Interpretations

In addition to the more general overall scores and the factors suggested above, the clinician may also interpret the performance of the patient on specific designs. These are generally similar to the overall considerations, but there are specific problems to look for in each design which are particularly applicable.

Figure A is one of the most frequent figures to show rotations in organic brain disorders. The errors on A are especially significant because of the simplicity of the figure. Psychoanalytic theorists have been especially interested in the combination of the circle (female) and the diamond (male). Increases in one compared with the other may suggest sexual problems related to male or female characteristics. Hammer (1955) suggested that overlap between the figures may indicate virility strivings. Gross distortion in this simple figure is generally associated with significant psychosis or organic brain dysfunction.

In Figure 1, any general difficulty has been associated with some kind of pathology in the adult. Dashes substituted for the dots may indicate aggression (including delinquency), lack of impulse control, or organicity. An inability to produce a horizontal line may be caused by right hemisphere brain dysfunction or by depression (downward slope) or denial (upward slope). Circles instead of dots suggest regression and poor impulse control. Perseveration (continuing the line of dots) suggests organicity, whereas only a few dots may indicate carelessness or lack of cooperation if the person is not psychotic or brain injured.

Figure 2 is also one of the easier items to reproduce. If the figure as drawn represents an arc, there are strong suggestions of egocentrism. Substitution of musical notes suggests psychosis or organic brain syndrome, as does perseveration. Irregular slope or shifting can be associated with extremely poor ego function or strong mood lability.

Figure 3 has been given numerous dynamic interpretations. Troubles with the figure have been associated with sexual problems. Compulsive care in reproduction may indicate anal fixations. Flattening or rounding of the point may indicate difficulty handling aggression, whereas reduced size or preoccupations with details may indicate a fear of emotional expression. Substitution of circles or dashes may suggest significant ego dysfunction as seen in brain damage or psychosis.

Figure 4, when rotated, is generally indicative of brain damage or psychosis. Enlargement of the square is associated with neuroses, whereas a lack of closure may suggest schizoid symptoms or more severe disorders. An extra loop suggests impulsivity, while flattening of the loop suggests a flattened affect. The separation of the two figures suggests hesitancy, self-doubt, and usually anxiety.

Figure 5, if drawn with an unusually long straight line, is suggestive of a need to emphasize masculinity. Drawing the line through the half circle may indicate immaturity or a feeling of being overwhelmed. Obsessive compulsiveness may be associated with counting the dots, even to the point of worrying about the number of dots rather than the shape of the design. Rotation, substitution of circles or dashes for the dots, substitution of lines for dots, or squaring of the hoop may be associated with organicity or psychosis.

Figure 6, when drawn with sharp angles rather than sinusoidal curves, suggests aggression and possible organicity. Incorrect placement of the crossing may indicate instability or, if the upper curve is left mostly above the horizontal curve, denial. Decreasing size of the curves indicates flat affect or a neurotic condition. Drawing the figure as a face or adding a dot for an eye suggests paranoid delusions. Excessive erasure indicates ambivalence or lack of self-assuredness, whereas perseveration suggests brain damage. Drawing straight lines suggests aggression, and problems with femininity in women. Reduction in overall size suggests intellectualization, whereas exaggeration of curves suggests overemotionality. Two U-shaped curves substituted for two crossing curves may indicate fearfulness and interpersonal problems.

Figure 7, if performed correctly, generally contradicts organicity involving the right hemisphere, although other forms of brain dysfunction may still exist. Difficulties with the angles have often been associated with brain dysfunction, as have closure problems, difficulties in sizing, and rotation over 45 degree. Problems in closure may relate to interpersonal difficulties, as may difficulty with overlapping. Problems related to the general phallic shape of the figure may imply sexual dysfunction or overconcern.

Figure 8, when correctly produced, also argues against significant right hemisphere dysfunction. Problems with the angles may be associated with brain dysfunction or regression of the ego back to early childhood states (the figure requires a mental age of about 11 years). Overlapping of the figures has been associated with homosexuality or other emotional disturbances. Elongation of the figures' points or their elimination may be associated with sexual problems, particularly with castration fears. Rotation is generally indicative of organicity or psychosis.

Interpretive Strategies

As described above, there are a number of interpretive strategies one can use with the Bender. In each case, the conclusions generated by each method are only tentative. The information from specific scoring systems, the scoring factors, and the separate designs must be integrated to form a picture of the individual. Initial hypotheses indicated by only one or two signs are generally rejected in favor of those symptoms that are the most pervasive and, thus, most likely characteristic of the individual. The process is very much like that described for the MMPI in this regard. It is especially necessary to weight evidence from other tests when deciding the difference between emotional conditions and those suggesting organic brain dysfunction since there is considerable overlap in the signs relevant to each group.

Except for more simple discriminations (no impairment versus some kind of impairment), the use of the Bender requires extensive experience in both scoring and interpretation. As the test represents a cross between objective and projective tests, the user must decide which approach (or combination) is appropriate to the setting in which the test is employed, and then follow appropriate interpretive strategies and validity checks to evaluate such a system. As described later, the Bender is best used to generate and confirm hypotheses in coordination with other tests and clinical interviews.

ADVANTAGES AND DISADVANTAGES

Supporters of the Bender (e.g., Hutt, 1969) outline a number of important advantages for the test. These advantages include the following: (1) it can be used as a buffer or warm-up test, as it is not threatening to most patients and may be enjoyable to many; (2) it is useful as a supplementary technique that provides a good source of nonverbal material more reliable than many other projective techniques; (3) it provides information otherwise difficult to obtain from uneducated or culturally deprived individuals; (4) it is a useful measure of emotional states when the person otherwise denies problems; (5) it is sensitive to malingering; (6) it is useful as an adjunctive technique in the diagnosis of brain damage; (7) it is useful in discriminating borderline psychotic disorders; and (8) it is a useful research tool.

There are also significant disadvantages to the Bender. First, when used alone, it has tended to be overinterpreted, with clinicians possibly accepting hypotheses as certainties without adequate verifying information. The ease and speed with which the test is given can reinforce this tendency in situations where a quick evaluation is needed. It is necessary, as a result, to emphasize that the test must be used as part of a test battery including a complete clinical interview and evaluation rather than as a single test. Used in conjunction with such tests as the MMPI and various measures of organic brain dysfunction, it can add a great deal to a battery in terms of possible hypotheses and in confirming or contradicting the results of other tests. Its short administration time makes it an excellent test in this role.

A second problem is the lack of an accepted and verified manner of interpreting the test. This leaves a great deal up to clinical judgment and experience and allows for extensive disagreements among "experts." As there is no clear evidence supporting any one system, the new clinician usually begins with a system favored by his or her supervisors and ends with one that often takes a little from many systems. While this can result in a highly workable system, it can also serve to give continued support to unprovable hypotheses and clinical superstitions. It also makes it very difficult to change the mind of the interpreter, since, under these conditions, each clinical research study uses a different administration, different instructions, and different methods of analyses.

CLINICAL EXAMPLES

The use of the Bender as part of a neuropsychological battery is illustrated in the cases at the end of Chapter 8.

CHAPTER EIGHT

Neuropsychological Tests

Neuropsychological testing represents a major segment of the assessment work done by psychologists. Two of the major and most commonly used tests for brain dysfunction, the Benton and the Bender, have already been discussed; however, there are hundreds of tests beyond these which are used by some psychologists for the diagnosis of organicity. In her book on neuropsychological assessment, for example, Lezak (1976) presented a test index that covers seven pages of small print.

In this chapter, I examine those tests that are used by clinicians with some frequency, though not as frequently as the other tests presented in this volume. The chapter also examines tests for which there has not been a great deal of use but which the current literature suggests can be of significant value to the clinician. Finally, the chapter considers the issue of neuropsychological test batteries.

TOKEN TEST

The Token Test is a simple, easy-to-administer test using a minimum of material. It is intended to assess speech functions, and is consequently much more sensitive to left hemisphere damage. The test requires about a fourth-grade education, and is usually easy for the normal individual. (Its use in psychiatric populations has been limited, however, and it is likely that poorer "normal" performance would be found in such groups.)

The test has been found sensitive to aphasic disorders that are not apparent upon observation of the patient.

Administration

The test requires 20 tokens, varying in shape (circle and rectangle), size (small and large), and color (red, yellow, green, blue, and white), so that every possible combination is represented. The sets are normally made out of plastic but could be made out of other material as well. The test has 62 commands, each of which requires the manipulation of, or attention to, one or more of the shapes. For example, one may ask "Touch the green rectangle." In more complex items, the person might be instructed to "Put the red rectangle under the red circle." The complexity of the statement to which the individual can reliably respond is quickly established in this way. If an item is missed initially, it is repeated. If correct the second time, the individual gets full credit for the item. A shorter 39-item version of the test was developed by Spreen and Benton (1969) working from Boller and Vignolo's (1966) original items.

Discriminative Validity

The test is able to discriminate aphasics from normals about 90 percent of the time (Boller, 1968; Hartje, Kerstechensteiner, Poeck, & Orgass, 1973; Orgass & Poeck, 1966). As noted above, however, there are no clear indications of the test's effectiveness when given to a psychiatric population. This fact currently limits the use of the test in many neuropsychological settings. Within this limitation, the test can be an extremely useful addition to any screening battery investigating the possibility of organic defect.

PURDUE PEGBOARD

The Purdue Pegboard, published as a test of fine motor skills by Science Research Associates, has been shown to be an extremely useful, quick test of neuropsychological function. The test allows the clinician to assess right- and left-hand motor function, an area in which deficits commonly occur in brain injuries. Motor function is an especially valuable area to assess since specific deficits in the right hand can usually be localized to the left hemisphere and specific deficits in the left hand to the right hemisphere. Since the test is short, averaging under five minutes, it can fit easily into a larger test battery.

Administration

The patient is given a long pegboard with two rows for pegs. The examiner then requires the patient to begin by placing the pegs in the board with the left hand, then the right hand, and finally both hands. The subject is given 30 seconds for each trial. The patient's score is the number of pegs placed in each trial.

Discriminative Validity

A series of studies (Costa & Vaughan, 1962; Costa, Vaughan, Levita, & Farber, 1963; Fernald, Fernald, & Rines, 1966) have revealed generally good hit rates for the test when comparing normal and brain injured patients. Brain damage was generally represented by scores below 13 on the right hand, 11 on the left hand, and 10 for both hands. The cutoff points are reduced to 10 for both the left and the right hands and 8 for both hands for patients over 60. Overall accuracy averages about 80 percent for the test. Significantly poor performances are seen with psychiatric populations, however; Fernald et al. (1966) reported only a 34 percent hit rate in a psychiatric group. Our experience has not been so negative, as we have found that psychiatric patients can be motivated to do better. Test results must be interpreted with caution in such patients, however, especially those showing psychomotor retardation. A specific deficit in one hand compared with the other is a much more reliable sign in such patients. A right-hand score equal to or less than the left-hand score, for example, is generally indicative of a left hemisphere problem, whereas a left-hand score 25 to 30 percent below the right-hand score suggests right hemisphere dysfunction. As with the Token Test, this is an excellent addition to a screening battery for organic function when the test's limitations are considered.

STROOP COLOR AND WORD TEST

Several recent publications have demonstrated the usefulness of the Stroop Color and Word Test in the diagnosis of brain damage. The Stroop has been found to have several advantages: It is easy to give and easy to score; it is sensitive to most brain injuries, especially to frontal lobe injuries, which are often difficult to detect by neuropsychological tests; and it takes less than five minutes to administer.

Administration and Materials

The Stroop test consists of three 8½ x 11 inch pages. Each page consists of five columns of 20 items. Each item on Page 1 is one of these words: Red, Green, or Blue. The words are repeated in a largely random order. Page 2 consists of 100 items, as does Page 1, but each item is the sequence XXXX. On this page, each XXXX is printed in red, green, or blue ink. Page 3 consists of the words on Page 1 printed in the colors on Page 2, with the limitation that a word and the color in which it is printed may not match. Thus, the word Red may appear in blue or green ink, the word Green in red or blue ink, and the word Blue in red or green ink.

The instructions for the test are simple (Golden & Anderson, 1978). On Page 1, the subject is instructed to read down each column as quickly as possible, pronouncing the words presented there. On page two, the instructions are the same, but the subject is told to name the color of each XXXX. On Page 3, the subject is instructed to name the color of the ink in which the word is printed rather than the word itself. The subject is given 45 seconds on each page. The score is the number of items correctly finished within the time limit on each page. These are converted into T scores using tables in the test manual.

Discriminative Validity

Golden (1976) found that the Stroop could reliably differentiate between normal, psychiatric, and brain damaged patients. Specifically, on Page 2, normal patients tended to complete 70 to 90 items, psychiatric patients completed 60 to 80 items, and brain damaged patients generally scored below 60. The three scores of the Stroop can be used to localize a lesion as well: good scores on Pages 1 and 2, along with a poor score on Page 3, are indicative of frontal injuries, especially to the left hemisphere. Right hemisphere injuries are characterized by normal scores on Page 1 with depressed scores on Pages 2 and 3. Left hemisphere (nonfrontal) injuries are characterized by poor scores on all three pages of the Stroop (Golden & Anderson, 1978; Perret, 1974).

The Stroop score is also useful in the diagnosis of dyslexia. Specifically, equal scores on Pages 2 and 3 are never seen in literate adults. Thus, if Page 3 is within 10 percent of Page 2, there is a high possibility of dyslexia, as this implies that the normal interference problem (the words interfering with color naming) has not occurred, and that there is a lack of word reading responses.

The Stroop is an excellent addition to other screening batteries because of its speed and the usefulness of the test in diagnosing lateralized and frontal injuries.

MEMORY FOR DESIGNS TEST

The Memory for Designs Test (F. K. Graham & Kendall, 1960) consists of 15 designs that must be reproduced from memory. The test is similar to the Benton in this sense; however, the Memory for Designs does not have a copy phase as does the Benton, and the figures are considerably simpler as well.

Administration

Each design is shown to the patient for 10 seconds. The patient is then asked to reproduce it on a single sheet of paper.

The scoring system is relatively simple: Designs completely forgotten or reproduced with one error or less are scored 0, two or more errors without loss of the essential design are scored 1, loss of the essential design is scored 2, and rotations or reversals are scored 3. The total score is the sum of the individual scores. Scores in the range 0 to 4 are scored normal (one could get this by forgetting all the designs completely), scores 5 to 11 are considered borderline, and scores 12 and above are considered organic.

Discriminative Validity

The scoring system of the Memory for Designs, since it does not penalize lapses in memory, is closely related to that of the Bender (McIver, McLaren, & Phillip, 1973). The discriminative rates for the test are, as a result, highly similar to those yielded by the Bender. Brilliant and Gynther (1963) reported hit rates of 88 percent for psychiatric controls and 63 percent for the organic group. Other studies have presented results basically in the 70s (Grundvig, Ajax, & Needham, 1973; Grundvig, Needham, & Ajax, 1970; McManis, 1974; Shearn, Berry, & Fitzgibbons, 1974). Watson (1968) reported problems with differentiating chronic psychiatric from brain damaged patients with the Memory for Designs.

Although the Memory for Designs appears accurate in basic discriminations, it does not yield the rich clinical material that the Bender and Benton can. The test does not take significantly less time, nor does it have as well-established norms as the Benton for the memory components. Although some prefer the test over the others presented, I do not see that it is superior to those tests. There appears to be no clear reason, other than personal preference, for substituting the Memory for Designs for the Bender or Benton.

BENTON VISUAL RETENTION TEST

The Visual Retention Test was originally devised by Benton (1945) as a measure of neuropsychological function. The test is commonly called the Benton Visual Retention Test, or referred to simply as the Benton. The test assesses visual construction skills, visual memory, and visual perception. Since its introduction, the test has become a major measure of neuropsychological function and is in wide use throughout the country.

Administration

There are three sets of 10 cards for the Benton Visual Retention Test; each constitutes an equivalent form (Form C, Form D, Form E). Each set of cards has two designs with only one figure each, while each of the remaining eight designs has three figures that differ in size. Each set of cards can be administered in one of four ways.

Administration A. The first administration technique begins with giving the patient 10 blank sheets of paper that are 5½ x 8½ inches in size, the exact size of the cards on which the designs are drawn. The patient is also given a pencil with an eraser. The subject is instructed to study each of the cards presented to him or her for 10 seconds, after which the patient is asked to draw the design from memory just as it is on the page. Unlike the Bender, the design book is placed at an angle of about 60 degrees to the horizontal in order to facilitate viewing by the patient.

If the subject begins to draw before 10 seconds and the withdrawal of the picture, the patient should be told that although the current picture may be easy, others will be harder and the patient should get used to studying the picture for 10 seconds. Before the third card, the first with three designs (see, e.g., Figure 8-1), the patient is reminded not to forget to reproduce everything in the design. If the subject fails to reproduce all figures in design 3, then these instructions are repeated for design 4. During any administration, the subject is permitted to erase or correct. The examiner does not routinely reassure the patient about the quality of his or her performance, but may do so if the patient asks. All drawings are done on a fresh sheet of paper so that there is only one drawing per page.

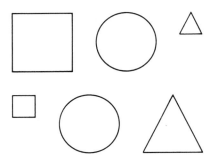

Figure 8.1 Examples of two sets of figures similar to items from the Benton.

Administration B. The same instructions are followed, except the patient is only allowed five seconds to memorize the figures.

Administration C. The patient is given paper and pencil as in A, but this time is told that he or she will be shown the card on which there is one or more figures that should be copied as exactly as possible. The card is left in the patient's view and removed only after the drawing has been completed. These instructions are repeated if the subject requests additional instructions. Slow patients may be urged to work a little faster, especially if maximal effort is not being put forth by the patient. In all other respects, this administration is identical to Administration A.

Administration D. Administration D is like Administration A, except the patient is told that he or she will see the card for 10 seconds, and after a wait of 15 seconds, will then be allowed to draw the design from memory. Unlike in Administration A, the patient is given only one sheet of paper at a time and only at the end of each 15-second delay period. Comments before designs 3 and 4 are the same as above. If the patient attempts to begin a conversation during the waiting period, the examiner should suggest that he or she concentrate on remembering the design. Benton (1945) noted that some patients may sketch the design during the waiting period with their fingers.

This is allowed as long as no visual record is left of the patient's "sketch."

Scoring

There are two scoring systems used for the Benton. The first system, number of correct answers, is the easiest to use and most appropriate for individuals using the Benton as a quick screening test. The second system, number and type of errors, is somewhat more complex and difficult to learn. This system is best used when a detailed analysis of the patient's performance is desired.

Number Correct. In this system, the patient's drawings are each scored as 1 (correct) or 0 (wrong). Any error in a drawing makes the entire design earn a score of 0. Benton (1945, 1955) presented clear instructions for identifying errors, which makes this system quick and efficient. Possible scores range from 0 to 10. Number correct can be determined for all administrations, using the same criteria.

Number of Errors. In any design with less than perfect performance, the patient has made one or more errors that may be coded according to a system devised by Benton. The error score for any one figure can vary considerably, depending on the patient's performance. As a result, error scores show more variance than do number of correct reproductions scores. The error score is not more efficient in identifying the presence of brain dysfunction, but it can be considerably more useful in analyzing the nature of a dysfunction.

Benton identified six categories of errors: omissions, distortions, perseverations, rotations, misplacements, and size errors. Each of these categories is discussed separately.

The error of omissions refers to leaving out any figure, or drawing only one or more lines that have no resemblance to the missing figure. If the subject leaves a space for the figure or places a line in the proper place, this indicates that the person remembers a figure was included, whereas the failure to leave a place or state the figure was there suggests that the person either failed to perceive or immediately forgot the figure in its entirety. If this type of error occurs in designs 1 and 2 (which have only one figure each), the error is scored as *M*. If a major (large) figure is forgotten in designs 3 through 10, the scoring is *MR* or *ML*, depending on whether the figure was on the left or the right. If the subject fails to indicate that a figure was omitted in some way, the scoring is *MR* or *ML*. If a peripheral figure is forgotten, the scoring is *PR* or *PL*. If the subject adds a figure that is not scorable as a distortion or perseveration (see below), the error is coded *Add.*

Distortions represent inaccurate drawings of figures in the design. If the error is made on designs 1 or 2, the scoring is *SM*. On the other designs, the scoring is *SMR* or *SML* when a major figure is involved, or *SPR* or *SPL* when a peripheral figure is involved. This system is used only when the distortion involves simple substitution (e.g., a circle for a square). In all other cases where fragmentation, multiple reproduction, or misplacement of an internal detail occurs the *S* in the scoring is replaced by an *I.*

Perseverations involve substituting or adding a figure from the previous design into the current design. Perseverations also are scored if an inappropriate figure is placed from one design to the next and then on to further designs (e.g., a square from design 3 is carried forward to designs 4, 5, and 6). Perseveration also occurs when one figure in a design is drawn to be identical to a major figure in the same design. Benton (1945) noted that perseveration is never scored along with an *Add* or substitution error for the same figure, and a rotation cannot be scored for the perseverated figure. Misplacement or size errors, however, may be scored. Scoring symbols for this class include *PerM* (perseveration on design 2 from design 1), *PerMR* and *PerML* for major figures, and *PerPR* and *PerPL* for peripheral figures.

Rotations are scored for rotating the figure more than 24 degrees from the original position. These errors are scored for the degree of rotation present: 180 degrees, 90 degrees, or 45 degrees. The single exception is when a figure is rotated to rest on a side rather than an angle. This is scored as *St.* Other rotations are scored as 180M, 90M, and 45M for the first two designs; 180MR, 180ML, 90MR, 90ML, 45MR, 45ML, StMR, and StML for rotated figures; and the same with P substituted for M for peripheral figures. For figures with mirror image transformations, (Mir) is added after the rotation code, for example 90MR(Mir).

Misplacements are errors in the spatial relationships of the figures within a design. If the positions of the two major figures are exchanged, this is coded *Rev.* The failure to show an overlap between overlapping figures is coded *NOv.* Showing overlap between two nonoverlapping figures is coded *Ov.* If an overlap should be present but occurs at the wrong place, the error is coded *WOv.* If a right peripheral figure is placed to the left of, between, above, or below the major figures, this is coded *MisPR*; the same problem with a left peripheral figure is coded *MisPL.* Displacement of a peripheral figure upward or downward is coded *UPR* or *UPL* for upward problems or *DPR* or *DPL* for downward errors.

Size errors are problems with the sizes of the figures. If the right major figure is less than $3/5$ of the height of the left major figure, the error is coded *SzMR* whereas the opposite problem is coded *SzML.* If the peripheral figure is greater than $3/5$ of the larger major figure, the error is coded *SzPR* or *SzPL.*

There are 27 fundamental errors possible overall, with the remaining codes referring to the involvement of peripheral or major figures and the location on the right or the left. Benton (1945) estimated that up to four or five errors may be present in a single design, while up to 24 may be found in a poor protocol. Although higher scores are theoretically possible, they rarely occur. The error system is more complicated than the correct number system; however, it is generally easy to score with experience and familiarity with the symbols.

Several additional rules are important when using the error system. First, if an error can possibly be scored as a rotation or distortion, the error is classified as a rotation. Only one misplacement error can be scored for a single feature of the design. For example, one cannot simultaneously score a misplacement for a right peripheral figure and an upward displacement of the same right peripheral figure. When a perseveration is scored, a substitutive, additive, or rotational error should not be scored for the same figure. Misplacement or size errors can be scored, however. If a peripheral figure is displaced relative to one major figure but not the other, no misplacement of the peripheral figure should be scored.

Normative Data. One of the strengths of the Benton (1955) is its normative data. Adult norms are provided for Forms A and B that take into account both IQ and age. Norms are given for both errors and number correct. Form B norms are derived by subtracting one point from the Form A norms. Similar normative data is presented for Form C, although users of the manual will find these norms on page 75 rather than in the manual's norm section. Norms are also available for an eight-item version of Form C; however, such a version saves only about one minute, making its use rather questionable since some diagnostic power is lost. No norms are currently available for Form D.

Discriminative Validity

Benton (1945) emphasized the role of such factors as motivation, depression, autistic preoccupation, poor motor skills, and faking on the test results. It is important that such possibilities be examined and test interpretation be suitably cautious if any of these conditions is likely to interfere. This is an important part in the interpretation of any test results.

Benton suggested that the best measure of organicity is the deviation of the patient's score from his or her expected score. For the number correct score, a value two or more points below expectation was seen in 69 percent of the organic group and in only 16 percent of the normal group. A value three points below expected was seen in 57 percent of the organic group and in only 4 percent of the control group, making such a score a likely indication of brain damage in an otherwise normal individual. Using error scores, nearly identical results were obtained. Benton noted that the accuracy of the test changes with the location, severity, and chronicity of the injury. Like other visual-construction tests, the Benton is most sensitive to diffuse injuries and right hemisphere lesions.

Other studies have reported results of the same magnitude. The hit rates for the test have generally been in the range of 80 to 90 percent for controls and 60 to 70 percent for organic patients (Brilliant & Gynther, 1963; Crochelet, 1970; Cronholm & Schalling, 1963; L'Abate, Friedman, Vogler, & Chusid, 1963; Sterne, 1969, 1973; Von Kerekjarto, 1961; Zwann, De Vries, & Van Dijk-Bleker, 1967).

Of important interest in examining the Benton is the performance of psychiatric patients. Neurotic patients are generally able to perform at normal levels and present no diagnostic problems when the possibility of organicity is being studied. Schizophrenic patients, however, show significant deficits on the Benton when compared with normal controls (Nikols, 1963). An examination of the performance of schizophrenics reveals a wide range of behavior, apparently related to motivation and the degree of cognitive dysfunction. Despite this, the Benton appears to be better than the Bender or the Memory for Designs tests in the discrimination of brain damaged and schizophrenic patients. Benton noted that in addition to the differences in the standard scoring, schizophrenics give more truly bizarre responses than do organic patients who have no emotional disturbance. Thus, the presence of bizarre responses indicates a schizophrenic process. The reader is cautioned to remember, however, that one may be both brain damaged and schizophrenic.

Variable performance is also seen in depressed patients, the degree of deficit varying with the severity of the depression and the ability of the examiner to motivate the patient. Depressed patients generally do poorly on tasks requiring motor skills. As a consequence, interpretation should be cautious except, of course, when the performance is in the normal range.

Benton (1974) also addressed the question of simulators. A series of studies by Benton and Spreen (1961a, 1961b) compared the performance of deliberate malingerers with that of brain damaged patients. They found that simulators scored significantly less well than the organic patients, who generally scored within five points of their expected level on the number of correct measure. Simulators also showed more distortion errors and tended to demonstrate fewer omissions, perseverations, and size errors. Simulators may also be noted by comparing their test performance to the skills in nontest interactions, especially if one is allowed to observe them in an inpatient setting.

Qualitative Considerations. Research on the Benton has suggested that three kinds of errors are more likely in brain damaged than in normal populations. The first is the omission of a peripheral figure, especially without any indication by the patient that he or she is aware that such a figure exists. Benton stated that this is even more significant after the patient has been exposed to several designs, each with a peripheral figure. This finding can be associated with a reduction of visual field width associated with parietooccipital lesions. An important problem is the unilateral omission of figures, usually on the left side. This phenomenon, called unilateral neglect, is often associated with right hemisphere lesions, especially those in the posterior areas of the hemisphere.

Rotations are common in brain injured patients, but are also seen in normals. In normals, however, the errors tend to be stabilizing errors in which a figure, drawn to sit on an angle, is rotated so it sits on a flat side. The presence of other types of rotation errors are thus likely to be more discriminating.

Size errors are also relatively more common in brain injured patients. Normals may vary their figures in size, but they do get the basic relationships among the major and peripheral figures correct. The brain injured patients, however, may fail to do this, and show striking enlargements or shrinkages of specific items.

Good Performance. As is true with other tests of brain dysfunction, a good score does not rule out the possibility of a brain lesion. As noted earlier, some 30 percent of all brain injured patients will be missed by the Benton. In general, these are more likely to be left hemisphere or frontal lesions than lesions in the right parietal area. Even lesions in the right parietal area, if there has been significant time for recovery, may present with few or no deficits. Thus, good performance must be interpreted to mean that there is no evidence for a brain lesion, although one may still be present. Because of this situation, it is better to use the Benton in conjunction with alternate tests of brain function that are more sensitive to those areas that the Benton is not likely to pick up.

Advantages and Disadvantages

The primary advantage of the Benton is the availability of well-normed alternate forms that can be administered in several different ways. Thus, a patient can be given both Forms A and B in order to directly investigate a possible nonverbal memory problem without confounding the analysis with such variables as the person's current drawing level. The presence of alternate forms allows the test to be repeated without the patients remembering the figures from a previous administration. In addition, the Benton is as effective or more effective than other drawing tests (with or without a memory component) in discriminating among normal, brain damaged, and psychiatric patients (Benton, 1974; Watson, 1968).

There are few strong disadvantages to the Benton. It is appropriate for a wide range of ages, and has been shown to be useful in a wide range of circumstances. Its main deficit has been the tendency of some to use the Benton in an inappropriate manner. This usually involves using the test as a final arbiter of the presence of organicity, rather than as part of a more comprehensive screen.

HOOPER VISUAL ORGANIZATION TEST

The Hooper Visual Organization Test (Hooper, 1983), commonly referred to as the Hooper, was designed to be an objectively scored test that could discriminate between brain damaged patients and patients with functional disorders. Hooper stated that a visual organization test was chosen for this purpose because such tasks are sensitive to brain dysfunction and relatively independent of language and intelligence.

Administration

The Hooper may be given as an individual or group test. The test consists of 30 items, each of which is the drawing of a simple object cut into pieces and mixed up. The patient's task is to visually organize the pieces and name the object. It closely resembles the Object Assembly subtest of the WAIS except for the additional demand of Object Assembly on motor construction skills.

The patient is shown the 30 pictures singly. The patient can write down his or her answer in a booklet, or this can be done by the examiner. There is no time limit on items, although after one minute subjects are usually prompted to guess. The manual for the test lists acceptable answers for full credit and, in the case of some items, half credit. The examiner may give credit for alternate answers at his or her discretion, however.

Interpretation and Validity

Hooper classified scores in the following manner: no impairment is indicated by scores between 25 and 30; mild impairment is represented by scores of 20 to 24.5 and is seen in mild organic disorders, severe emotional disturbance, or schizophrenia; moderate impairment includes scores from 10.0 to 19.5 and is seen in cases of organic brain syndrome, as well as in schizophrenics whose performance can be recognized by neologistic or bizarre responses; and scores below 10.0 represent severe impairment and are seen in severe organic or schizophrenic disorders, which can again be discriminated by the qualitative aspects of the record.

Hooper described four classes or errors that are useful in making a qualitative analysis. In isolate responses, the patient reacts to a concrete aspect of one piece rather than making the abstract integration. This response is seen in both organics and severe schizophrenics. Perseveration is using a response appropriate for an earlier item. This response is characteristic of schizophrenics, but has been seen in organics as well. The final category is neologistic responses, in which the patient forms words with no meaning to the examiner, such as "Megaloon."

Discriminative Validity

Hooper presented one study in which 100 percent accuracy was achieved in a schizophrenic group (not including chronics) and 79 percent accuracy in an organic group using a cutoff of 20. A second study by the author in a state hospital produced less significant results: 64 percent in a chronic brain syndrome group versus 78 and 67 percent in two chronic schizophrenic groups. Neurotics and patients with personality disorders, however, were able to do the test without difficulty. Lezak (1976) concluded that many brain damaged individuals can complete the Hooper without difficulty; as a consequence, the Hooper may not always indicate the presence of brain damage. Poor scores may not indicate brain damage, although they do indicate disruption in the patient's thought processes.

Advantages and Disadvantages

Our own experience has indicated that the Hooper is not very sensitive to many localized forms of brain injury. The good results come, instead, from populations with diagnosis of chronic organic brain syndromes. Thus, if one is looking for less obvious lesions, the Hooper would not be the test of choice.

The Hooper could be useful, however, in discriminating the reason for poor Object Assembly performance if one needs to discriminate between visual and visual-motor skills. It can also be used as part of a screening battery that does not include other visual discrimination tests.

OTHER NEUROPSYCHOLOGICAL TESTS

A number of other individual tests discussed in this book can be and are used for neuropsychological evaluation. These include the WAIS subtests (as discussed in chapter 1), the Shipley-Hartford and Raven's Matrices (chapter 2), achievement tests (chapter 3), personality tests (chapter 4), the Bender-Gestalt (chapter 7), the Benton (chapter 8), the individual subtests of the Halstead-Reitan (chapter 9), and the individual subtests and items from the Luria-Nebraska Battery Neuropsychological Exam (chapter 10). These tests are discussed in the indicated chapters.

TEST BATTERIES

The current literature supports the premise in this chapter that no one test of organicity is sufficient for the diagnosis of an organic disorder. Also, no single combination of tests has received widespread support as "the" best battery. Several important considerations can, however, be described for an organic test battery.

Screening Batteries

Most psychologists who test for organicity do so as a screening of a patient population to identify individuals who need further testing or who should be referred to a neurological consultant. Such batteries, since they are given to large numbers of persons, must be relatively short. A second type of screening battery, done on a smaller group of referred patients, is able to be somewhat longer (since fewer people are tested) and needs to be more discriminating (since all the patients referred would be expected to have some signs of neurological problems).

For both types of batteries, it is important to put together a set of tests that are not overlapping. Giving the Benton, the Bender, and the Memory for Designs tests, for example, would be little better than giving only one of them, since they each tap the same skills and generally identify the same patients. A better battery might be the Stroop Color and Word Test, the Canter Background Procedure, and the Token Test. These three tests cover a wide range of skills and are likely to show brain damage in almost any area of the brain. Similar batteries may be chosen from among the many tests available for diagnosing brain dysfunction.

Longer batteries can be more efficient than shorter batteries in screening. A longer battery might include the three tests described above plus the Purdue Pegboard (as a motor measure), the Seashore Rhythm Test (a measure of nonverbal auditory skills discussed in the next chapter), and the Speech Perception Test (a verbal auditory procedure discussed in the next chapter). Such a battery would take about an hour to administer.

Golden (1976) suggested a battery consisting of four WAIS subtests—Object Assembly, Block Design, Similarities, and Digit Symbol—along with the Stroop Color and Word Test, Speech Perception, the Rhythm Test, and the Aphasia Test (see next chapter). He found the battery to have an accuracy of about 90 percent. Optimally, the battery took about 1½ hours to administer.

These batteries, of course, are not the only ones possible. One should be careful to evaluate the usefulness of any set of tests chosen, however, as all combinations will not work as well, even when they appear to be logically sound.

Extended Diagnostic Batteries

In addition to screening for brain dysfunction, psychologists are also engaged in forming detailed descriptions of the deficits resulting from a brain injury, as well as localizing brain injury and identifying its nature and extent. Such decisions require extensive test batteries. These batteries can be individualized for each patient depending on the goals of the evaluation.

When this technique is used, a great deal of weight is placed on the clinical judgment of the examiner, who must select the proper tests or risk misidentifying the nature of the patient's problems. Such batteries are also more difficult to interpret since the relationships of the tests in the battery may not be known except on a theoretical basis.

The alternate method of putting a battery together is to use a comprehensive standard battery. Such batteries generally include measures for all significant neuropsychological skills—intelligence, perceptual motor, auditory, tactile, and visual skills; verbal skills; nonverbal skills; and basic motor skills (see Golden & Anderson, 1978). Two batteries, differing greatly in construction but with the aim of fulfilling these conditions, are discussed in the two following chapters.

CASE EXAMPLES

Case 1. Case 1 was originally seen on a medicine ward for a variety of complaints including headache, fatigue, depression, and general listlessness. The patient, a 35-year-old male, was uncooperative and displayed a number of bizarre symptoms. A psychiatric consultation was requested as a result. The psychiatrist, in turn, suggested psychological testing for an organic brain syndrome.

The patient was given the tests listed in Table 8-1, with the results indicated in the table. On four subtests from the WAIS, the patient performed normally on two verbal tests (Similarities, Vocabulary), and showed extensive impairment on two performance tests (Block Design, Picture Arrangement). The Picture Arrangement score was especially significant, as it was substantially below all the other scores, a finding common in right frontal injuries. On the Reitan-Indiana Aphasia Test (discussed more completely in the next chapter), the patient showed no deficits, except for an inability to draw a cross. The patient's performance on the Token Test was normal. On the Stroop Color and Word Test, the patient showed normal performance for word reading, and was slightly impaired on color

TABLE 8-1   Results for Case 1

Similarities	12 (scale score)
Vocabulary	10 (scale score)
Block Design	7 (scale score)
Picture Arrangement	3 (scale score)
Aphasia Test	1 (errors)
Memory for Designs	6 (points)
Stroop Test:	
Word	95 (items)
Color	63 (items)
Interference	15 (items)
Token Test	0 (errors)

naming, and substantially impaired on the interference page. The patient's Memory for Designs fell within the borderline range.

Overall, the pattern of deficits clearly suggested brain damage that was probably worse in the right hemisphere and most likely involved the frontal areas. Neurological procedures were later able to identify a previously unsuspected hematoma (sac of blood exerting pressure on the brain) primarily over the right frontal area but involving the left frontal as well. The patient's "psychiatric' symptoms were due to the effects of the brain dysfunction.

Case 2.   Case 2, a 37-year-old man with a history of significant alcoholism, was screened for possible organic damage. As can be seen in Table 8-2, the patient was able to do the copy phase of the Benton (Administration C) without error, but missed 4 of the 10 designs on Administration A with a total of five errors, suggesting some impairment of memory function. According to age and intelligence (which was normal), the patient would be expected to get 8 right on the memory administration. Thus, the subject performed at a level of 2 below his expected score, a borderline finding seen in both brain impairment and normals a significant percentage of the time.

TABLE 8-2   Results for Case 2

Benton Visual Retention Test		
Administration C:	0 errors	10 correct
Administration A:	5 errors	6 correct
Purdue Pegboard		
Right 11		
Left 11		
Bender-Gestalt		
Borderline		
Stroop Color and Word Test		
Word 96		
Color 76		
Interference 26		

The patient showed some impairment on the Purdue Pegboard, scoring equally well with the right and left hands. We should expect the right hand to do better generally. On the Bender, the patient scored at a low normal level, close to the cutoff score of the Pascal and Suttel (1951) system. Finally, the patient scored normally on the Stroop test, on both the Word and Color pages, but showed significant losses on the Color-Word score.

Overall, the data seems to suggest someone functioning at a borderline level with some indications of minimal frontal atrophy, especially in the left hemisphere and possibly in the right, as suggested by the Purdue Pegboard, the Stroop, and the borderline Benton. As one can see, had only some of these tests been given, conclusions for the patient may have been significantly different, an important consideration in putting together a screening battery. In this patient, later CAT scan results suggested minimal frontal atrophy consistent with the test results.

Case 3. Case 3, a 31-year-old male, was seen for evaluation three years following a brain injury suffered in an automobile accident. The patient earned the test scores reported in Table 8-3. As can be seen, the patient's performance IQ is significantly below his verbal IQ (27 points). No subtests were particularly impaired compared with the others, except for a score of four on the Digit Symbol.

The patient was given several visual-motor tests. The Memory for Designs (Figure 8-2) was awarded a score of four (in the normal range). The Bender (Figure 8-3) showed a significant number of dysfunctions, as did the Bender taken with background interference (Figure 8-4). (The reader should compare the reproduced figures to those in Chapter 7.) Note the heavy use of the margin as a point of reference and the general poor drawing skills. There are extensive overlap errors, especially on the interference Bender.

The patient also showed severe memory disruption (MQ of 74) compared with the expected MQ, which should have been equal to the patient's overall IQ. Finally, on the Purdue Pegboard the patient achieved very poorly with the left hand. These results clearly point to an overall widespread impairment of the right hemisphere of the brain.

TABLE 8-3   Results for Case 3

Wechsler Adult Intelligence Scale
   Performance IQ   82
   Verbal IQ   109
   Full-Scale IQ   97

Purdue Pegboard
   Right   15
   Left   6

Benton
  (see Figures 8-3 and 8-4)

Memory for Designs
  4 errors (see Figure 8-2)

Wechsler Memory Scale
  74 (MQ)

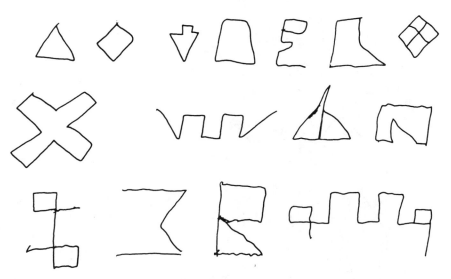

Figure 8-2.   Memory for Designs performance of the same subject whose Bender performances are shown in Figures 8-3 and 8-4. This was given a normal diagnosis using the Memory for Designs criteria. Note evidence of tremor.

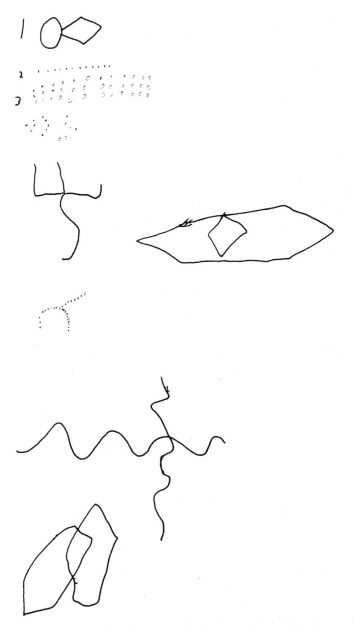

Figure 8-3. Bender results from the case example under regular administration.

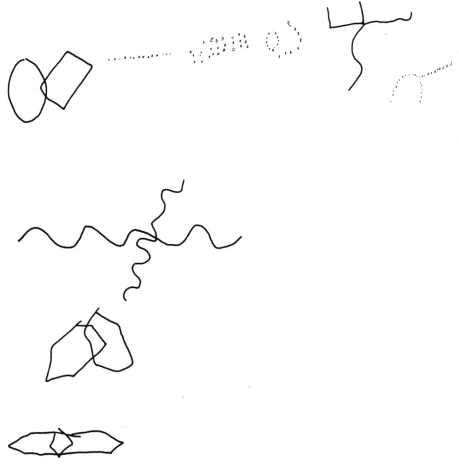

Figure 8-4. Bender results from the case example taken under background interference conditions. Note the substantially greater impairment in the drawings in this example, as well as the "hugging" to the edge of the paper in both examples. These reproductions should be compared with the actual figures presented in the Bender chapter.

CHAPTER NINE

The Halstead-Reitan Neuropsychological Battery

The Halstead-Reitan Neuropsychological Test Battery began with the work of Ward Halstead in 1935 at the University of Chicago. Halstead exhaustively studied the behavior of brain injured patients, developing and discarding hundreds of tests in the process. The results of his initial investigations were published in his 1947 book *Brain and Intelligence.* In this book, Halstead introduced some of the tests that have become an integral part of the neuropsychological battery.

Subsequent to the publication of the book, one of Halstead's students, Ralph Reitan, established a neuropsychology laboratory at the University of Indiana Medical Center. Beginning in 1951, Reitan established a test battery designed to measure a broad range of abilities. He included only tests thought to be valid indicators of brain dysfunction. The major goal of this test battery was the development of a variety of principles of inference that would allow the diagnosis of the individual subject (Reitan, undated).

Reitan began with Halstead's basic battery and supplemented it with a number of additional tests in order to broaden the scope of the battery. Over the past 25 years, Reitan has published a number of important studies that validated or modified the battery. This initial work of Halstead and Reitan has led to the adoption of the battery across this country and around the world. Its acceptance has been illustrated by the numerous studies appearing in major psychological and medical journals on the validity of the battery, and by the popularity of workshops in the use of the Halstead-Reitan Battery presented by Reitan and others.

PURPOSE OF THE NEUROPSYCHOLOGICAL EXAMINATION

Smith (1975) suggested four major purposes for the neuropsychological battery: (1) to aid in neurodiagnosis, (2) to establish baselines to measure future performance, (3) to make prognostic statements about clients, and (4) to aid in planning rehabilitation.

Neurodiagnosis

As an aid in neurodiagnosis, the neuropsychological examination can be useful in confirming a neurological diagnosis. A number of neurological conditions exist for which a diagnosis is questionable. Such cases include patients for whom there is a question between a neurological cause (e.g., head trauma) and a functional disorder (e.g., schizophrenia). In other cases, there are questions of the origin of learning disabilities.

Baseline

Neuropsychological testing is useful for examining the effects of treatments affecting brain function. If tests are given before treatment has commenced — whether it is drug treatment, surgery, or educational intervention — then later testing can establish any improvement or subsequent decline.

Prognosis

Neuropsychological tests can aid in estimating the degree of recovery a patient is likely to show. Although this area has not been investigated as fully as is necessary, initial research results suggest that neuropsychological tests can be a valuable aid (Meier, 1974). This information would be especially useful in counseling clients and family in planning rehabilitation programs and using limited rehabilitation resources.

Rehabilitation

It has become increasingly recognized that a primary purpose of neuropsychological testing is the planning and evaluation of rehabilitation programs for brain injured patients (Golden & Anderson, 1978). Luria (1963) suggested that an extensive neuropsychological examination is necessary to identify the behavioral nature and scope of a brain injury. With such information, rehabilitation programs may be designed that treat directly the major deficits of the patient.

As described by Luria (1963, 1966) and Golden and Anderson (1978), the process of rehabilitation planning closely parallels the process of neurodiagnosis by neuropsychological tests. Our knowledge of the effectiveness and use of these techniques is limited as yet, but the initial data suggests good potential for such techniques (Gudeman, Golden, & Craine, 1978).

APPARATUS, ADMINISTRATION, AND SCORING

The Halstead-Reitan Neuropsychological Battery consists of a number of independent tests. Unlike most of the other tests included in this volume, the exact procedures that make up the battery differ somewhat among neuropsychological laboratories. Most users of the battery include the following tests, however: (1) Wechsler Adult Intelligence Scale (or its earlier form, the Wechsler-Bellevue), (2) Minnesota Multiphasic Personality Test, (3) Halstead Category Test, (4) Speech-Sounds Perception Test, (5) Seashore Rhythm Test, (6) Tactual Performance Test, (7) Trail Making Test, (8) Reitan-Klove Sensory-Perceptual Examination, (9) Reitan-Indiana Aphasia Examination, (10) Lateral Dominance Examination, and (11) Halstead Finger Tapping Test. The Wechsler Adult Intelligence Scale and the Minnesota Multiphasic Personality Inventory are discussed elsewhere in this volume. The remaining tests are reviewed individually here.

Halstead Category Test

The Halstead Category Test was designed to measure an individual's capacity to deduce general principles from experience with specific items. The test consists of 208 slides, each of which suggests a number from one to four. When subjects are shown a slide, they must decide what number the slide suggests by attempting to guess the principle represented by the slide. For example, the first slide contains the Roman numeral I. Almost all subjects deduce that this slide suggests the number one. After the subjects decide on an answer, they press one of four levers numbered from one to four. If the subject guesses the correct answer, the pressing of the correct lever causes a pleasant door chime to ring, reinforcing the subject's guess of the underlying principle. If the subject's guess is incorrect, the pressing of the lever is followed by a loud, disagreeable buzzer, which indicates that the subject must utilize a different underlying principle in order to get the correct answer.

The test consists of seven different subtests, each with its own undelying principle. For example, the first group of items suggests the correct answer by presenting the Roman numerals I, II, III, and IV. In the second set, the correct answer is determined by the number of items on the page. If two circles were shown, for example, the correct answer would be two. In the third set, four items are always presented; however, one of the items is unique in some manner. The correct answer for this set is the position of the unique item. Thus, if the unique item is the third figure, the correct response would be three.

The items for the Category Test are presented on a small viewing screen contained in a projection box. Because this apparatus is somewhat clumsy, different investigators have devised alternate ways of presenting the items. There is no alternate method that is generally accepted at present.

At the beginning of the test administration, the subjects are told that items will be presented that suggest a number from one to four. The subjects are told that the bell indicates a correct choice, and the buzzer indicates an incorrect choice. Finally, they are told that they must deduce the one principle that runs through each subtest. At the beginning of each subtest, the subjects are again told that there is a principle that they must deduce, and that it may be the same as or different from the principles underlying the other subtests. Before the last subtest, the subjects are told that the answer to each item is the same as the answer when the subjects previously saw the slide.

The most serious administrative problem with the Category Test is the length of the procedure. Although a normal patient might finish the test within an hour, a brain injured patient may take two hours or more. Despite the Category Test's value in making diagnostic decisions, this extreme length makes many clinicians reluctant to use it. The length may also cause severe fatigue in a patient; answering may become random, or a subject may sometimes be unwilling or unable to finish.

Fatigue during the test may be lessened by giving the subject breaks between subtests, although this may adversely affect performance on subtest seven because of the increased time the subject must remember the items. This technique may also considerably increase the length of the testing session. A second method to control fatigue is to employ a short form of the test, which uses fewer items. At present, however, there is no short form of the test that has been shown to be equivalent to the longer form for interpretation purposes.

A third alternative is to limit the length of the test to a set time period. We have found that the prorated score after one hour of testing correlates highly ($r = .85$) with the overall score achieved by the subject. This procedure has the effect of eliminating the more difficult, later items for the subjects unable to complete them accurately. This technique does as well as the longer test in discriminating among brain injured, schizophrenic, and normal patients, although it does tend to underestimate the number of errors that will be made by severely brain injured patients.

It is useful in some cases to employ a testing the limits procedure in which the subject unable to do the test initially has the items repeated along with hints and suggestions that might lead the subject to the correct principle. Such a procedure sometimes illuminates the qualitative problems that the patient may have.

The score for the Category Test is the number of items missed. If all items are not completed, the total score is prorated by the formula:

$$\frac{\text{Number of Errors}}{\text{Number of Items Attempted}} \times 208$$

Speech-Sounds Perception Test

This test, one of Halstead's original examinations, consists of six sets of 10 items. For each item, the subject hears a nonsense word (e.g., feep) that must be matched with one of four written alternatives (e.g., teep, feep, feek, teek). All the nonsense words are formed by adding a consonant before and after the vowel pair "ee." Thus the discrimination is between different consonant sounds.

The test is administered by telling clients that they will hear nonsense words that must be matched against their written equivalents. The three sample items on the tape correspond to the first three items of the first set. If the subjects successfully match the sample items, the test is then given by playing the tape. If the subjects fail to understand the instructions, they are repeated. After the test items have begun, the examiner has no role as all items are presented by the tape.

The score for the Speech-Sounds Perception Test is the number of errors made out of 60 items. Inspection of the items missed is sometimes useful as an aid in determining specific speech sounds that give the patient more difficulty.

Seashore Rhythm Test

The Seashore Rhythm Test was taken by Halstead (1947) from the Seashore Battery of Musical Abilities. The test consists of 30 items, each of which is a pair of rhythmic patterns presented by tape. The client must indicate whether the two patterns in each item are the same or different. The subject indicates this by placing an "S" or a "D" in the appropriate space on the answer sheet.

The test is administered by telling the client that he or she will hear two rhythmic patterns, one after the other. The client is told that it is necessary to tell if the patterns are the same or different. Following this, the sample items are presented. After each sample, the client is told to write "S" or "D" as appropriate. The examiner also writes "S = Same" and "D = Different" on the answer sheet to avoid misunderstandings. If the subject understands the directions, the tape is started and the 30 items presented.

Once the test has begun, it cannot be stopped even if a subject should become confused because of the speed at which the items are presented. This procedure makes the test more sensitive to brain damage, but it also interferes with interpretation, as poor performance may be due to an inability to pay attention or to work at a normal speed rather than an inability to remember and match rhythmic patterns. If this appears to be the case, it is often informative to repeat the items slowly by stopping the tape recorder. This procedure allows a more detailed analysis of the results. The score for the test is the number of items missed under normal administration.

Tactual Performance Test

The Tactual Performance Test is a modification by Halstead of a standard Goodard-Sequin formboard. The formboard consists of a board with 10 spaces, each corresponding to a wooden geometric figure. In the standard formboard task, the subject attempts to place each geometric shape into the corresponding cutout. In this modification, the formboard is placed on a base that holds it at a 45 degree angle to the horizontal, and the subject is required to do the test blindfolded. Many of the skills demanded by the Tactual Performance Test are, consequently, quite different from those required by the standard, visual formboard test.

Since no visual skills are to be used in this test, it is imperative that the subject never be allowed to see the board or the geometric shapes. The subject, consequently, must be fully blindfolded before any test apparatus is presented. It is extremely important to ensure that the subject is not able to see in any direction.

After the subject is blindfolded, the board and blocks are placed directly before the subject. The examiner then tells the subject the task that is to be done and shows the subject the outline of the board. Then the subject is allowed to begin the test. Three trials are run: dominant hand only, nondominant hand only, and both hands together. Throughout the examination, the examiner keeps the shapes directly before the subject.

A number of problems may arise in the course of the three trials. First, subjects may attempt to use both hands during the single hand trials. Whenever this occurs, the subject should be immediately stopped from using the extra hand. In some cases, this may require the examiner to hold the alternate hand in the patient's lap.

A second problem is the wandering of the subject's hand(s) from the board to the base supporting the board or the table. When this occurs, the subject should be told and stopped. Similarly, the subject's hand(s) may be on the board but ignoring a whole section, such as the upper third. In these situations, the subject should be told to feel the whole board so that this error may be corrected.

There may also be problems with blocks already placed. The most common problem occurs when a subject accidentally knocks out a block that has already been correctly placed. In these cases, the examiner should replace the block for the subject and tell the subject that this is being done. A rarer problem is caused by the client who forces a block into the wrong hole. This is difficult to do, but not impossible if a subject persists. In these cases, the examiner should have the subject feel the block and the space, explaining that they are not the same. The examiner is not to explain why they are not the same, however.

Problems may also develop with subjects who are fearful of being blindfolded. This is more common in settings where psychiatric as well as organic clients are seen. This problem may be handled by shortening the time period for each trial (see below) and allowing the subject to remove the blindfold between trials. When this is done, the examiner must ensure that the subject does not see the board or blocks. In some patients, even these measures may be ineffective and it will be impossible to test a subject while blindfolded. These subjects can be tested without the blindfold, although the interpretation of the results under this condition is greatly altered.

A similar kind of problem occurs with the patient who cannot work for long periods of time or gets dizzy after being blindfolded for several minutes. In each case, the examiner may respond by shortening the length of each trial or providing rest periods. If such rest periods are provided within a trial, it is necessary to note this on the protocol and take it into consideration during the interpretation.

If a subject is unable to use one hand at all, all three trials should be given using only the good hand. As might be expected, this procedure also considerably affects interpretability of the results.

The final problem is the length of each trial. As can be seen above, there are specific problems that limit the time during which a patient can be tested. In addition to those considerations, there are subjects who would take 30 minutes or more on each trial if allowed. This is an inordinate amount of time to spend on a single trial within a test battery. Reitan (undated) suggested that 15 minutes is a reasonable cutoff in most cases, although in some, where the subject tires easily or becomes frustrated, he suggested a time limit of 10 minutes. Russell, Neuringer, and Goldstein (1970) suggested a general time limit of 10 minutes for each trial.

We have found that the 10-minute limit yields as much information as the 15-minute time limit, as well as saving a significant amount of testing time. For subjects unable to work 10 minutes, one should attempt to get at least a 5-minute sample. The shorter the time period, however, the less reliable the results produced.

After the three trials have been completed, the blocks and board are put away and the subject's blindfold removed. The subject is then given a clean sheet of paper and instructed to draw an outline of the board and to then draw each of the shapes as closely as possible to the spot where it actually was. After this phase of the test, the examiner should examine the sheet. If any of the shapes are not clear, or if the subject is unable to draw, the subject can indicate by verbal description and pointing what a shape is and where it goes. There is no penalty for poor drawings if the subject can indicate the shapes and positions in these alternate methods.

Several scores are generated for the Tactual Performance Test. First, there are three time scores, one for each trial. These are added together to yield a total time score. Two additional scores are derived from the drawings after the test: one for Memory, a point being given for each correct shape remembered, and one for Location, a point for each correct shape placed in a correct position.

Trail Making Test

The Trail Making Test consists of two parts (Part A and Part B), each consisting of 25 circles distributed randomly on an 8½ x 11 inch piece of white paper. In Part A, there is a number, from 1 to 25, written inside each circle. In Part B, there is either a number, from 1 to 13, or a letter, from A to L, written inside each circle.

Before beginning Part A, the client is shown a sample page that has seven circles on it, each numbered between one and seven. The client is given a pencil and told to connect the circles, beginning at number one, to the circle labeled number two, to the circle labeled number three, and so on, until the end is reached. The client is also told to work as quickly as possible. If the subject completes the sample correctly, the test page is presented and completed.

If the subject fails to complete the sample correctly, the errors are explained. For example, one might say, "You did not complete the circles in order. You are to go from one to two to three rather than from one to two to four." If the subject cannot complete the sample even after explanation, the subject should be guided through the correct sequence. Then the subject is allowed to try alone. This process can be repeated until the subject successfully completes the sample or until it becomes clear that the subject is unable to complete the test.

When the actual test for Part A begins, the instructions are repeated and are followed by the command to begin. The client is watched closely by the examiner. Any time a mistake is made, this is immediately told to the patient, who is then allowed to continue from the point where the error was made. For example, the examiner might say, "You skipped a number," or "You failed to draw your line all the way to the last circle." The test is completed when the client correctly reaches the last circle. The score for the test is the time in seconds between the examiner's saying "begin" and the client's correctly reaching the last circle.

After Part A is completed, the subject is given the sample from Part B. The client is told to connect the circles by going from one to A to two to B (doing first a number, then a letter, then a number again). The subject is then allowed to do the sample. If it is correctly performed, the examiner presents the test page. If an error is made, the examiner follows the same procedures described for Part A.

Except for the change in basic tasks, the test for Part B is conducted exactly as the test for Part A. Scoring for both parts is identical as well. In some cases, the examiner will find the subject unable to complete a section of the test (usually Part B). In these cases, the subject can be stopped after 300 seconds.

Reitan-Klove Sensory-Perceptual Examination

This examination consists of a number of separate procedures designed to measure sensory function.

The first test is for tactile imperception. The subject's hands are placed palm down on a table, and the examiner touches the right and left hands using a random sequence. The subject must report which hand is touched. During these trials, the examiner determines the pressure needed to get a consistent, accurate response from the subject.

The method of reporting may be changed if the subject

cannot say "right" or "left" reliably. For example, the subject could raise the hand that was touched, or could point to the word "right" or "left" after opening his or her eyes. The method of reporting is not important as long as only tactile input is used by the client.

Some subjects are unable to keep their eyes closed, especially those with right hemisphere injuries (Fisher, 1956). These subjects may be blindfolded, or their arms hidden from them behind a curtain or through a board. Again, the method is not important as long as the subject is denied visual feedback.

After these initial procedures, the subject is then touched on the left hand alone, right hand alone, or both hands together in a random order. Each type of touch should be repeated four times. The purpose of this procedure is to see if the subject can report the simultaneous touch on both hands. The failure to do so is a suppression. Suppressions are rare but of important diagnostic value. If the apparent suppression is due to a failure to sense the touch on one side because of inadequate pressure, however, the interpretation of the suppression changes considerably. Consequently, it is important to correctly use the pressure determined in the initial phase of the examination.

Additional suppressions can be determined for the right hand/left face combination and the left hand/right face combination. This is done by repeating the procedures used for the right and left hands discussed above.

A similar procedure may be used with auditory stimuli. The patients are told to keep their eyes closed, and the examiner stands behind them. The examiner tells the subject that he or she will make a noise in the right ear (touching it) or the left ear (touching it). The subject must report in which ear the noise is made. The examiner makes the noise by rubbing two fingers together. The examiner determines the necessary level of loudness, and then alternates the four left, four right, and four simultaneous trials as was done for the tactile stimuli.

To determine suppressions for visual stimuli, the subject must fixate on the examiner's nose. If the subject cannot do so consistently, items can be presented only when the subject is fixating; this must be determined on a trial-by-trial basis by the examiner. The visual trials are conducted by having the examiner sit three feet in front of the sitting client. The examiner extends his or her hands, and tells the subject it will be necessary to identify whether the hand on the (patient's) right or the (patient's) left is moved. Then the sequences used for the tactile and auditory procedures are employed. The procedures are administered three times with the examiner's hands above eye level, the examiner's hands at eye level, and the examiner's hands below eye level.

Some patients may have a loss in peripheral vision. Examiners must then reduce the distance between their hands so the subjects are able to report unilateral stimuli on both sides accurately. Some subjects may have a complete loss of one visual field (homonymous hemianopsia), which makes it impossible to test for suppressions, or partial loss in the upper and lower visual field on one side (upper or lower quadrantanopsia). In cases of partial loss, either above or below eye level, trials are omitted, depending on the locus of the loss.

In all testing for suppressions, irrespective of the modality, the client is never told there may be bilateral stimulation, although most subjects soon realize this. In some cases, suppressions may appear to occur because the subject is not paying attention or gets confused. It is useful, in these cases, to redo the trials for that procedure to ensure the reliability of the results (Goldstein, 1974). For all suppression procedures, scores are the number of suppressions separately recorded for left and right. If more than four trials are given, this is indicated.

After completing the suppression procedure, the examiner begins the Finger Agnosia procedure. This tests the ability of the subject to identify which finger is touched by the examiner. In this test, subjects close their eyes, or are prevented from seeing their hands in an alternate manner. The fingers of the subject's hands (first right, then left) are touched four times each in a random order. The subject reports by saying the name of the finger touched (i.e., thumb, forefinger, middle finger) or a number assigned to the finger (one through five). The system of naming or numbering the finger is determined before the procedure, and should be the method the subject prefers. If a subject cannot use a verbal response, the subject might respond by raising the appropriate finger or touching it with the other hand. Scoring is the number of errors out of 20 trials (five fingers × four touches).

The next procedure is Fingertip Number Writing. The examiner writes on the subject's hands numbers (three, four, five, or six) that the subject must identify. The examiner begins the procedure by writing the numbers three, four, five, and six on the subject's palm and identifying each number. If the subject requests, the examiner can modify how the numbers are written. Then the subject closes his or her eyes (or any of the other procedures discussed above for limiting visual information can be used), and the examiner writes numbers on each finger of the right hand, proceeding from the thumb to the little finger. This is repeated four times. The number to be written at each trial is given on the scoring form. The procedure is then repeated for the left hand. The score for each hand is the number of errors out of 20 trials.

In the Coin Recognition procedure, the examiner places a penny, a nickel, and a dime into the subject's right hand and then into the left hand. The subject must identify each coin by touch alone, and is not allowed to rub it on other objects or do anything except feel the coin. If the subject is able to identify coins in one hand alone, the examiner places a coin in each hand simultaneously, either two pennies, two nickels, or two dimes. The subject is not told the coins are the same. The score is the number of errors made for each hand.

The Tactile Form Recognition Test uses four shapes cut out of plastic: square, triangle, circle, and cross. These shapes are available to place in the patient's hand, and are also mounted at the top of a board with a hole in it. The subject alternately places the right and left hand through the hole. The examiner then places a plastic shape in the subject's hand. The subject feels the shape and points to the correct shape mounted on the board with the other (free) hand. The subject first places the right hand through the board. All four shapes are placed in the subject's hand, one at a time. The order of presentation of the shapes is given on the scoring forms. The procedure is then repeated with the left hand, the right hand again, and the left hand again. Two scores are determined: the number of errors for each hand and time measures. Time measures for each item are calculated by measuring the time from placement of the shape in the palm of the subject's hand to the subject's answer. These times are summed to get a total right-hand and a total left-hand time.

Aphasia Screening Test

This test consists of a survey of the major forms of aphasia. A booklet of items, containing pictures and words to be recognized or read, is necessary to administer the test. The test requires the subject to (a) name objects; (b) spell words; (c) draw shapes, including a Greek cross; (d) read letters and numbers; (e) read words; (f) read sentences; (g) write words; (h) pronounce words; (i) write sentences; (j) explain concepts; (k) do arithmetic, on paper and in his or her head; (1) discriminate body parts; and (m) tell right from left. Items must be presented exactly as described in the manual, and any deviation from the correct answer is counted as an error.

Two systems of scoring exist. In the first, the score is the number of items in which there is an error. In the second, a weighted scoring system is used. More points are scored for items seen as more significant. The weights for each item are presented in Russell et al. (1970).

Lateral Dominance Examination

This is a set of procedures that attempt to establish the hand, eye, and foot dominance of the individual and the relative functioning of the right and left hands.

The first items on the test determine the subject's ability to follow the test's instructions. The subject is asked to do such things as "show me your right hand." The next section attempts to determine the subject's hand dominance. The subject is asked to demonstrate how to do seven things such as "throw a ball." The examiner notes which hand the subject uses. The subject is asked to write his or her name, and the examiner notes the hand used and the time it takes. The subject is then asked to write his or her name using the other hand, and the time to do this is also recorded.

The subject is then asked to show how he or she would look through a toy telescope or shoot a toy rifle. The examiner notes the eye used in the first item, and the shoulder used in the second. The subject is then asked to show how a bug would be stepped on and a football kicked. The examiner notes the leg used.

The next procedure is the Miles ABC Test of Ocular Dominance. The subject must look through V-shaped scopes at various items. The subject does now know that only one eye can look through the scope at a time. The examiner holds the stimulus items directly below his or her eyes; the subject looks through the scope, and the examiner determines the eye used. Ten trials are given. The score is the number of trials in which the right eye is used and the number of trials in which the left eye is used.

The final procedure is grip strength. This requires a dynamometer, preferably one that can be adjusted to the size of the patient's hands. The subject takes the dynamometer in a hand. The hand is extended downward, and the subject is instructed to squeeze as hard as possible. Two trials are given for each hand. If the two trials differ by more than five kilograms (11 pounds), additional trials are given until two trials within five kilograms are available. These two trials do not have to be consecutive. The final score for each hand is the average of the two trials selected.

Halstead Finger Tapping Test

The Tapping Test uses a counter with an arm that is mounted on a flat board. The arm can be pressed down by the subject's index finger, and then returns to its original position. The subject is told to place his or her whole hand on the board with the index finger on the arm of the counter. The examiner instructs the subject to tap the key down, allow it to return to its starting position, and then tap it down again as quickly as possible. The proper method is demonstrated by the examiner.

The subject is then given five 10-second trials with each hand, starting with the preferred hand. During each trial, the subject taps the arm as many times as possible. The subject is given a rest after the third trial. Additional rest periods may be included if the subject appears fatigued.

The scores on each hand must be within five taps to be acceptable. If this is not the case, additional trials are given until five trials within five taps are obtained. This is usually achieved within eight trials. The final scores are the averages of the five trials selected for each hand.

One major problem in this test is the tendency of some subjects to move the whole hand or arm instead of only the index finger. In these cases, the subject should be informed of his or her failure to follow instructions, and the trial should begin over again. In those few cases in which the subject is unable to tap with the hand and arm immobilized, the examiner must attempt to get as close an approximation as possible. Since these subjects generally do quite badly, even with the nonstandardized administration, this does not significantly affect the interpretation of the results.

CLINICAL INTERPRETATION

Category Test

The Category Test has been found to be the most sensitive test in the Halstead-Reitan to the presence of brain dysfunction. Numerous studies have found that the test is highly effective in differentiating brain injured from normal subjects. Wheeler, Burke, and Reitan (1963) found that the test was able to achieve a hit rate of nearly 90 percent. The optimal cutoff point for the test has been found to lie between 50 and 51 errors (Halstead, 1947).

Impairment in the Category Test may reflect a number of underlying deficits in the ability to sustain attention, remember past performance, learn from reward and punishment, concentrate, evaluate past performance, analyze visually presented material, understand spatial relationships, and in the flexibility to handle a complex, changing problem. It is this complexity of skills demanded by the test that makes it sensitive to brain impairment of all kinds.

It can be difficult to identify the specific reasons for poor performance on the Category Test in an individual subject. In many cases, the reasons are multiple and impossible to separate. In other cases, comparison of Category Test performance with performance on other tests in the battery can yield information on the underlying deficits. For example, if tests of visual-spatial performance are normal, this can be ruled out as a cause of the deficit. If visual-spatial deficits are prominent, and Category Test performance is impaired on the subtests demanding strong spatial skills (subtests five and six), this can be regarded as a major cause of the deficit.

In cases in which the Category Test is impaired and most other tests show normal performance, the deficit is generally in the patient's ability to evaluate his or her own performance, to learn from the combination of missed and accurately guessed items, and to form hypotheses relating feedback to the items. These are generally abilities associated with the frontal lobes (especially in the left hemisphere). Consequently, significantly impaired Category Test performance with otherwise generally normal performance may indicate the presence of a frontal lobe disorder. When the Category Test and other tests show impairment, this may indicate lesions almost anywhere in the cerebral hemisphere.

The same features that make the Category Test highly sensitive to brain injury make the test sensitive to many forms of thought disorder, especially schizophrenia. Several studies have found the test (and the battery as a whole) unable to differentiate chronic schizophrenics and organics. Other studies, however, have supported the ability of the Category Test and the Halstead-Reitan to differentiate schizophrenics and organics. The studies finding negative results usually used populations consisting of chronic, long-term schizophrenics on medication that affected their ability to perform on the Category Test. The more successful studies generally used more acute populations and controlled for the effects of medication and motivation in a schizophrenic population. Even in these cases, however, the accuracy of the Category Test is reduced. For example, Golden and Anderson (1978) found that is was necessary to raise the cutoff point for the Category Test from 51 to 64 errors when using an acute schizophrenic control group. The hit rate for the Category Test was consequently reduced to 70 percent.

A second factor in the poor performance of some non-brain injured subjects is the close correlation between the Category Test results and age and IQ. For example, Logue and Allen (1971) found a correlation of .71 with IQ. In clinical practice, it is important to take these factors into account when interpreting the meaning of a score on the Category Test.

Speech Sounds Perception Test

The Speech Sounds Perception Test measures the ability of a subject to discriminate speech sounds and match them to their written representations. Thus, subjects must have the ability to hear and code speech into phonemes, to match phonemes to their alphabetic equivalents, and to find the appropriate answer and underline it. Disability in any of these areas can adversely affect performance.

Halstead (1947) suggested that the test might be a measure of interference, because he found that subjects missed the second phoneme in an item much more often than the first. The first phoneme, he suggested, interferes with the second. Such a view, however, would predict that performance would worsen over the course of the test as interference built up from succeeding items. Golden and Anderson (1977) however, found that the opposite occurs – performance improves as the test proceeds.

Seashore Rhythm Test

Wheeler et al. (1963) found the Seashore Rhythm Test 75 percent accurate overall. Unlike Speech Sounds, the Rhythm Test is more effective in discriminating brain injured patients (82 percent) than normal controls (72 percent). As is common in tests highly sensitive to brain injury, the hit rates are considerably reduced when a psychiatric control group is used. Golden (1977) reported an overall hit rate of 70 percent using an acute psychiatric control group. The optimal cutoff point for the Rhythm Test is between four and five errors.

Tactual Performance Test

The Tactual Performance Test is highly sensitive to the presence of brain injury because of the complex pattern of skills demanded. The test requires adequate motor control in both the right and the left arms, as well as kinesthetic and proprioceptive feedback, which enables subjects to locate and move their arms in space without visual feedback. In addition to these basic skills, the subject must also be able to plan a logical and efficient approach to the test in order to place the blocks quickly. Finally, the Location and Memory scores place great demands on incidental and spatial memory. The test is effective because most brain injuries involve impairment to one or more of these many abilities.

Six scores are derived from the Tactual Performance Test that can be used in interpretation. The first score is the total time it takes to finish the three trials. Using a cutoff of 15.7 minutes (942 seconds) is highly effective in discriminating between brain injured and normal patients (Halstead, 1974; Reitan, 1955b). Even in the difficult discrimination between acute schizophrenics and brain injured populations, the test is 70 percent effective (Golden, 1977).

The Location score has also been found to be one of the most sensitive discriminators of brain injured and normal subjects. Wheeler et al. (1963) reported an 85 percent hit rate in a normal population and a 64 percent hit rate in a control population; with psychiatric controls, Golden and Anderson (1978) reported 77 percent accuracy in the brain injured group and 67 percent accuracy in the controls. As these figures suggest, this score is much less affected by schizophrenia than is the Category Test or Rhythm Test. The Memory score is also highly effective: 74 percent hit rate in normals, 77 percent in brain injured patients, and 80 percent in psychiatric controls. The optimal cutoff point for Memory is between five and six items correct; for Location, it is between four and five correct.

In addition to these scores, the raw scores for the right-hand, left-hand, and both hands trials are also useful. A comparison of the right hand's and left hand's performance is useful in establishing the hemispheric localization of an injury. If the right hand's score is 40 percent or more longer than the left hand's score, this is suggestive of a left hemisphere injury. If the left hand's score is not at least 30 percent better than the right hand's score, a right hemisphere injury is suggested. Overall poor performance on all measures is suggestive of a right hemisphere or diffuse injury.

The Tactual Performance Test may also be used to locate an injury in the anterior (front) or posterior (back) areas of the hemisphere. If the Tactual Performance Test on the right hand is performed more poorly than tests of motor skills (Finger Tapping, strength), posterior injury is suggested. If the relationship is reversed, anterior injury is suggested. Similar conclusions may be reached about the status of the right hemisphere using the left hand's performance. Anterior injuries involving the prefrontal lobes, however, can often be seen in poor performance on the Tactual Performance Test that is not accompanied by the tactile deficits normally seen in posterior injuries or by the motor deficits seen in other frontal injuries.

Trail Making Test

The Trail Making Test, especially Part B, is a highly sensitive test of brain dysfunction. Part A requires basic motor and spatial skills from a patient, as well as the ability to count. Part B requires each of the abilities used in Part A, as well as the ability to remember and follow a complex plan (alternating numbers and letters) and to be cognitively flexible in executing the plan.

Extensive research has found the Trail Making Test to be very effective in discriminating brain injury patients and normal controls, with hit rates of about 85 percent. The optimal cutoff point for Part A is between 39 and 40 seconds; for Part B, optimal cutoff is between 91 and 92 seconds.

Comparison of the performance on Parts A and B yields valuable information. If Part A performance is impaired and Part B performance is better (B is less than twice A), the problem is basically due either to a spatial deficit (right hemisphere) or to a dominant hand motor deficit (usually left hemisphere). If Part B performance is impaired compared with Part A performance (B is greater than three times A), the deficit involves handling verbal material (left hemisphere) or planning and flexibility (frontal lobe). Left frontal disorders may be seen in poor performance on Part B and on the Category Test without impairment on most other tests. Poor performance on both Part A and Part B suggests either a diffuse injury or a massive involvement of one hemisphere (such as a massive hemorrhage).

A number of studies have questioned the usefulness of the Trail Making Test in psychiatric populations. A good score on the Trail Making Test usually rules out brain damage in a psychiatric population, but a bad score does not necessarily indicate brain damage. Goldstein and Neuringer (1966) emphasized the importance of looking at the qualitative dimensions of performance in psychiatric populations. They found that brain injured patients were less likely to, show bizarre behavior when given the test. Schizophrenics were more likely to give up on the test. Organics who failed often had trouble with the alterations required. Using these signs, the authors reported 83 percent accuracy in the schizophrenic group and 70 percent accuracy in the brain injured group. Golden and Anderson (1978), limiting his population to acute schizophrenics and using procedures designed to eliminate problems of motivation and bizarre behavior, found the test had an overall accuracy of 80 percent. In general then, it appears that subjects who can be motivated to do the test can be discriminated accurately; most of the loss of accuracy comes in the inability to get adequate performance samples from some chronic schizophrenic patients.

Reitan-Klove Sensory-Perceptual Examination

The presence of lateralized sensory-perceptual dysfunction almost always indicates some kind of damage to the central nervous system. This damage, however, may be in the spinal cord or the brain stem instead of in the cerebral hemispheres, especially in subjects in whom the only deficits are sensory and motor in nature.

As was observed earlier, suppressions are rare but extremely significant. Golden (1977) found that over 90 percent of the subjects with reliable suppressions were in the brain damaged group, irrespective of the modality in which the suppression occurred. A suppression almost always suggests a destructive lesion in the hemisphere opposite the side of the injury (e.g., right tactile suppression implies a left hemisphere injury). Tactile suppressions imply damage to the opposite parietal lobe, auditory suppressions suggest damage to the opposite temporal lobe, and visual suppressions are related to damage in the opposite occipital lobe. Because of the significance of these signs, it is imperative that the examiner ensure that suppressions are reliable and not due to wandering attention on the part of the subject.

Finger agnosia is most common with injuries of the parietal lobe. The most severe form of finger agnosia problems is seen in left parietal injuries. In the classic form, the subject is unable to perform this task on either hand, showing extremely poor performance (generally at chance levels). In the less severe forms, left parietal injuries may be reflected in a Finger Agnosia deficit on the right hand relative to that on the left hand. Generally, the errors on the right hand must exceed the errors on the left hand by three or more errors for the results to be reliable. Conversely, making three or more errors on the left hand than on the right hand implies right parietal involvement.

Fingertip Number Writing can be analyzed in much the same way as Finger Agnosia; however, Fingertip Number Writing is a more sensitive test than Finger Agnosia. Consequently, injuries near the parietal lobe (e.g., a tumor in the temporal lobe) may affect Fingertip Number Writing more severely than Finger Agnosia. When both are down equally, the injury is likely to be in the parietal lobe itself. Because of the sensitivity of this test, a decline in Tactual Performance scores without an effect on Fingertip Number Writing is often indicative of a frontal rather than a parietal disorder.

The Coin Recognition Test is difficult to interpret, since many clients are unable to recognize coins, even when presented singly. If this is the case, the test cannot be interpreted. If the person can accurately distinguish coins singly but not together, however, this is indicative of an injury to the parietal areas of the hemisphere opposite the side of the errors, especially if other tactile signs are present as well. Impairment on this test alone should be interpreted cautiously.

The Tactile Form Recognition Test is a more reliable measure of the inability to recognize objects by touch (astereognosis). More errors with one hand than the other strongly indicates brain injury in the opposite parietal lobe. Errors with both hands suggest a diffuse brain injury or an inability to comprehend instructions, as is seen with some injuries to the left hemisphere as well as with severe functional disorders.

Aphasia Screening Test

Aphasia symptoms are a common result of brain injury. It is especially common to see severe aphasic disorders in individuals with cerebrovascular disorders of the left middle cerebral artery. Consequently, all valid tests of aphasia are generally highly effective in identifying many brain injured patients. Reitan (1959) found that the number of aphasia symptoms were directly related to the likelihood of brain damage. Twenty percent of the patients with no errors had brain damage, 38 percent of the patients with one error showed brain damage, 86 percent of the patients with two errors had brain injury, and 100 percent of the patients with four or more errors were brain injured. Using the weighted scoring system proposed by Russell et al. (1970), Golden and Anderson (1978) found that 90 percent of the left brain injured patients had seven or more errors, whereas only 55 percent of the diffuse and 41 percent of the right hemisphere patients had seven or more errors. Only 27 percent of the psychiatric patients had that many errors.

The Aphasia Test may also be used to localize brain injury. If errors involve the drawing items alone, the injury is likely to be in the right hemisphere. If only verbal items are missed, the injury is probably in the left hemisphere. If both types of items are missed, the injury is likely to be in the left hemisphere or diffuse. Mathematical items may be missed by patients with injuries in either hemisphere.

Halstead Finger Tapping Test

Motor functions have long been recognized by clinical neurologists as a significant sign of brain dysfunction. This is especially true when one hand performs significantly worse than the other hand. Performance by the dominant hand that is not at least 5 to 10 percent better than the nondominant hand is generally considered significantly impaired; performance by the nondominant hand that is 20 percent or more below that of the dominant hand is considered poor (Golden & Anderson, 1978). Lateralization of the injury is to the hemisphere opposite the impaired hand.

Most research on Finger Tapping has looked at the level of performance rather than the comparison of the left and right hands. Wheeler et al. (1963) found their brain damaged patients showed impairment in level of performance 79 percent of the time, whereas half the control group also showed impairment. Golden (1977) found similar results for a brain injured group, and somewhat better results for the psychiatric controls (58 percent). In general, the literature suggests that impairment on this motor task is usually seen in brain injured patients, but is also frequently seen in control individuals. The test is probably more reliable when the results show a lateralized deficit on one hand compared with the other. The optimal cutoff point for the dominant hand is between 50 and 51 taps; for the nondominant hand, it is between 45 and 46 taps.

Lateral Dominance Examination

It is usually assumed that the hand with which a subject writes is the dominant hand. Most subjects give consistent results: the hand used for writing is used for other tasks as well. Foot dominance is determined by the demonstrations involving the football and the bug. Eye dominance is assessed by the ABC Test of Ocular Dominance. Scores of eight or more to either the left or the right eye suggest the dominance of that eye; if the scores are seven and three, six and four, or five and five, neither eye has clear dominance.

The meaning of mixed dominance, where eye, hand, and foot dominance do not match, is unclear. Although it may be associated with brain injury, especially cases of early brain injury, it can also be caused by peripheral factors such as weakness in one eye or arm. Mixed dominance has little meaning by itself; however, if it is combined with other signs suggesting early brain injury (see chapter 1 on WAIS), then it can be used as an additional piece of confirming data.

If an individual is left-handed or mixed dominant, the clinician must evaluate the possibility that verbal functions are located in the right rather than the left hemisphere. In such individuals, many of the score relationships discussed here are reversed, except for those relating to motor and sensory function. In cases where dominance for one side is incomplete, psychological skills such as speech may be represented in both hemispheres. Thus, interpretation is more difficult and more tentative in such individuals.

Strength of grip measures can be interpreted in much the same manner as finger tapping. If the dominant hand is weaker or less than 5 percent better than the nondominant hand, this suggests an injury to the dominant hemisphere. Conversely, if the strength in the nondominant hand is 20 percent or more below the strength of the dominant hand, this may indicate an injury to the nondominant hemisphere. Norms for dynamometers differ with the instrument used.

Impairment Index

The Impairment Index was designed by Halstead (1947) to reflect overall performance on his battery of tests. When Reitan began using the battery clinically, he dropped two of Halstead's tests from his battery and from the Impairment Index. Reitan's revised Impairment Index included the Rhythm Test, Speech-Sounds Perception Test, Finger Tapping Test, Category Test, and Tactual Performance Test (Total Time, Memory score, and Location score). Others have also prepared impairment indexes, including, along with the Halstead tests, the Trail Making Test, the Aphasia Test, the Sensory-Perceptual Exam, and other tests. Each of these impairment indexes was calculated in a similar manner. The index equalled the number of tests in the index that fell beyond a predetermined cutoff point divided by the total number of tests included in the index. For example, Reitan's Index equal led the number of tests impaired divided by seven. Each of these indexes had a minimum score of zero (*no impairment*) and a maximum score of one (*all tests in the brain injured range*).

Subsequently, other systems have been suggested. Russell et al. (1970) rated the performance on each test on a zero (*good performance*) to five (*poor performance*) scale. The Impairment Index was then the average of these ratings. Kiernan and Matthews (1976) suggested converting all scores into T scores and averaging the T scores. The latter has the advantage that T scores can be corrected for age effects, an important factor in several of the tests.

Although this array of different methods for calculating the Impairment Index would appear to make evaluation of it impossible, the results with each index have been remarkably similar. Wheeler et al. (1963) reported that the original Reitan Impairment Index was 90 percent effective in discriminating brain injured and normal subjects. Similarly, Kiernan and Matthews (1976) reported between 72 and 84 percent accuracy in a more difficult to discriminate population. The results of other studies have been in the same range, with most studies reporting discriminations of 80 to 95 percent accuracy. The differences between studies have been largely related to the composition of the control and experimental groups.

As might be expected from the discussion of the individual tests, the more schizophrenic the control group, the poorer the results that are achieved. With groups of chronic schizophrenics, the differentiation between controls and brain injured patients may be minimal. Several studies, however, have identified some of the factors responsible for this, including lack of motivation, the medication patients are taking, lack of cooperation, history of electroconvulsive therapy, and failure to rule out brain damage as a possible cause in many chronic schizophrenics.

INTERPRETATION OF INDIVIDUAL TESTS

Several major methods of interpretation are employed in examining the effectiveness of the separate tests within the Halstead-Reitan. The first method, the level of performance approach, establishes an optimal cutoff point. Performance worse than the cutoff is classified as brain injured while better performance is classified is normal. The accuracy of these classifications is expressed as hit rate. By chance, the hit rate for a given test is 50 percent. Consequently, hit rates must be significantly above this level for a test to be considered useful.

The second approach is a comparison of performance on one side of the body as compared to the other. This method is generally employed with tests of motor and sensory function. More impairment on one side of the body is taken to indicate brain injury. A similar method compares scores representative of left brain function (verbal skills) to those representative of right hemisphere (nonverbal skills). Significant impairment on one as compared to the other implies brain dysfunction of some kind.

DETERMINING THE PRESENCE OF BRAIN DYSFUNCTION

The presence of brain damage can be inferred in several different ways. The first method involves the Impairment Index. Scores greater than .4 have been found to be highly associated with brain damage. This procedure will miss 10 to 20 percent of the cases with actual brain damage. In general, the cases missed include very mild or fully recovered cases of brain dysfunction, as well as cases of idiopathic epilepsy (cases of epilepsy with no demonstrable etiology). This also includes cases in the areas of the brain which are largely "silent" in the sense that no current test can measure deficits caused by injury in those areas.

In a similar manner, 10 to 30 percent of the cases identified as brain damaged will not be. This can be due to a failure to perform adequate age corrections in older populations. Misidentifications may also occur in psychiatric populations, especially with chronic schizophrenics. This can be minimized by insuring optimal testing conditions: shorter sessions to control for attentional difficulties, discontinuation of medication that interferes with performance on psychological tests, and reinforcements to motivate the client to cooperate. It is also necessary for the clinician to recognize those situations when adequate test data has not been collected and to refuse to reach conclusions based on such data.

Errors may also occur in subjects with low intelligence. Such discrimination is especially difficult since low IQ scores are associated with many forms of brain damage, especially those which occur early in a child's life or result in generalized destruction of the brain. It is important in these cases to be aware of the performance expected of individuals at various IQ levels who are not brain damaged. Those who are brain damaged generally show poorer results, more lateralized motor and sensory deficits, as well as patterns suggestive of a given brain locus or process (see next sections).

IQ can also be used to avoid missing cases of brain injury in high IQ subjects. These subjects may show normal or superior performance after a brain injury and may be missed when examining the level of their performance. Using the IQ, however, can tell the clinician that the "normal" performance is substantially below what would be expected of a given client, a clue which can lead to the correct diagnosis.

In addition to the Impairment Index, performance on other tests may point to brain dysfunction. For example, Reitan (as reported earlier) has found that four or more errors on the Aphasia Test almost always indicate central nervous system dysfunction, except when there are peripheral nerve or muscle disease. The presence of reliable suppressions is almost always related to brain dysfunction, usually of a serious nature.

Conclusions reached by these first two methods should be checked against the last method of inferring brain dysfunction. This method examines the data for patterns of results indicating a particular locus of dysfunction or a specific cause of the dysfunction. This method allows the clinician to recognize brain dysfunction in mild cases, as well as to rule out deficits caused by other problems such as spinal cord damage or schizophrenia.

LATERALIZATION

Lateralization involves the analysis of neuropsychological test results to discover if a brain injury is located in a specific hemisphere. This process requires a knowledge of the effects of brain damage in each hemisphere of the brain and the probable meaning of the performance on any single test or combination of tests within the battery.

Left Hemisphere

The major measures reflecting left hemisphere involvement are verbal tests. Impairment on the Speech-Sounds Perception Test, the verbal items on the Aphasia Test, the Trail Making Test (Part B), and the verbal tests on the WAIS, as well as a lower Verbal IQ than Performance IQ, are suggestive of left hemisphere involvement.

Results of any motor or sensory test indicating poor right-hand or body performance implies left hemisphere involvement. On Finger Tapping or grip strength, the right hand should be about 5 to 15 percent faster or stronger than the left hand. Poor right-hand performance on the Tactual Performance Test is also indicative of left hemisphere involvement, especially when the left-hand performance is 40 percent or more better.

Right Hemisphere

The major measures of right hemisphere involvement are poor ability to draw (especially the Greek cross on the Aphasia Test), poor performance on the WAIS spatial tests (except Digit Symbol), poorer performance on the Rhythm Test than on Speech Perception, equal or poorer performance on Part A than on Part B of the Trail Making Test, and poor performance on Digits Backward (with normal performance on Digits Forward) on the WAIS Digit Span.

Deficits of the left hand or the left side of the body on motor or sensory tests indicate right hemisphere dysfunction. If the left hand is nondominant, left-hand tapping speed should not be less than 85 percent of the right-hand tapping speed. On the Tactual Performance Test, the left-hand speed should be at least 30 percent faster than the right-hand speed. Overall poor performance on the Tactual Performance Test suggests right hemisphere or diffuse dysfunction, as does poor performance on the Memory scores of the Tactual Performance Test.

Diffuse and General Indications

Scores of several tests are general indicators of brain damage and do not suggest a specific lateralization. These are the Category Test scores and the Total Time and Location scores of the Tactual Performance Test. The WAIS Digit Symbol subtest also is considered a general indicator.

Poor performance on both Parts A and B of the Trail Making Test, poor performance with both the right and the left hands in a sensory or motor task, low IQs, and generally poor performance on the WAIS suggest diffuse impairment. Poor overall performance on all tests also indicates a diffuse disorder.

LOCALIZATION

In cases that are found to be lateralized, the injury is often localized within the hemisphere. Localization is the process of determining the locus of the injury within the hemisphere. This is done in much the same way as lateralization is determined, by matching the test results to general deficits expected from the involvement of each lobe.

The following discussion highlights the major deficits associated with each common locus of injury. It should be recognized that in actual practice the results vary considerably across individuals. In addition, lesions are not confined to the neat boundaries used in describing research results. Finally, the behavioral effects of a lesion are not necessarily restricted to the physical boundaries of a lesion. For example, a tumor may interfere with the function of other areas of the brain by pressing against them or by disrupting cerebral circulation (Smith, 1975). Any localization, as a consequence, must be considered approximate and a better measure of the behavioral effects of a lesion than of its physical boundaries.

Frontal Lobes

Many small lesions in some areas of the frontal lobe may show little behavioral deficit, whereas other lesions may disrupt behavior on a global basis. Bilateral lesions may cause especially marked disintegration of all voluntary behavior. Thus, lesions relatively near each other in these areas may cause markedly dissimilar results.

Lesions of the left prefrontal areas, the most forward parts of the brain, may result in deficits on tests of categorizing and flexibility. Thus performance on the Category Test and the Trail Making Test (Part B) may be impaired, while performance on other tests in the battery is normal. Such injuries rarely cause deficits on the WAIS or on motor and sensory tests (Smith, 1964, 1966a). The right hand's performance on the Tactual Performance Test is impaired in a few cases, but no other sensory symptoms are present.

As the lesion moves back toward the central sulcus, the patient is more likely to show severe deficits on Finger Tapping and in motor speech tasks (speaking and writing). Grip strength may be affected, as may all tests that have a significant motor component (e.g., the WAIS Digit Symbol). The right hand's performance on the Tactual Performance Test will be affected, but the left hand's trial will not be relatively impaired. Performance on Speech Sounds and Rhythm will generally be intact.

If the lesion is in the right prefrontal areas, there may be no deficits, although Category Test impairment may occur. McFie (1969, 1975) has associated poor performance on Picture Arrangement with right frontal deficits; in other cases, Digits Backward may be affected (Mahan, 1976). Deficits may sometimes be seen in complex spatial tasks (Block Design and Tactual Performance Test, but not in overall IQ (Benton, 1968; Smith 1966b). As the lesion is moved back, deficits on Finger Tapping (left hand) are seen. In some cases, there are deficits on the Rhythm Test.

Temporal Lobes

The temporal lobes are primarily concerned with auditory functions. The presence of auditory suppression is related to severe injury in the opposite temporal lobe.

The left temporal lobe is responsible for phonemic decoding (Luria, 1966). With such an injury, low scores often are seen on Speech-Sounds. Performance on Rhythm may be impaired, but not as severely as on Speech-Sounds. Numerous aphasia symptoms may be seen in speaking, reading, writing, or any task that requires phonemic discrimination. Digit Span may often be impaired, as may Similarities (McFie, 1975).

Lesions to the right temporal lobe often cause Rhythm deficits, although this is not always the case (Fedio & Mirsky, 1969; Reitan, undated). Deficits may also be seen in Object Assembly, Picture Arrangement, and Digit Symbol (McFie, 1975; Meier & French, 1966).

Visual deficits may occur due to deeper lesions, since the optic tracts pass through the temporal lobe. If the lesion is in the left temporal lobe, this may cause right upper quadrantanopsia, loss of the upper right visual field. In the right temporal lobe, a lesion may cause left upper quadrantanopsia.

Temporal lobe disorders may also show motor and sensory deficits because of the proximity of the motor and sensory areas of the brain. Generally, these motor deficits are mild. The sensory deficit is seen on the most sensitive tests of sensory function: Fingertip Number Writing and the Tactual Performance Test. In many cases, temporal lobe injuries seem to be a cross between a frontal lobe and a parietal lobe injury.

Parietal Lobes

The parietal lobes are involved in tactile input and the integration of auditory, visual, and tactile input. Because of the importance of these functions, parietal deficits are generally quite clearly evident on neuropsychological tests.

Deficits in either parietal lobe generally cause sensory deficits on the opposite side of the body. Depending on the severity and precise location of an injury, there will be deficits on the tactile suppression test, the Tactile Form Recognition Test, Finger Agnosia, Fingertip Number Writing, and the Tactual Performance Test. The Tactual Performance Test will be more impaired than the Finger Tapping Test; however, Finger Tapping will be impaired to some degree, as will other motor tasks, since these require kinesthetic/proprioceptive feedback (motor deficits due to sensory loss is termed ataxia).

Left parietal deficits result in right-sided sensory losses and a loss in IQ. Deficits will be seen on the Arithmetic, Digit Span, and Block Design subtests of the WAIS (McFie, 1969). Part B of the Trail Making Test will be poorly performed. Subjects may demonstrate a variety of aphasic symptoms: inability to name objects (dysnomia), reading deficits (dyslexia), writing problems (dysgraphia), and arithmetic problems (dyscalculia). Lesions of the parietal-temporal-occipital junction may cause a complete loss of verbal skills (global aphasia).

Heimburger, Demyer, and Reitan (1964) found that the presence of Gerstmann's syndrome was usually associated with left parietal injuries. Gerstmann's syndrome includes finger agnosia, agraphia, acalculia, and right-left confusion.

Lesions of the right parietal lobe may result in complete deterioration of performance on the Tactual Performance Test, and/or a specific loss in the left hand, as well as minor motor deficits. Right parietal lesions also cause deficits in drawing, especially of the Greek cross (construction dyspraxia) (Wheeler & Reitan, 1963). Deficits are also found on the Trail Making Test (especially Part A), Block Design, and Picture Arrangement, and on arithmetic items that demand "carrying" and spatial orientation (Golden, 1977; McFie, 1975).

A major symptom of right parietal injury, as well as of other right hemisphere injuries, is unilateral spatial neglect. In this disorder, patients ignore the left side of stimulus items. They draw only the right side of the Greek cross, or read only the right half of a sentence.

Parietal lobe injuries may also cause lower quandrantanopsia, loss of the lower visual field. The loss would be in the left visual field in a right parietal injury, and in the right visual field in a left parietal injury. In lesions that involve both the parietal and temporal lobes, there may be a complete interruption of the optic tracts. This causes homonymous hemianopsia, a complete loss of the opposite visual field.

Occipital Lobes

Occipital lobe lesions may also cause homonymous hemianopsia, because the occipital lobes are the termination of the optic tracts in each hemisphere. When the deficit is in the right occipital lobe, there is often unilateral spatial neglect, as described above. Less extensive deficits in the occipital lobes may cause irregular deficits in the visual field (scotomas).

Occipital deficits may result in visual agnosia, an inability to recognize objects by sight. This interferes with performance on such tests as Picture Arrangement, Object Assembly, and Picture Completion. If the deficit is in the left occipital lobe, there may be a loss of the ability to recognize visual verbal stimuli. This can result in an inability to read (dyslexia) or can seriously impair reading speed.

ORGANIZING TEST DATA

With the information outlined above and in chapter 1, all the poor results on the Halstead-Reitan Battery can be classified as indicating left, right, or diffuse brain injury. For example, the normative data presented previously and in Table 9-1 can be used to classify the data in the sample case presented in Table 9-2.

The Category Test score in Table 9-2 suggests significant brain dysfunction. The score is placed in a summary column (Table 9-3) labeled "Diffuse/General" impairment. The Speech-Sounds score suggests left hemisphere damage and is placed under the left hemisphere column. The Rhythm performance is normal and is not included in the table. (Some clinicians prefer to include the good tests as well; these can be included by putting the name of the test on the form with brackets around the test name.)

TABLE 9.1 Ranges for Brain Injured Performance on the Halstead-Reitan*

Test	Brain Injured Range
Category Test	>50 errors
Tactual Performance Test – Total Time	>942 seconds
Tactual Performance Test – Memory	<6 correct
Tactual Performance Test – Location	<5 correct
Rhythm Test	>4 errors
Speech-Sounds Perception test	>7 errors
Finger Tapping Test (Dominant)	<51 taps
Finger Tapping Test (Nondominant)	<46 taps
Impairment Index	>0.4
Trail Making Test (Part A)	>39 seconds
Trail Making Test (Part B)	>91 seconds
Suppressions (all modalities)	>0
Finger Agnosia	>2 errors
Fingertip Number Writing	>3 errors
Tactile Form Recognition	>0 errors
Grip Strength (Dominant)	<40 kg.
Grip Strength (Nondominant)	<35 kg.
Aphasia Exam	>6 points or 72 errors

*Norms adopted from Halstead (1947), Reitan (undated), Russell, Neuringer, and Goldstein (1970), Golden (1977), and Golden (1978).

The total score on the Tactual Performance Test is placed in the general column. Since the right-hand score is 100 percent worse than the left-hand score, these scores are placed under the left hemisphere column. The Location score is placed under the general column.

The Finger Tapping performance of the right hand fails to exceed the left-hand performance. Consequently, this is placed under the left hemisphere column. Both Finger Agnosia and Fingertip Number Writing show clear right-hand deficits and are also listed under the left hemisphere column.

The Wechsler scores show relative deficits on Digit Span and Arithmetic. These are both listed under the left hemisphere column. Of the WAIS performance tests, Block Design, Picture

TABLE 9.2 Sample Case (right-handed, 25 year old, 12th-grade education)

Category		Tactile Form Recognition	
78 errors		Right	28 secs/0 errors
Speech-Sounds		Left	28 secs/0 errors
14 errors		Wechsler Adult Intelligence Scale	
Rhythm		Vocabulary	12
2 errors		Comprehension	10
Tactual Performance Test		Similarities	10
Right Hand	600″	Digit Span	7
Left Hand	300″	Arithmetic	7
Both Hands	240″	Information	11
Location	3	Digit Symbol	6
Memory	7	Picture Completion	10
Total	1140″	Block Design	8
		Picture Arrangement	8
Finger Tapping		Object Assembly	10
Right	48 taps	VIQ	96
Left	48 taps	PIQ	90
Suppressions		FSIQ	93
None		Aphasia	
Finger Agnosia		Dyslexia	
Right	8 errors	Mild Dysarthria	
Left	3 errors	Mild Dysnomia	
Fingertip Number Writing		Trail Making Test	
Right	12 errors	Part A	22 secs
Left	5 errors	Part B	108 secs

Arrangement, and Digit Symbol are relatively impaired. Block Design and Picture Arrangement are listed under the right column. The PIQ and VIQ do not differ sufficiently to suggest lateralization to either hemisphere, nor are they significantly impaired. They are listed under the general column, however, since they are important for analyzing the overall level of performance.

Three verbal aphasic symptoms were found and are listed in the left hemisphere column. On the Trail Making Test, Part

TABLE 9.3   Organization of Scores for the Sample Case

Left Hemisphere	Diffuse/General	Right Hemisphere
Speech Sounds (14)	Category (78)	Block Design
TPT (R = 600, L = 300)	TPT total (1140″)	Picture Arrangement (8)
Finger Tapping (R = L = 48)	Location (3)	
Finger Agnosia (R = 8, L = 3)	VIQ = 96, PIQ = 90	
Fingertip Number Writing (RT = 12, L = 5)	Digit Symbol (6)	
Trails B > Trails A (B = 108, A = 22)	<Vocabulary (12)>	
Dight Span (7)	Impairment = .71	
Arithmetic (7)		
Dyslexia		
Dysarthria		
Dysnomia		

B is impaired, whereas Part A is normal. Consequently, they are listed under the left hemisphere.

The Impairment Index is calculated last. Of the tests used by Reitan, five are impaired: Category, Speech-Sounds, Tactual Performance Test Total and Location, and Finger Tapping. Thus the impairment index is 5/7 or .71. This is listed in the general column.

An examination of the final summary sheet suggests several initial conclusions. First, despite a normal IQ, the Impairment Index and the many poorly performed tests clearly suggest that this is a case of brain impairment. Second, the overwhelming weight of the data suggests a left hemisphere difficulty.

Once a working hypothesis such as this is formed, the clinician must examine all the results to see if they are consistent with this hypothesis. The right hemisphere column lists only two tests, Block Design and Picture Arrangement. Since both of these tests may be affected by left hemisphere damage, these scores are not inconsistent with the hypothesis. The results in the general column also are not inconsistent with the hypothesis, and no tests were performed well that should be impaired given such an injury.

In a number of circumstances, however, results might have been found that contradicted the hypothesis. For example, if a left hemisphere injury was hypothesized and the left hand performed the Tactual Performance Test much worse than the right, it would be necessary to change the hypothesis.

Overall one of several major hypotheses may be made in a given case:

1. Overall good performance with no significant deficits.
2. Good performance in one hemisphere but significant impairment in the other.
3. Impaired performance in both hemispheres but one considerably worse than the other.
4. Equally impaired performance in both hemispheres.
5. Scattered deficits; both hemispheres have apparent focal deficits.
6. Motor and sensory performance impaired on one or both sides, with cognitive performance intact.
7. Cognitive performance impaired but motor/sensory abilities intact.

If the final decision involves a significant deficit in one hemisphere, a worse deficit in one hemisphere, or scattered deficits, the data is examined to see if there is a suggestion of localization within the hemispheres.

In the case presented in Table 9-2, there are significant right sensory deficits; impairment on the Tactual Performance Test (right hand); impairment on Block Design, Arithmetic, and Digit Span; and impairment in the Trail Making Test (Part B). These deficits closely describe the deficits associated with left parietal disruption. This would be the most likely site for a lesion in this patient. It should be noted that this technique is applicable to any neuropsychological test battery.

PROCESS

Process identification is important in differentiating among neurological conditions, as well as among neurological conditions and psychiatric disorders that cause symptoms similar to those of brain dysfunction. Process analysis can also aid the psychologist in recognizing neurological conditions that do not produce strong changes in level of performance but make reliable changes in pattern of performance. These two abilities are highly important in reducing the number of errors made in neuropsychological diagnosis. The skill of accurately recognizing neurological process is based on familiarity and experience with neuropathological disorders and their neuropsychological correlates. Some of the basic dimensions of those correlates are described here.

Schizophrenia

As has been seen, the discrimination of schizophrenia and brain damage has been a major concern in clinical neuropsychology. The use of a test battery and ensuring optimal test conditions reduces some of the problems involved in such a diagnosis. Even under optimal conditions, however, sizable numbers of schizophrenics show a level of performance indicative of brain dysfunction.

Patients with disorders suggesting localized, focal problems can be ruled out, because schizophrenia is not likely to produce focal deficits. Patient profiles with scattered motor, sensory, and cognitive disorders, as well as personality test results suggesting psychosis, must be compared to diseases known to produce such patterns (e.g., Parkinson's disease, multiple sclerosis, multiple tumors). Multiple sclerosis, for example, may produce motor, sensory, and cognitive deficits, along with an elevated schizophrenia score on the MMPI. The pattern is predictable, however, and can be separated from other diseases. If a profile cannot be related to any known disorders, schizophrenia becomes likely.

The schizophrenic with diffuse deficits generally shows a pattern different from that of generalized neurological disorders. Tests measuring higher cognitive skills and attention are severely impaired, whereas basic skills are intact. Some tests that would normally be impaired in a generalized disorder are performed adequately. It is this contradictory pattern and the personality test results that define the schizophrenic pattern.

In cases in which a question remains as to diagnosis, retesting within an examination is useful. The results of the psychiatric patient are inconsistent, whereas the brain damaged patient does not show sudden regaining of skills over short periods of time.

Several cautions are in order when attempting to make these discriminations in difficult cases. First, it is necessary to rule out all possible neurological diagnoses. The patient referred for a neuropsychological examination generally presents conflicting features. It is unfair to the patient and referral source to rule out possible alternatives without careful examination.

Second, qualitative dimensions of the patient's behavior must be observed. As Goldstein and Neuringer (1966) observed, the schizophrenic is more likely to be bizarre and unmotivated rather than unable to do a test. Behavior within a test can be revealing. The schizophrenic may be able to perform a problem at one point, for example, but not at another.

Third, the effects of drugs and low motivation must be eliminated. If a patient cannot be accurately tested, no valid conclusions can be reached. Many failures reported in the test literature are the result of this significant but often overlooked factor.

Tumors

Tumors occur in a variety of forms, each of which varies in the manner it affects neuropsychological test results. There are several common findings, however. All tumors create an area of focal deficit surrounded by an area of more diffuse and less severe deficit. The area of focal deficit varies greatly in severity; the effects may be extremely mild in some tumors, extremely severe in others. In the most severe tumors, brain tissue is destroyed and suppressions are seen if the tumor is in a sensory reception area of the cerebral hemispheres.

The surrounding deficits may also vary in severity. They are nonexistent in some tumors, and in others, the entire function of the brain may be disrupted. These secondary effects may be the result of increased pressure, edema (swelling of the brain), or disturbances in cerebral circulation.

An abscess, a pocket of pus in the brain caused by infection, may result in similar symptoms, as may a hematoma, a pocket of blood within the brain, or an aneurysm, a ballooning of a section of an artery of the brain. Metastatic tumors result from the spread of cancer from other parts of the body to the brain. They are identified because they are usually multiple, causing pockets of focal deficit throughout the brain.

Head Traumas

Head traumas are often characterized by a focal deficit in one hemisphere and a somewhat more diffuse and less severe deficit in the opposite hemisphere. The severity of these deficits may vary considerably. In cases in which there is unconsciousness, the severity generally correlates with the length of time it takes a person to awake.

Head trauma may also lead to localized or more severe bleeding in the brain. There are usually more severe and permanent deficits in these injuries; if the bleeding is severe, the area of injury may be extended considerably. In some cases, hematomas (pockets of blood) may form, sometimes several months after an injury due to slow bleeding in an artery.

Cerebrovascular Disorders

Disruption of the cerebrovascular system is a major cause of brain injury. A common disorder is infarction of an artery, resulting in a lack of oxygen in tissue served by the artery. A common site for infarction is the middle cerebral artery, which supplies the motor, temporal, and parietal areas of each hemisphere. These infarctions can result in partial or complete loss of motor and sensory functions on one side of the body. If the left middle cerebral artery is involved, there will also be extensive verbal deficits. If the right middle cerebral artery is involved, there will be severe spatial deficits (e.g., Block Design, drawings) and losses on the Rhythm Test. Similar results, in a more severe form, will be caused by hemorrhage of these arteries. In this case, there will also be clear suppressions.

Many cerebrovascular disorders occur after the onset of arteriosclerosis. Since arteriosclerosis causes diffuse brain impairment, patients with cerebrovascular disorders may present a picture of diffuse impairment throughout the brain accompanied by an area of severe focal deficit.

Aneurysms are the result of a ballooning on a part of an artery. Aneurysms cause mild focal deficits where they are located. Their effects rarely extend beyond this, however, unless they hemorrhage. Aneurysms typically have Impairment Indexes of .4 to .6, whereas infarctions have indexes of .6 to 1.0 and hemorrhages have indexes of .9 to 1.0.

In many cases, cerebrovascular disorders and tumors produce similar results. For example, a severe tumor near the middle cerebral artery may be difficult to distinguish from an infarction or hemorrhage.

Epilepsy

Epilepsy is generally a secondary result of another neuropathological condition, often caused by the irritation of the brain by a scar, tumor, or other space-occupying disorder. There is also a large class of epilepsies labeled idiopathic (i.e., of unknown origin). A series of studies on epilepsy (Klove & Matthews, 1966, 1969, 1974; Matthews & Klove, 1967) found that epilepsy with known causes showed more severe impairment on the Halstead-Reitan than those labeled idiopathic. At present, however, there is no way to identify the presence of epilepsy by the test battery. Epilepsy is always a possibility, especially in clients with focal lesions.

Alcoholism

Chronic alcoholics have significant deficits on the Halstead-Reitan (Gudeman, Craine, Golden, & McLaughlin, in 1977). These deficits occur on tests of frontal lobe activity (Category Test, Trail Making Test [Part B]), spatial skills (Tactual Performance Test, Rhythm, Block Design, Picture Arrangement, Object Assembly), and left-sided motor skills (Finger Tapping). The severity of the deficits depends on the chronicity and severity of the alcoholism.

Presenile Dementia

The presenile dementias (Alzheimer's and Pick's diseases are the major forms) result in generalized deterioration of brain function, including deficits on those tests thought to be resistant to brain damage (e.g., Vocabulary). The Impairment Index in these disorders is usually 1.0.

Parkinson's Disease

Patients with Parkinson's disease show significant impairment (including a tremor) on tests of drawing and impairment on the Category Test, although WAIS scores tend to be normal (Reitan & Boll, 1971). Motor and tactile skills are down on the Tactual Performance Test and the Finger Tapping Test. These deficits may be bilateral or unilateral. Patients may also have very small writing in an attempt to reduce motor problems. In the later stages of this disorder, there may be generalized impairment across Halstead's basic tests.

Multiple Sclerosis

Multiple sclerosis (MS) is a degenerative disease of the central nervous system. MS produces sensory and motor symptoms that are often inconsistent, and may show periods of exacerbation and remission. The patients usually show a higher Verbal than Performance IQ, and show deficits on Finger Tapping, the Tactual Performance Test, and other sensory tests. There may be mild cognitive losses reflected as a borderline score on the Category Test. Auditory problems are rare, but visual deficits may be caused by involvement of the optic nerve (Goldstein & Shelley, 1974; Matthews, Cleeland, & Hopper, 1970; Reitan, Reed, & Dyken, 1971; Robbins, 1974). MS patients may also show peaks on the Hypochondriasis and Hysteria scales of the MMPI, a pattern characteristic of conversion hysteria (Cleeland et al., 1970). Because of the MMPI profile and the inconsistent symptoms, MS is sometimes mistaken for a psychological disorder.

REHABILITATION

Luria (1963) suggested that when one area of the brain is destroyed, it interrupts the functional systems responsible for behavior. Recovery of any lost abilities depends upon reformulation of the functional systems responsible for those behaviors. The reformulation may take place in one of three ways. First, another area may substitute for the lost area. This is more likely in situations in which both hemispheres of the brain are involved in a task. For example, both parietal lobes can be involved in spatial tasks; consequently, loss on one side can be compensated for by increasing the participation of the opposite parietal in the appropriate functional system.

One can also involve new areas of the brain by providing an alternate method of doing a task. The task may be done by involving more basic systems of the brain. For example, the patient may have injury to the motor speech areas and be unable to say the letter "p." Such patients, however, are often able to perform the more basic motion of blowing through pursed lips. Starting at this point, such a response may be shaped into saying "p."

Finally, a functional system may be reformed by including higher centers of the brain. A subject with lesions in the motor area, for example, may be unable to tap his or her finger on command; however, if the patient is told to tap out his or her age, the patient is able to do this since this task involves the higher cortical centers to a greater extent.

The emphasis in each of these situations is that the overt behavior is maintained, although the manner in which the brain executes the behavior is changed. The formation of an effective new functional system depends upon the integrity of the areas that must form the new functional system. Consequently, the neuropsychologist must be interested not only in what deficits are present, but also in what strengths are present.

Whichever mechanism may be operating in a given case, it is the job of the rehabilitation neuropsychologist to provide training that enables the brain to efficiently form the most workable alternative functional system. The major technique is to provide a situation in which the brain receives accurate feedback on its performance. This feedback allows the brain to assess the accuracy of its attempts to reformulate the functional system. The tasks must be designed so that the feedback is clear. The lack of clear feedback is one factor limiting the spontaneous improvement that a subject makes without therapy.

PLANNING REHABILITATION PROGRAMS

In order to reach the goals described above, it is necessary to use the neuropsychological examination to fully document the deficits caused by a brain injury. It is important to recognize that all deficits, whether a direct result of a brain injury or of other factors, must be considered if the maximally effective rehabilitation program is to be designed.

The identification process can be done in two ways. First, analysis of neuropsychological test results can reveal underlying deficits. This requires a knowledge of the skills demanded by each test, and a comparison of the patient's performance on tests with overlapping requirements. Second, a knowledge of the locus and cause of a brain injury can be related to experimental information on how the brain works (see Golden & Anderson, 1978; Luria, 1966, 1973). Combining the information from these two approaches can lead to a detailed analysis of the areas in which a subject is impaired.

In addition to considering the status of the patient's cognitive abilities, it is also necessary to evaluate the patient's emotional status. The client's emotional status can significantly affect the efficiency of rehabilitation programs. In some cases, emotional problems are so severe as to preclude a successful program. In many cases, treatment of the emotional disorder is necessary either as a prelude to treatment or as an integral part of the treatment (see chapters 4 and 5).

Several considerations help to set the priorities for rehabilitation. The major goal is the organization of a program so that maximal performance levels may be achieved by the patient with a minimum expenditure of staff and patient effort. Beginning therapy in an area dependent upon skills that have not yet been learned is an inefficient approach, as is putting a patient with low motivation in a program that requires great effort before the motivational problems have been treated.

It is important to determine which deficits, if any, may be due to emotional disorders that the patient may be showing. In order to do this, it is necessary for the psychologist to compare the disabilities expected from the client's neurological disorder with those shown. If there are deficits beyond what would be expected, these can be due to the client's emotional status. This is important, since deficits that are due to the patient's emotional reaction may be very resistant to normal rehabilitation treatment.

It is also necessary to assess the importance of the deficits to the patient's life. Some deficits are more relevant to a patient's occupation, and some more important to a patient psychologically. For example, I saw one patient whose motor strength and coordination tested as normal, but who felt he was weak. Although he had many more severe problems, it was found that a strength-building program aided considerably in getting the patient's cooperation and making him feel that therapy was important.

Finally, the neuropsychologist needs to consider in which areas progress can be made most successfully. Early and obvious success in a rehabilitation program can be a powerful reinforcer to the patient and his or her family. This is a considerable aid in enlisting the patient's full effort in the rehabilitation program.

ADVANTAGES AND DISADVANTAGES

The primary area in which the Halstead-Reitan has been found to be ineffective is in the chronic schizophrenic population. Numerous testing and interpretation problems exist with this battery, as well as with other neuropsychological tests, for this population. The Halstead-Reitan is an effective tool for acute or milder schizophrenic populations, however.

A second disadvantage to the test battery is the time it takes to administer. In many settings, it is not possible to provide the manpower necessary to administer a test procedure that may require a full working day or more to complete. In other cases, the patient is not capable of such sustained activity (although properly placed rests during the tests will reduce this problem). Many clinicians feel that it is more appropriate to use a shorter, individually chosen test battery (Golden & Anderson, 1978; Lezak, 1976).

The use of individualized, shorter examinations also has disadvantages, however. First, it is possible to miss an important deficit if the battery is not selected properly. Since there are no guidelines for such test selection, the accuracy depends on the skills of the individual clinician. Second, this approach does not allow the collection of data on the effectiveness of a test battery, or research on how interrelationships among tests may relate to a given locus or neurological process. Thus, all interpretation must remain largely qualitative and clinical.

Another disadvantage is that many of the tests in the battery depend on motor skills. This is especially evident in the spatial tests (e.g., Block Design, Tactual Performance Test, drawing tests, Trail Making Test [Part A], and Object Assembly). Subjects with severe central or peripheral motor impairment often cannot be tested adequately as a result of this problem. It is necessary in these cases to use alternate tests of these skills that do not demand motor ability, such as Raven's Matrices (see chapter 4).

Finally, the battery does not cover all possible neuropsychological deficits. Although most of the major deficits required for interpretation are included (as evidenced by the success of the battery), some problems are missed. As a result, many investigators have extended the scope of the battery by adding additional test procedures. The Wisconsin Neuropsychological Laboratory, for example, developed an additional set of tests aimed primarily at detecting brain stem injuries (Norton & Matthews, 1972). Others have found the Peabody Picture Vocabulary Test useful for patients with expressive speech problems (see chapter 3). In many cases, specific tests may be added to the battery for individual cases. (See Lezak, 1976, for a review of many tests available in experimental and clinical neuropsychology.)

Adding additional tests has the drawback of further increasing the time required for the battery, although doing so undoubtedly provides a more comprehensive and effective examination. This problem has been partially dealt with by shortening the tests within the Halstead-Reitan in the ways suggested in this chapter, and by developing shorter forms or alternate tests.

The major advantage of the Halstead-Reitan over other neuropsychological batteries and procedures is the extensive validation and experimental work available on the test battery. This work allows the clinician to depend on the proven relationships within and between tests to reach conclusions about diagnosis rather than depending on clinical judgment derived from experience and the literature on each individual test. This ability to identify complex test patterns and relationships, such as those identified for alcoholism or multiple sclerosis, greatly increases the value of the test battery. Any standard or individualized test batteries attempting to replace this test would have to develop similar, extensive information.

CASE EXAMPLES

Case 1. FR was a 62-year-old, right-handed male with a ninth-grade education. He was referred for neuropsychological testing because of a gradual loss of sensation in his right side over the preceding three weeks. The neuropsychological examination was part of a more extensive neurological investigation.

Table 9-4 presents the patient's test results. As can be seen

TABLE 9-4   Results for Case 1

Wechsler Adult Intelligence Scale		
Information	7	
Comprehension	7	
Arithmetic	6	
Similarities	6	
Digit Span	2	
Vocabulary	6	
Digit Symbol	3	
Picture Completion	10	
Object Assembly	8	
Block Design	8	
Picture Arrangement	6	
Verbal IQ	81	
Performance IQ	100	
Full-scale IQ	79	

Peabody Picture Vocabulary
IQ   88

Speech Perception
36 errors

Rhythm
13 errors

Finger Tapping
Right   0
Left   37

Tactual Performance Test
Left   10:00 (2 blocks in)
Left   10:00 (2 blocks)
Left   10:00 (2 blocks)
Memory   1
Location   0

Trail Making Test
Part A   84 seconds
Part B   discontinued

Category
120 errors

Finger Agnosia
Right 9 errors
Left 0 errors

Fingertip Number Writing
Right 11 errors
Left 5 errors

Tactile Form Recognition
Right 2 errors
Left 0 errors

MMPI
normal

Impairment Index
1.0

Aphasia symptoms: dysnomia, spelling dyspraxia, dysgraphia, dyslexia, dyscalculia, dysarthria.
Dominance: right hand, right foot, left eye.
Suppressions: right hand, right ear.

from general indicators, the patient's performance was quite impaired. He missed 120 items on the Category Test, was unable to place all 10 blocks of the Tactual Performance Test on any of the trials, and failed to remember the location or shape of any of the forms on the Tactual Performance Test. He earned an Impairment Index of 1.0, indicating that all tests on which the index is based were impaired. He also showed severely depressed performance on the Wechsler tests most sensitive to brain damage (i.e., the Digit Symbol and Digit Span Tests).

In examining the scores for laterality, several are outstanding. The right-hand tapping was highly impaired compared with tapping of the left hand. The right hand was also more impaired on all tests of tactile sensitivity (Finger Agnosia, Fingertip Number Writing, Tactile Form Recognition). The patient was unable to do the Tactual Performance Test with his right hand. He also showed reliable suppressions on the right hand and in the right ear. Part A of the Trail Making Test was slow, but the patient was unable to finish Part B. Both the Speech-Sounds Perception and Rhythm tests were down severely. The patient had numerous signs of aphasia. Performance IQ was significantly greater than Verbal IQ. All of these signs indicate left hemisphere involvement.

It must be recognized that there was a localized lesion in the left hemisphere, probably in the left temporoparietofrontal area. There was not a complete loss of speech skills, however, which suggests that the parietal involvement may be limited.

It is likely, given this evidence, that there had been a serious hemorrhage in the left middle cerebral artery. This is based on the localization of the deficit, the severe effects overall, as well as the suppressions and complete loss of motor movement in the right arm. A secondary possibility would be a tumor. The neurological diagnosis for the patient was hemorrhage of the left middle cerebral artery.

Case 2. MM, whose results are presented in Table 9-5, was a 26-year-old, right-handed male who complained of severe headaches and vomiting. MM's score on the Category Test was normal, although just below the cutoff point. His Tactual Performance score, Location score, and score on Part B of the Trail Making Test were all within the normal range, although there was a minor deficit on the right hand. There was a normal performance on all the tests developed by Halstead. The only deficit on the WAIS was a low score on Digit Span, possibly due to the patient's tendency to be distracted easily. Overall, the performance was good enough to argue against any kind of tumor

TABLE 9-5   Results for Case 2

Wechsler Adult Intelligence Scale		Tactual Performance Test	
Information	9	Right	4'35"
Comprehension	14	Left	2'57"
Arithmetic	13	Both	1'23"
Similarities	9	Memory	7
Digit Span	7	Location	5
Vocabulary	12	Category	
Digit Symbol	14	45 errors	
Picture Completion	10	Trail Making Test	
Block Design	12	Part A	33"
Picture Arrangement	10	Part B	75"
Object Assembly	11	Speech Perception	
Verbal IQ	104	6 errors	
Performance IQ	114	Rhythm	
Full-scale IQ	109	3 errors	
Impairment Index		Tapping Test	
0		Right	58
		Left	53

Aphasia symptoms: none.
Sensory symptoms: none.

or space-occupying disorder. When neurological tests were completed on this patient, including CAT scan, the final diagnosis was schizophrenia with hypochondriacal delusions. The patient was referred for psychiatric treatment.

Case 3.   PS was a 22-year-old, right-handed female with one year of college. The referral was for assessment of residual brain damage after a trauma five months prior to the testing. The results for PS are listed in Table 9-6. Overall IQ showed a deficit in intelligence compared with the levels expected of a normal college student. The Category Test score was borderline, but indicative of brain dysfunction. The overall Tactual Performance Test time was well into the brain injured range, as were the Impairment Index, Tactual Performance Test location

TABLE 9-6 Results for Case 3

Wechsler Adult Intelligence Scale		Tactual Performance Test	
Information	8	Right	10'10"
Comprehension	7	Left	6'30"
Arithmetic	7	Both	5'00"
Similarities	10	Memory	8
Digit Span	4	Location	17
Vocabulary	7	Category	
Digit Symbol	6	52 errors	
Picture Completion	9	Rhythm	
Block Design	5	10 errors	
Picture Arrangement	4	Speech Perception	
Object Assembly	7	4 errors	
Verbal IQ	86	Tapping Test	
Performance IQ	76	Right	41
Full-scale IQ	81	Left	25
Peabody Picture Vocabulary		Trail Making Test	
(IQ)	67	Part A	36"
Tactile Form Recognition		Part B	252"
Right 1 error		Finger Agnosia	
Left 9 errors		Right 4 errors	
Grip Strength		Left 3 errors	
Right (kg)	21	Fingertip Number	
Left (kg)	16	Writing	
Impairment Index		Right 0 errors	
.72		Left 3 errors	

Aphasia symptoms: mild dysnomia, right-left disorientation reversal of key drawings, mild construction dyspraxia.

---

score, and Part B of the Trail Making Test. All these indicators suggested that moderate brain dysfunction remained.

A number of signs pointed to a right brain focus. On the WAIS, the Performance IQ was 10 points below the Verbal IQ. The patient's lowest scores were on Digit Span (where Digits Backward was much worse than Digits Forward), Picture Arrangement, and Block Design. The Rhythm Test was significantly impaired, while the Speech-Sounds Perception Test performance was normal. The left hand was considerably reduced (39 percent) in tapping speed compared with the right hand, although both hands were slow. There were signs of left-hand deficits on Fingertip Number Writing, while the right-hand performance remained normal. Grip strength of the left hand was also some 24 percent weaker than that of the right hand, although both were considerably below the mean for college women on our instrument (45 kg). PS also had mild construction dyspraxia, including a reversal of her key drawing on the Aphasia Examination.

There were a number of good right brain scores as well: The left hand on the Tactual Performance Test performed quite well compared with the right hand; the Trail Making Test (Part A) was within normal limits; the memory score of the Tactual Performance Test was quite good; and the left hand on the Tactile Form Recognition (astereognosis) Test was normal.

There were also signs of left brain involvement. PS showed several aphasia symptoms, although none were severe. Her receptive vocabulary, as measured by the Peabody Picture Vocabulary Test, was also down considerably. This suggested a problem in attaching names to pictures. The decrease in the Verbal IQ from her expected level was also indicative of left brain involvement. She missed one item on the right hand of the Tactile Form Recognition Test. There was a slight impairment of the right hand on the Tactual Performance Test compared with the left hand. The Finger Agnosia score suggested somewhat more impairment on the right hand than the left hand, although the difference was not large enough to suggest any localization. Part B of the Trail Making Test was severely impaired, compared with Part A, which was normal.

In conclusion, then, the overall pattern of results indicated diffuse brain impairment with a more severe focal area in the right frontotemporal area. This was seen through the greater impairment in left finger tapping than on the left-hand Tactual Performance Test. There were relatively good scores on Object Assembly and the sensory tests. There were also good scores on Part A of the Trail Making Test and the memory score of the Tactual Performance Test. There was only mild construction dyspraxia and good learning across trials on the Tactual Performance Test. All of these argued against a primary focus in the parietal area. In addition, the severe impairment of Rhythm and Picture Arrangement (the lowest WAIS score) and Digits Backward argued for an anterior right brain focus.

In the left brain, the deficits were primarily in the parietal area. The right hand on the Tactual Performance Test was worse than expected when compared with the Finger Tapping Test. There were mild dysphasia symptoms, tactile errors, and both expressive and receptive vocabulary problems. Auditory reception was normal on Speech-Sounds Perception. The severe deficits on Part B of the Trail Making Test suggested a difficulty in handling verbal symbols. The relatively good Category Test argued against a focus in the left frontal lobe. Indeed, the Category Test was normal for a person with an IQ of 81. It was likely that the primary focus of the head injury was either in the right anterior or in the left posterior areas with the countrecoup effects responsible for the deficits in the opposite hemisphere.

The neurological report noted that PS was struck above the right eye during a car accident. She had severe surface lacerations in that area and the right side of her face, with no other external evidence of trauma.

CHAPTER TEN

A Standardized Version of Luria's Neuropsychological Tests

Several alternative approaches exist to the Halstead-Reitan as a comprehensive measure of neuropsychological tests. One alternative is based on the work of the Russian neuropsychologist A. R. Luria. Luria (1966) used items selected for their qualitative importance in diagnosing the patient. Rather than using more global measures, such as the Bender or the Category test, Luria employed specific measures designed to look at the exact dimensions of the performance of a brain injured patient. Thus, rather than test receptive speech skills with a test such as Speech-Sounds Perception, Luria gave a series of items to test the ability of the patient to understand single letters, groups of letters, words, sentences, sentences with inverted grammatical constructions, and sentences with contradictions. Using this procedure, Luria was able to identify those specific areas in which a patient is unable to function. Such information can then be used for localizing, identifying, and rehabilitating the neurological patient (as described in the last chapter).

One disadvantage with Luria's testing procedure that has interfered with its use in the United States has been the lack of standardized procedures and materials for administering the test. The latter deficit was corrected by the publication of *Lu-*

ria's Neuropsychological Investigation by Christensen (1975). This publication made standardized material available for Luria's batteries; however, standardized administration or scoring procedures were not provided by Christensen. These were developed in a series of articles by Golden and his associates (Golden, Hammeke, & Purisch, 1978; Hammeke, Golden, & Purisch, 1978; Lewis et al., 1979; Marvel, Golden, Hammeke, Osmon, & Purisch, 1979; Osmon, Golden, Purisch, Hammeke, & Blume, 1979; Purisch, Golden, & Hammeke, 1978). These studies have largely confirmed the results of Luria's observations using unstandardized procedures, and suggest that these procedures can be highly effective in identifying and localizing brain dysfunction.

ADMINISTRATION

The standardized version of Luria's Neuropsychological Investigation contains 269 items. Each item is administered separately and represents a specific aspect of function. With a few exceptions, each item differs in some respect from all other items on the test. The items vary along such dimensions as complexity, degree of difficulty, mode of stimulus input (auditory, verbal, tactile), mode of answering (open ended, motor, speech, multiple choice), whether it is timed or untimed, and amount of information available. In this way, 11 major areas of neuropsychological performance are explored: motor skills; rhythmic and pitch abilities; tactile abilities; expressive speech skills; receptive speech abilities; reading, writing, and arithmetic skills; memory skills; visual-spatial skills; and intellectual ability. An example of a page of items from the protocol can be seen in Figure 1 of the manual.

It is usually recommended that the administration of the Luria-Nebraska Neuropsychological Battery (LNNB) be preceded by information about the client. This can focus on problems the patient perceives he or she is having, as well as giving the clinician the opportunity to observe difficulties the patient has in such areas as speech (both receptive and expressive), memory, and intelligence. This can aid in giving the clinician a focus for problems that may arise during the examination.

Test Materials

The materials necessary for the two forms of the test battery are similar but not identical. Both forms require a small portable tape recorder capable of administering the items on the C2 (Rhythm) scale. Both forms also use the Patient Response Booklet for items that require written responses from the client, such as drawings of figures or writing samples.

The set of test materials contains all the stimulus cards needed for the test and a cassette tape used in administering the C2 scale. A number of common household objects are also required for the administration and must be supplied by the user.

Test Setting

The battery can be administered at bedside with the client in a reclining position; however, it is preferable for the client to be seated upright, with a hard surface available for presenting materials and for writing responses. The examiner should be seated opposite the client and should present the visual materials in the midline of the client's visual field.

The battery may be given in a series of sessions. The examiner may vary the length of these sessions as necessary depending on the ability of the client to concentrate and the build-up of fatigue in the individual. By carefully observing the ways in which the client is able to handle the testing situation, a great deal of important qualitative information can be gained, some of which is scored within the qualitative scoring system of the LNNB.

Repeating or Paraphrasing Items

Item instructions may be repeated or paraphrased as necessary to allow the client to understand. Instructions generally are not repeated more than twice; unless the examiner judges that this will improve client performance. When instructions are paraphrased, changes should reflect such factors as the client's cultural language background and any impairment in understanding that may have been caused by brain damage. On most items, instructions can be written or communicated in a system other than oral speech. Where appropriate, the examiner may demonstrate what is requested of the client to ensure that the client understands the task; the demonstrations should not use the items actually employed in the battery. For all scales except C2 (Rhythm), C5 (Receptive Speech), and C10 (Memory), the item stimuli may also be repeated as necessary, unless prohibited by specific item directions. It is permissible to readminister any item in the battery, with the exception of specific C5 (Receptive Speech) and C10 (Memory) items. In these cases, the entire item, not only subsections, is to be readministered.

Encouraging, Questioning, and Instructing the Client

It is the goal of the LNNB to get the maximum possible performance out of the client. Thus, before initiating testing, the client should be informed that he or she will be asked to do a number of things and answer a number of questions, some of which may be very simple and seem silly, whereas others may be very difficult. Despite the fact that some items may seem silly and meaningless to the client, it is important that the client try to do his or her best, responding to the task as quickly as possible, but at the same time making sure that accuracy and quality are maintained. This may take constant encouragement on the part of the examiner, who should be exhorting the client as necessary. In those cases in which the client does not seem to be putting forth full effort, the examiner should discover the reason for this and aid the client in whatever way is necessary to allow the client to maximally perform. In this regard, it is very important for the examiner to be familiar with and skilled in dealing with clients from the diagnostic group being seen. It is especially important that the examiner be skilled in working with clients who either have emotional problems or are suffering from acute neurological disorders, as these groups tend to be the most difficult to test in an adult population.

When the client gives an answer that is inadequate but not wrong to any item on the battery, the examiner may further query the client (e.g., "Can you tell me more?") until the examiner is clear that the client's intent was clearly right or wrong. Leading questions are not permissible for the objective scoring; however, for the qualitative scoring, the examiner may add questions when necessary to clarify the nature of any errors or unusual behavior on the part of the client.

SCORING

Each item is scored in one of a number of ways, depending on the item content. The scoring techniques include accuracy, speed, quality of response, time to make a response, trials to a criterion level, and number of responses. After a raw score is determined for each item, it is translated into a scaled score of zero one, or two. A score of zero indicates normal performance, a score of one indicates weak evidence of brain disorder, and a score of two indicates strong evidence of brain disorder. The administration protocol of the test contains the normative data necessary to determine the scaled score for any given raw score on each item.

Determining Scaled Scores

After the individual responses to each item have been converted into item scores (zero, one, or two), the item scores are summed within each scale to yield summary scale indexes. For all scales, one simply adds together the scores of the items that make up each scale. With the addition of the summary, localization, and factor scales, items may each be on multiple scales. Raw scores are converted into T scores with a mean of 50 and a standard deviation of 10 using the appropriate tables in the manual. High scores reflect more pathology, as with such tests as the MMPI.

Qualitative Scoring

Those who have had experience with the LNNB items, as well as those aware of Luria's basic theory, notice early in the use of the battery that all items can be missed for multiple reasons. A score of an error on the LNNB (as with all quantitative tests) may arise from a wide range of difficulties: The client may fail to understand the instructions, may perseverate, may ignore the left side of the stimuli, and so forth. In addition, clients may get an answer correct and still show signs of brain dysfunction. For instance, the client may give the correct answer to an intelligence item but show signs of dysarthria in giving the answer. Similarly, a client may understand instructions for motor items only after several repetitions and demonstrations.

In the earlier versions of the LNNB, users were discouraged from keeping track of such material and related observations and using this information in interpretation, as is generally done with many standardized tests. However, then this valuable information was unavailable both for quantitative description of the basic deficit as well as for scientific study. Therefore, in addition to the quantitative scoring system, the qualitative scoring system is now available. The qualitative scoring categories catalog the client's "test behavior." Comparisons may then be made between the frequency of the client's qualitative signs in each category and the frequency of these qualitative signs for normals and various groups of brain damaged clients. The purpose of the qualitative scoring is to provide a systematic method of reporting the major categories of behavior not regularly scored on the battery, enabling the examiner to better describe the nature of a client's deficits and to make users more sensitive to these categories of behavior. In preliminary use, the scores have been useful in further heightening the ability of the battery to specify the nature of a client's disorder, as well as to correctly classify cases as brain dysfunction that may have been previously missed.

In the actual scoring of qualitative errors, there is, of course, a wide range of nearly infinite possibilities aimed at gaining a better understanding of the "why" behind a given error on the battery. It is the ability to make these qualitative observations with some reliability that makes the Luria-type items used on the LNNB especially useful. By integrating the qualitative and quantitative information, a more definitive, clearer understanding of the client may be generated.

The qualitative scoring also allows for the analysis of behavior not directly associated with performance on any single item. For example, a client who, between items, continues to repeat stimuli from the previous items may be scored for perseveration. Using only the quantitative scoring system would provide no way of indicating that the client was engaging in this type of behavior.

There are 66 basic qualitative categories that may be scored on the LNNB. These categories have been divided into 11 conceptual groupings or areas: Motor Functions, Sustained Performance, Self-Monitoring, Self-Cuing, Visual-Spatial Functions, Peripheral Impairment, Expressive Language, Dysarthria, Receptive Language, Speed, and Option Card.

GENERAL SCALE DESCRIPTIONS

After the scores for each item are determined, the following 11 primary summary scales are scored. These summary scale scores are the sum of the individual scaled scores on each item within a given area.

Motor Functions

This scale includes both simple and complex motor skills. The items on the scale involve simple timed motor tasks, simple motor tasks without visual feedback, simple motor tasks that are produced by imitation, simple and complex motor movements directed by verbal commands, and bilateral motor coordination. In addition, the scale evaluates mouth and tongue movements, including simple movements and series of movements, and the ability of the subject to spontaneously draw and copy simple geometric shapes.

Rhythmic and Pitch Skills

The first half of this section evaluates pitch skills: The ability to determine whether two tones have the same pitch, to determine which of two tones is higher, and to reproduce increasingly complex tonal sequences. The second half of the section evaluates rhythmic skills: identifying the number of tones in a sequence, identifying whether rhythmic patterns are the same, and producing rhythmic patterns on verbal command.

Tactile Functions

This section evaluates simple and complex tactile and kinesthetic functions. All items in this section are given to the subject while he or she is blindfolded. The subject must identify where he or she is touched, state whether a touch is sharp or blunt, discriminate between a hard and soft touch, identify numbers and letters written on the hands, reproduce a movement of one arm that is flexed by the examiner, and identify common objects by touch alone.

Visual (Spatial) Functions

This section evaluates basic visual and spatial functions, except for construction skills, which are evaluated in the motor section. The items require subjects to recognize simple objects presented to them, to identify photographs and line drawings, to identify objects presented in a mixed-up jumble, to discern pictures in which only part of the gestalt is visible, to solve problems similar to those found in Raven's Matrices (chapter 2), and to work with three-dimensional piles of blocks and two-dimensional rotations.

Receptive Speech

This section evaluates the subject's ability to correctly understand a wide variety of material presented auditorially. The initial section evaluates the subject's skills in understanding simple phonemes, phonemic combinations, series of phonemes, and phonemes presented in different pitches. The second part of the section evaluates simple word comprehension; comprehension of simple sentences; and comprehension of sentences involving contradictions, prepositions, possessive constructions, spatial relationships, logical relationships, inverted grammatical structures, and complex or compound constructions.

Expressive Speech

This section evaluates an individual's skill at expressing material orally. This includes the repetition of phonemes and the repetition of successively more difficult words. The section also evaluates the subject's ability to repeat increasingly complex sentences, as well as to repeat automatic and simple sequences (such as the days of the week). The section also measures a subject's ability to spontaneously discuss a topic in response to pictures, a story, and a theme. Finally, the subject must organize words into intelligible statements.

Writing

This section evaluates basic writing skills, including simple spelling and the ability to copy letters and words from cards, from memory, and from dictation. Spontaneous writing skills are also evaluated.

Reading

The Reading section parallels the Writing section. The subject must reproduce sounds from letters; name individual letters and their sounds; and read words of varying complexity, sentences, and short stories.

Arithmetic

This section covers a wide range of skills related to mathematical abilities. These skills include number recognition (both Arabic and Roman numerals), the comparison of numbers, simple arithmetic skills (addition, subtraction, multiplication, and division), and simple algebraic problems. Two items require the subject to subtract 7 and 13 from 100 continuously, which are similar to the tasks seen on most mental status exams.

Memory

This section evaluates a wide range of mnestic processes. Subjects are reexamined on their ability to memorize a list of items over several trials, to memorize pictures and other non-verbal stimuli, to memorize short verbal lists with and without interference, to memorize a story, and to associate verbal labels with pictures.

Intellectual Processes

This section, which covers a wide range of intellectual processes, includes a number of items similar to those on the WAIS Comprehension, Picture Arrangement, Arithmetic, Similarities, and Vocabulary subtests. In addition, subjects must explain the theme of a picture, describe what is funny about a picture, and make logical comparisons.

In addition to these basic 11 sections, three additional summary scores are calculated. The Left Hemisphere score consists of all items in the Motor and Tactile sections that require the use of the right hand alone. The Right Hemisphere score consists of all items in the Motor and Tactile sections that require the use of the left hand alone. The final scale, Pathognomonic, consists of 31 items that are especially sensitive to brain damage. These items, rarely missed by non-brain injured patients, are missed by brain injured patients much more frequently than other groups of patients.

After raw scores are determined for each summary index, they are plotted on the profile sheet (see the example in the case presentations at the end of this chapter). From the left-hand column of the profile sheet, T scores (with a mean of 50 and a standard deviation of 10) can be read for each score. These T scores can be averaged across all 14 indexes to yield a

Total score, which can act as a quick summary of the individual's level of performance.

CLINICAL INTERPRETATION

In interpreting the LNNB, little confidence is placed in formal interpretations of elevations on individual scales alone. The test is intended to be given as a whole, with pattern analysis, item analysis, and qualitative analysis serving as the major interpretive steps.

Levels of Interpretation

When interpreting the LNNB, or other similar batteries, it is important to be aware that the many levels on which the battery can be interpreted depend on the needs, as well as the skill and knowledge, of the user.

The first level is primarily concerned with ascertaining whether significant brain injury exists in a given client as a screening procedure to differentiate neuropsychological from other possible disorders. The second level of interpretation involves simply describing what the client can and cannot do, without drawing any conclusions or reaching any integrative statements. The third level of interpretation takes the second level to the next logical step: identification of the probable underlying causes responsible for the client's overall behavior. Finally, the fourth level of interpretation involves the integration of all findings and conclusions into a description of how the brain of the individual is functioning. This is a difficult task in most cases, since the result of brain damage is affected by a variety of factors.

Identifying Brain Damage

Use of the Critical Level. The first step in identifying when a profile is statistically abnormal and likely to be indicative of brain damage is based on establishing a valid critical level for the client. The critical level represents the highest

LNNB score that can be considered normal for the battery. In contrast to some other tests, this cutoff level is variable with the LNNB, and is adjusted for both age and education. This represents an attempt to recognize that individuals with different backgrounds have different premorbid levels of functioning.

Once the critical level has been accurately established, determining the probability of brain damage is relatively simple. The scales on the battery that exceed the critical level are counted, yielding the number of abnormal scores. The scores that are considered at this point are the basic clinical scales (C1 through C12) and the Pathognomonic (S1) scale. In general, three or more scores above the critical level are thought to be indicative of brain damage, whereas zero or only one elevated scale suggests the absence of brain damage. Two elevated scales are considered borderline. If the critical level has been chosen correctly, the accuracy of this decision is about 85 to 90 percent. The accuracy increases with the accuracy of the critical level.

As noted above, use of these procedures will misidentify 10 to 15 percent of the brain damaged individuals as normal. Other techniques may be used to identify some of these clients. These are detailed in the test manual.

INTERPRETING SCALE AND ITEM PATTERNS

Scale Patterns Associated With Specific Forms of Damage

An analysis of the items within and across the Luria scales allows for a qualitative understanding of the patient's basic deficits. Our interest here is not simply in classifying the person as brain injured or as having a given form of brain injury, but in identifying patterns of item performance that suggest specific problems or underlying deficits. This information, in turn, can be used with a comprehensive theory of brain function (e.g., see Golden & Anderson, 1978; Luria, 1973) to localize and identify brain disorders. While the possible combinations of item patterns and skills measured are endless, the items on the scales are arranged in groups. By examining these individual groups and the differential performance of a patient on these groups, a substantial start can be made in the area of qualitative and pattern analysis focused on discovering why the patient missed a particular set of items within each scale. This is further analyzed by examining how the patient may have missed or performed on a single item, much as Luria himself did. The following is a basic review of the item patterns on each scale and the more common scale patterns that suggest specific problems.

C1 (Motor Functions). The C1 scale is one of the most complex scales on the LNNB. A wide variety of motor skills reflects both right and left hemisphere performance. The first four items involve simple movements of the hands. These items are especially sensitive to disorders in or near the posterior frontal lobe.

Items 5 through 8 are fairly simple motor movements that are performed when the patient is blindfolded. They require kinesthetic and tactile feedback for correct responses. Consequently, this section of the scale tends to be more sensitive to injuries in the parietal lobes. Items 9 through 20 are again simple motor movements, but with spatial organization required. These items are sensitive to both frontal lobe disorders and disorders of the right hemisphere, especially those that interfere greatly with optic spatial organization. Items 21 through 27 require complex movements of various kinds. These items are very sensitive to injury both to the motor area of the frontal lobes and to the prefrontal areas that are concerned with the organization of behavior. They can also be affected strongly by lesions of the premotor area.

Items 28 through 35 concern oral movements organized in much the same way as the previous sections on hand movements. Items 28 and 29 reflect simple oral movements, Items 30 and 31 involve oral movements on the basis of kinesthetic feedback, and Items 32 and 33 measure complex oral skills. These items are sensitive to disruption of the frontal lobe areas and the parietal areas in the same way as are movements of the hand. However, they are also sensitive to disorders of some of the cranial nerves, and may therefore reflect problems in the brain stem or problems of generalized cerebral dysfunction. Items 34 and 35 show the ability of the client to perform simple oral movements on the basis of verbal instructions. These items can be affected both by impairment to the motor areas and by impairment in understanding of speech as reflected in the temporal-parietal areas of the brain.

Items 36 through 47 assess construction dyspraxia. Items that are performed very poorly often reflect severe spatial disorganization characteristics of injuries to the right hemisphere or to the left parietal area. Drawings that are accurate but done slowly may simply reflect motor dysfunction of the dominant hand and the opposite cerebral hemisphere (or, sometimes, compulsiveness). Items 48 through 51 measure the ability of the client to respond to speech regulation of the motor act. In each of these items, the client must keep in mind the instructions given, interpret them, and then respond appropriately. These items require involvement of the temporal-parietal areas of the left hemisphere, which are needed to understand what is required, and the frontal lobes, which are responsible for the verbal command of motor movements. Individuals with frontal disorders can often understand what is supposed to be done but are unable to execute the proper motor movements to respond to the request.

Elevations on the C1 scale are best interpreted in comparison with elevations on the C3 (Tactile Functions), the S2 (Left Hemisphere), and the S3 (Right Hemisphere) scales. When C1 is elevated but C3, S2, and S3 are not, this is suggestive of difficulties with complex motor tasks. Usually these deficits are caused by injuries to the right hemisphere or the frontal lobe of either hemisphere. This comparison can be very useful in initially localizing a deficit in the anterior-posterior dimension. Clients displaying pure parietal lobe dysfunction rarely achieve a C1 T score above 60, although specific items involving kinesthetic feedback are most frequently missed. On examination, the items on the battery usually show a clear pattern in these posterior injuries that is highly effective in localizing a given disorder.

When all four of these scales (C1, C3, S2, and S3) are highly elevated, generalized impairment of motor and sensory areas is suggested, but this is often in the context of diffuse deficits. If only these four scales are affected, then peripheral disorders affecting motor and sensory skills need to be considered, as well as the possibility of subcortical diseases, such as multiple sclerosis, which may leave cognitive skills intact.

If C1 is greatly elevated over C3, combined with elevation on the S2 or S3 scale, there is a suggestion of an anterior lesion in the hemisphere suggested by the higher of the S2 and S3 scales. For such an elevation to be considered significant, one of the two hemisphere scales must be at least 10 points above the other, and the larger the difference, the more likely the result is meaningful (assuming that there are not peripheral disorders). If C1, C3, and one of the hemisphere scales are elevated, especially if the difference is 20 points or greater between the lateralization scales, this is highly suggestive of strong involvement of the sensorimotor area in the brain (around the central sulcus) or its related subcortical area, although the pattern disappears if the motor symptoms remit over time. The scale is not sensitive to motor deficits limited to the lower limbs, nor is it particularly sensitive to those subcortical disorders that do not generally affect voluntary motor behavior.

C2 (Rhythm). The C2 scale is much more simply organized than the C1 scale. Items 52 through 54 involve the analyses of groups of tones. The client must compare two groups of tones, saying whether one is higher or lower. Items 55 through 57 require the client to reproduce tones. Whereas the initial items involve the perception of tonal qualities – an ability usually localized in the temporal lobe of the right hemisphere or, in some cases, the temporal lobe of the left hemisphere – these latter items involve the expression of tonal relationships, an ability assigned by some to the frontal lobe of the right hemisphere. It is not unusual for clients with right frontal disorders to show specific deficits on these expressive items. Items 58 through 61 involve the evaluation of acoustic signals. The client must identify the number of beeps in groups of sounds. The last two items in the C2 scale involve the perception and reproduction of rhythm. Item 62 measures the ability of the client to reproduce rhythmic patterns. This item requires both the perception of rhythmic patterns, a function localized in the right temporal area, and the reproduction of sounds, usually using the dominant hand. Thus, the item can be missed by individuals with deficits in either hemisphere. Item 63 asks the client to make a series of rhythms from verbal commands. The combination of verbal and rhythmic content on this item also makes it sensitive to injuries in either hemisphere.

C2 is the most sensitive of all the basic clinical scales to disorders of attention and concentration. Performance on items 52, 54, 58, 59, 60, 61, and 62 is especially diagnostic for individuals who have difficulty in attention and concentration. When elevations of the C2 scale are the highest in the profile, they are most often associated with right hemisphere injuries that are usually more anterior. This is especially true when the highest scales are some combination of C2, C9 (Arithmetic), C10 (Memory), and C11 (Intellectual Processes). However, this pattern may be seen in left anterior lesions as well, although in those cases it is accompanied by at least subtle, if not gross, deficits in some form of verbal skills. When the C2 deficit is combined with C4 (Visual Functions) scale elevation, then the lesion may be either anterior or posterior, with a more posterior lesion becoming more likely with higher elevations on C4. In the case where the S3 (Right Hemisphere) scale is quite high over the S2 (Left Hemisphere) scale, the possibility of a lesion straddling the sensorimotor area and involving both the anterior and posterior areas of the hemisphere must be strongly considered. C2 elevations, generally below those of other scales, are not unusual in left hemisphere injuries. Very good scores on the C2 scale are generally inconsistent with severe right hemisphere damage outside the sensorimotor areas.

C3 (Tactile Functions). This scale is the most sensitive of the LNNB scales to injuries in the anterior parietal lobe of either hemisphere. Items 66 through 79 involve different levels of cutaneous sensation. Individuals must identify where they are touched, how hard they are touched, and so forth. Injuries to the anterior parietal area cause significant elevations on this scale, as do injuries to the middle parietal areas that Luria (1973) designated as the "secondary areas" of the parietal lobe. Individuals with damage in and around the angular gyrus may have particular problems with Items 74 and 79. Items 80 and 81 are directly concerned with muscle and joint sensations. They are sensitive to injuries not only in the anterior, but also in the posterior, parietal lobe. If these items are the only ones missed on the C3 scale, one should also look for specific errors on the kinesthetic items of the C1 (Motor Functions) scale. The last four items on the C3 scale involve the stereognostic perception. These items are scored for both the number of errors and time. Individuals who have had old injuries to the parietal lobe on either side may have difficulty meeting the time requirements. One should be careful in analysis of these items, as they are highly sensitive to the residual effects of brain injury even when other skills have improved.

The items on the C3 scale, along with the first 20 items on the C1 scale, make up the S2 (Left Hemisphere) and S3 (Right Hemisphere) scales. A difference in performance between the left and right hands on the C3 scale, the C1 scale, or both combined is highly indicative of lateralized brain dysfunction. Injuries that tend to be located in the posterior parietal or anterior prefrontal areas typically do not show extreme differences between the S2 and S3 scales.

Profiles with the highest scores on the C3 scale are interpreted in conjunction with the relative standings on the S2, S3, and C1 scales. If C3 is greatly elevated over C1 and one of the hemisphere scales is elevated significantly over the other, then this points to a posterior lesion in the hemisphere indicated by the elevated hemisphere scale. This generally remains true even when the C1 scale is equal to the C3 scale, especially if the C1 deficits arise from construction difficulty and sequencing rather than motor paralysis. Since all items of the C3 scale are included in the hemisphere scales, it is impossible (if the battery is scored correctly) to get a C3 elevation without elevations on one or both of the hemisphere scales. If both the hemisphere scales are elevated, however, either a bilateral injury or a severe left hemisphere injury must be considered. The deficit may be due to an inability to concentrate, which should also result in inconsistent behavior, or to an inability to integrate and identify all stimuli. When the deficit is purely spatial, such as in profiles with C3 and C4 (Visual Functions) elevations, the injury is likely to be right parietal-occipital, although this pattern may also reflect subcortical involvement of one or both hemispheres. When naming is strongly involved, left parietal deficits should be considered. All such hypothesized localizations assume a normally dominant left hemisphere.

C4 (Visual Functions).   The C4 scale evaluates a range of visual functions. Items 86 and 87 ask the client to identify objects by viewing either an object itself or a picture of an object. Since naming is a significant component of these items, they are extremely sensitive to left hemisphere disorders, especially in the temporal-parietal region. These items are included to provide a measure of the client's ability to name. If the client is not able to do these items, later items on the battery that are more sensitive to right hemisphere function may be missed simply because of left hemisphere involvement.

Later items require a great deal more visual-spatial perception than do these first two items, although naming is still required. Item 88 presents pictures that are difficult to perceive, Item 89 presents only the shading of a picture that the person must integrate into the picture, and Items 90 and 91 present objects that overlap one another and that the client with poor visual-spatial skills has difficulty identifying. Item 92 is a modification of items from the Raven Progressive Matrices (Raven, 1960). It is also a strong measure of visual-spatial organization and right hemisphere function. Items 94 through 96 involve spatial orientation (the ability to tell time and to recognize directions). These items tend to be specifically related to right hemisphere function as long as the client is able to perceive the questions. Item 97 requires the client to do three-dimensional analyses of pictures; this item is especially sensitive to right hemisphere functions, although deficits may also be seen in more moderate-to-severe left hemisphere injuries. Item 99 involves spatial rotation without any speech components. Individuals may point to the correct answer or circle it as necessary (or say it if this is not possible). This item is highly sensitive to visual-spatial skills. It is a very simple task, and normal subjects rarely make more than one mistake on it.

Profiles in which the C4 scale is highest, in combination with any secondary scale, generally reflect impairment in the right hemisphere or the occipital areas of the left hemisphere. The C4 scale can be elevated in other left hemisphere injuries, but rarely will it be the highest scale overall. In right hemisphere injuries, deficits on only more complex visual tasks suggest either a mild parietal involvement or injury to anterior areas. These lesions are usually accompanied by elevation on the C1 (Motor Functions) scale, suggestive of right hemisphere lesions. Subcortical lesions that interfere with visual processing can also cause patterns suggestive of right hemisphere injury, as can severe peripheral visual problems.

C5 (Receptive Speech). C5 items evaluate the ability of the client to understand receptive speech, from simple phonemic analysis to the understanding of complex sentences with inverted English grammar. Items 100 through 107 concern the understanding of simple phonemes. For Items 100 through 105, the individual hears simple phonemes and must then repeat or write them. It is important to note if individuals are able to either say or write phonemes but not to do both. The ability to repeat phonemes but not to write them suggests impairment in the area of the angular gyrus, whereas the ability to write phonemes but not say them suggests a disorder of expressive speech rather than of receptive speech.

Items 108 through 116 involve the understanding of simple words and sentences. The client must do relatively simple tasks of naming, pointing, and identification, and must define simple words. The intent of these items is simply to ensure that the client is hearing correctly and interpreting correctly what is said to him or her.

Beginning with Item 117 and continuing through the end of this scale to Item 132, the individual is given increasingly more difficult instructions. These items assess the client's ability to understand and to perform or answer as requested. All these items can be affected by damage to the left hemisphere, but several items can also be affected by right hemisphere dysfunction. For example, Items 118 through 120 require some spatial orientation on the part of the client. If the client appears to understand the sentence but disrupts the spatial requests made, the possibility of right hemisphere dysfunction must be suspected. Similarly, spatial orientation is required by Item 123.

Items in the set that require comparisons (Items 121, 122, 125, 126, 127, 128, 129, 130, and 131) are especially sensitive to damage in the parietal-occipital areas of the left hemisphere, although they may also be affected by the client's simple lack of understanding caused by injuries to the temporal lobe or the angular gyrus. None of the items on the C5 scale requires any reading skills, so receptive speech ability can be measured independently of the client's level of education and reading readiness. Good performance on this scale with poor performance on the C8 (Reading) scale is suggestive of damage to the occipital or temporal-occipital areas of the left hemisphere.

Overall, the C5 scale is much more easily elevated by damage to the left hemisphere. The scale may also be elevated by damage to the right hemisphere, especially the anterior temporal-frontal areas. There is evidence that this anterior damage in the right hemisphere does cause specific elevations on the C5 scale. It is possible that this elevation is due to the fact that the right frontal areas may play some role in understanding speech.

When this scale is the highest, as well as when it is significantly elevated above the critical level by at least 15 points, deficits are usually associated with left hemisphere injury. Lesser elevations, caused by difficulty with the more complex items, can appear as the highest scale in right anterior injuries. This can be especially true in mild elevation combinations of C5 and C10 (Memory), C5 and C2 (Rhythm), C5 and C4 (Visual Functions), or C5, C11 (Intellectual Processes), and C9 (Arithmetic). In the most significant elevations, however, left hemisphere involvement is generally indicated.

C6 (Expressive Speech). The C6 scale evaluates the individual's ability to repeat simple phonemes and words and to generate automatic as well as more complex speech forms. Initial items (Items 133 through 142) simply require the repetition of sounds or words spoken by the examiner. Beginning with Item 143, the client must repeat the same list of words and sounds by reading them rather than hearing them.

Beginning with Item 154, the client must repeat increasingly more difficult sentences. Item 157 requires simple naming of objects, and Item 158 requires the naming of body parts. Item 159 examines the ability to name from a description rather than from a visual presentation of the object. Items 160 through 163 ask individuals to count and say the days of the week, first forward then backward, all a form of automatic speech. Items 164 through 169 evaluate the ability to produce speech spontaneously under three conditions: after looking at a picture, after hearing a story, and after being given a topic to discuss. If other items on this scale are performed without difficulty, and yet the client experiences problems with Items 164 to 169, there is the possibility of either low intelligence or damage to the frontal lobe area, usually in the left hemisphere. The final section involves complex systems of grammatical expression: the client must fill in words that are missing in a sentence or make up a sentence from words that are given to the client.

In general, C6 scores are sensitive to injuries only in the left hemisphere. It is rare to see a high C6 score in individuals with unilateral right hemisphere injuries. Exceptions to this are individuals who had difficulty reading prior to their injury, or whose disorders have somehow interfered with auditory perception or have had generalized effects (e.g., pressure effects from a tumor). However, as regards the individual client, examination of the patterns of the items on the battery can easily eliminate these possibilities. In the absence of these types of conditions, elevation on the C6 scale, especially a T score above 70, is almost always indicative of a left hemisphere injury. In general, the left hemisphere injury involves the temporal-frontal area, especially the posterior two-thirds of the frontal lobe. However, if the client is basically able to say the words but has difficulty changing sounds or tends to slur speech, the possibility of kinesthetic damage must be considered. In these cases, the damage is to the parietal lobe; however, such individuals also show significant kinesthetic and tactile deficits on the C3 (Tactile Functions) scale and can be easily evaluated from that scale and from the kinesthetic items on the C1 (Motor Functions) scale. If the high scores are confined to the more complex items on the battery, the likely focus of damage is in the prefrontal area of the brain rather than the more posterior areas represented by other patterns of deficits.

Interpretation of this scale is generally similar to C5 (Receptive Speech). When the scale is elevated well over the critical level, some left hemisphere involvement is generally indicated. Very mild C6 elevations may be associated with right hemisphere lesions, with the major errors occurring in the last items of the scale (spontaneous speech, sequencing, and fill-in items).

C7 (Writing). The C7 scale involves an evaluation of the ability to analyze words phonetically in English and then to do copying of increasing difficulty. Initially, clients are asked to copy simple letters, then copy combinations of letters and words, and then write their first and last names. They are then asked to write sounds, words, and phrases from dictation. The final items on the scale require the client to write sentences about a given topic.

In general, disorders of writing localize to the temporal-parietal-occipital area, especially in and around the angular gyrus of the left hemisphere. However, specific disorders may indicate problems in other areas. For example, the ability to write from written material but not from auditory material suggests a specific lesion in the temporal lobe. Conversely, the ability to write from dictation but not from written material suggests a lesion in the occipital or occipital-parietal areas of the cerebral cortex. If the client is, in general, able to write but has difficulty forming letters and changing from one letter to another, there could be a problem in kinesthetic feedback in which the client mixes up letters that are formed by similar motor movements. If the client is simply unable to write at all due to paralysis, this, of course, is suggestive of a lesion in the motor strip area of the posterior frontal lobe. Finally, if the client writes at an angle to the page, suggesting some spatial problems, and has no other writing disorders, this can be related to right hemisphere dysfunction. Lack of the ability to read or write one's name is often indicative of a general dementia or, in some cases, a disorder of automatic writing that may occur with injuries in both hemispheres.

Deficits in which the concept of spelling is completely lost (e.g., "CAT" is spelled "DBG") are most likely associated with injuries to the left hemisphere, especially in the parietal or temporal areas. Deficits in which the correct letters are retained but placed in the wrong order have been seen in patients with a wide variety of injuries. Motor writing errors (Option 2) are generally associated with the hemisphere opposite the client's normal writing hand, although care must be taken if an injury caused the client to change writing hands. In these cases, writing may remain poor but reflects an injury in the ipsilateral hemisphere. Motor writing problems may arise simply as a result of motor problems, reflecting the functions of the motor areas of the brain, but may also arise in injuries involving kinesthetic and tactile feedback. See Luria (1966) for an extensive discussion of the specific qualitative behaviors associated with each of these conditions. Motor writing deficits in which the writing itself is motorically intact but spatially disrupted (at large angles to the horizontal, or in which words are written over one another) may reflect injuries to the right (or spatially dominant) hemisphere.

C8 **(Reading).** The C8 scale closely parallels the C7 (Writing) scale. The client is asked to generate sounds from letters that the examiner reads aloud. This generally measures the ability of the client to show integration of letters and auditory analysis functions of the temporal and parietal areas of the left hemisphere. The client is then asked to name simple letters, read simple sounds, and read simple words and letter combinations that have meaning. Generally, disruption of these skills implies lesions in the temporal-occipital area of the brain or in the temporal-parietal area of the left hemisphere. Finally, the client must read entire sentences as well as paragraphs. If the client is able to read simple words but not entire sentences or paragraphs, possible injuries include disorders of visual scanning that make it impossible for the client to grasp more than one word at a time. This is usually due to injuries in the secondary visual areas of the occipital lobe.

In a client who could read prior to an injury, deficits on the C8 scale are almost always associated with a left hemisphere injury, usually posterior. However, mild deficits with complex words may appear in highly educated individuals with left frontal lesions. The exceptions to this are deficits that occur because of spatial disruption (inability to follow a line, which shows most clearly in paragraph reading) or neglect of the left side (which should be corrected by the examiner if the test is administered correctly). Both suggest right hemisphere dysfunction.

C9 (Arithmetic). The C9 scale is the most sensitive of the LNNB scales to educational deficits. Even in normally educated individuals, this is the scale most likely to appear in a severely pathological range when there is, in fact, no problem.

The scale starts with the client simply writing down numbers from dictation in both Arabic and Roman numerals. Several items have been employed to get somewhat closer to the spatial dysfunctions that are possible. The Roman numerals IV and VI, for example, can easily be reversed to read VI and IV. Similarly, in Arabic numerals, the client is asked to write 17 and 71, and 69 and 96. It is not unusual for a person with a subtle dysfunction to be more likely to show the reversal in the Roman numerals because of less overall familiarity with these numbers. Thereafter, the scale asks the person to write down numbers of increasing complexity. As numbers become more complex, it is possible to see if the client places the numbers in the correct sequence, again looking for possible spatial deficits that can be caused by right hemisphere or left occipital-parietal dysfunction. In the next section of the scale, beginning with Item 210, the client is asked to compare numbers with each other, an operation that is basic to the left occipital-parietal area. In Items 212 through 214, the client is asked to do simple arithmetic problems. These are problems that most individuals can probably do from memory. Dysfunction in this area is suggestive of serious inability to understand what is being asked or of severe left hemisphere damage, especially in the parietal areas.

In Items 215 through 217, the client is asked to do more complex addition and subtraction problems that cannot be done from memory. Items 218, 219, and 220 deal with more difficult manipulations. The client must fill in a missing number or sign, or do a series of more difficult addition problems. Deficits here are often seen in people with low education and are not considered as serious as deficits in other parts of the battery. However, an individual with higher educational attainment should be able to do these. Often a left parietal dysfunction in a highly educated person does not show up until this section.

The last section includes presentation of classic serial 7 and serial 13. Concentration difficulties that may show up on these items can be associated with left frontal lobe dysfunction in the presence of normal arithmetic skills.

The C9 scale appears to be potentially sensitive to lesions in all parts of the brain, as well as to preexisting deficits. The scale has no localizing value except in the combinations indicated already, until an item analysis is done. In cases where the person cannot read or write simple numbers, left hemisphere injury is indicated; problems with only the spatial aspects of arithmetic suggest, but are not necessarily limited to, right hemisphere injury.

C10 (Memory). The C10 scale is basically involved with short-term and intermediate memory. No attempt is made to assess long-term memory functions. The first items on C10 look at the ability of the client to memorize a list of seven simple words and to predict his or her performance. The inability to predict is often seen in clients with frontal lobe dysfunction; therefore, these items can be significant, especially if the scores are extremely deviant. In the second section of the scale, Item 226 measures visual memory with interference. The client is asked to remember a card under the condition of having to count up to 100 aloud between acquisition and retrieval. Items 227 through 230 involve immediate sensory trace recall. The items test visual memory, rhythmic memory, and tactile visual memory. These items can be affected by both left and right hemisphere dysfunction, but are more sensitive to right hemisphere dysfunction. This is especially true when these items are missed while the more verbal items on the test are performed without difficulty.

Items 231 through 234 are measures of verbal memory. Items 231 and 232 involve simple verbal memory under two conditions of interference, and Items 233 and 234 are similar in that interference is supplied by additional material that the client must memorize. Several difficulties in short-term memory, especially due to injuries to the left hemisphere, are seen in these items. Injuries to the bilateral hippocampal area, which cause a loss of long-term memory coding, show up on the items involving interference. Finally, Item 235 is a measure of the individual's ability to associate the verbal stimulus with a picture. This item can be interfered with by either left or right hemisphere dysfunction and is sensitive to high-level disturbances in memory skills.

Overall, the C10 scale is most sensitive to verbal dysfunction because of its importance in a majority of the items. However, nonverbal dysfunction caused by right hemisphere lesions shows up in a moderately elevated C10 T score of about 60, with a specific pattern of items missed, as described above. It is important to look at the pattern of items missed before venturing the hypothesis of a possible lateralization for the elevation in this scale. Extremely high T score elevations of 80 or more are nevertheless almost always associated with either left hemisphere or bilateral dysfunction.

Along with the C2 (Rhythm) scale, the C10 scale is quite sensitive to subcortical dysfunction. Indeed, subtle subcortical dysfunction, especially of the temporal lobes, is often accompanied by deficits on this scale. Very high error scores generally point to involvement of the left hemisphere, whereas lower scores may reflect involvement of either hemisphere.

C11 (Intellectual Processes). Initial items in the scale involve the understanding of thematic pictures. The first two items ask the client to interpret a picture in his or her own words, and Items 238 through 241 ask the individual to put pictures into a series that makes sense, similar to the items in Picture Arrangement on the WAIS. Items 242 and 243 ask the client to tell what is comical or absurd about certain pictures.

These items are often missed entirely by individuals with frontal lobe dysfunction and those with right hemisphere dysfunction that interferes with interpretation of verbal schemes. Deficits of visual scanning can also be seen in individuals who are not able to appreciate the complexity of a picture and who, thus, tend to focus on one area. Luria (1966) presented a detailed analysis of the type of visual movements present in various kinds of brain disorders, such as injuries to the premotor area of the frontal lobes and injuries to the occipital cortex.

In the second section, Item 244 asks for interpretation of a story, Item 245 asks for interpretation of expressions, and Items 246 and 247 ask for interpretation of a proverb. Note that Item 247 allows multiple-choice answers, and Item 246 requires a verbal response. If the client succeeds on Item 247 and misses Item 246, there is a possibility that the individual's intellectual processes are intact but that expressive language functions have been impaired. Such individuals should be able to show a relatively normal performance on the C5 (Receptive Speech) items, which require little verbal output, while missing the items on the C6 (Expressive Speech) scale.

Item 248 involves simple concept formations and definitions, and Items 249 and 250 ask for comparisons and differences between objects in much the same way as do items on the Similarities subtest of the WAIS. Performance in this area is further evaluated by Items 251 through 254, in which the client must find the logical relationships between specific objects and the groups to which they belong. Item 255 evaluates the ability to determine opposites, whereas Items 256 and 257 investigate the ability to form analogies. The last items on the scale, Items 258 through 269, involve simple arithmetic problems very similar to those seen on the WAIS Arithmetic subtest.

Overall, the C11 scale is highly sensitive to disorders in both hemispheres but is most sensitive to disorders in the left hemisphere. Injuries in either the parietal lobe or the frontal lobe cause maximum dysfunction. Poor performance on the C11 scale, in the absence of poor performance on the C5 and C6 scales and in the absence of any significant psychiatric thought disorder, is generally associated with prefrontal dysfunction. The determination of laterality, however, must be made by investigating specific items to judge whether those initial items that are right hemisphere oriented suggest adequate visual interpretation skills. If these skills appear to be intact, then the scale is likely to be reflecting a left hemisphere dysfunction alone. If these are the only items missed on the scale, the possibility of isolated right frontal dysfunction must be seriously considered.

Although the scale can reflect impairment in either hemisphere, a high elevation combined with elevations on C2 (Rhythm), C4 (Visual Functions), C10 (Memory), and C9 (Arithmetic) generally points to right hemisphere dysfunction, whereas an elevation combined with elevations on C6 (Expressive Speech), C8 (Reading), and C7 (Writing) indicates left hemisphere damage. This scale is generally more affected by posterior than by anterior injuries, but is affected by both.

Summary Scales

S1 (Pathognomonic). This scale is most useful as a measure of the degree of compensation that has occurred since an injury. *Compensation* refers to those processes that allow the brain injured patient to recover from the effects of a brain injury. This includes functional reorganization of the brain, in which the patient uses intact areas of the brain to find alternate ways of doing tasks, and actual physical recovery, in which the effects of the brain injury diminish and psychological functions return more closely to normal.

The S1 scale is interpreted by both its overall elevation and its relationship to other scores. In cases in which the S1 scale is quite high (usually at least 20 points over the critical level) and is the highest scale overall, the injury is likely to be uncompensated. This pattern is most often seen in acute, severe brain injuries. It may also be seen in a chronic injury of such severity that further compensation does not occur. When S1 is quite high but at about the average of the other scores, compensation has probably taken place and the patient has shown some recovery. If S1 is high but remains the lowest score in the profile, the injury is likely chronic and has generally recovered to the degree that can be expected.

In cases where S1 is elevated but not extremely high (less than 20 points above the critical level) and is the highest score overall, then the injury may be recent and just beginning to recover. Alternatively, this may reflect a long-term injury in which there has been a general recovery but in which one or more areas of function remain for which compensation has not taken place (usually reflecting severe injury to a limited area). If S1 is elevated, but not highly, and is at the same level as other scores, this generally reflects an injury that has partially recovered but still shows some dysfunction that is generally more diffuse than focal. An elevated S1 that is not extremely elevated and that is the lowest score overall reflects an injury that is compensated but not recovered, although not as serious as the same pattern mentioned above when S1 is very elevated.

S2 (Left Hemisphere) and S3 (Right Hemisphere). These two scales were constructed to give initial measures of lateralization. The S2 scale consists of all items reflecting left-hand sensory and motor performance, whereas the S3 scale consists of all items reflecting right-hand sensory and motor performance. These items are drawn from the C1 (Motor Functions) and C3 (Tactile Functions) scales. The scores on these scales are sensitive to lateralizing disorders that involve the sensorimotor strip in the central part of the brain or those areas directly adjacent to the sensorimotor strip. Lesions that do not affect the sensorimotor area may not show up as a lateralized discrepancy on the S2 and S3 scales. Thus, lesions that are more posterior or more anterior tend to look as if they were non-lateralized.

Extreme differences between the S2 and S3 scales almost always indicate a lateralized disorder in which the sensorimotor areas of the brain are involved. In general, right hemisphere injuries involving the sensorimotor area produce an elevation on the S3 scale, but the S2 scale remains within normal limits (i.e., less than a T score of 60). However, in left hemisphere injuries, both these scales often are elevated above a score of 60T. Moreover, the S2 scale is 10 to 20 or more points higher than the S3 scale. Bilateral injuries, as a rule, elevate both scales, but with the scales within 10 to 20 T-score points of each other.

Both these scales reflect sensorimotor operations in the brain and only incidentally reflect some cognitive functions. In general, they are interpreted with respect to the C1 and C3 scales, as discussed previously. Differences between the scales of at least 10 T-score points are necessary before one should begin to take any lateralization suggested by the scales as more than a hypothesis to be investigated. Large differences (in excess of 20 points), in the absence of peripheral problems, generally suggest a lesion involving the sensorimotor area of the brain.

QUALITATIVE ANALYSIS

The LNNB lends itself to a qualitative analysis, as well as the quantitative analysis discussed in this chapter. The consideration of the qualitative factors becomes the next step in the diagnostic process. Here, the interest is not in whether a client got a certain score on a certain item, but rather in how that score was achieved. One of the great advantages of this battery (inherent in its design, as well as in the administration and testing the limits techniques suggested) is that the same test procedures lend themselves to both quantitative and qualitative analyses. The two approaches complement one another and allow the user of the LNNB to enjoy the best of both methods, thus avoiding that continuing, yet ultimately futile, argument over which approach is better or which approach should be the one employed.

In scoring qualitative errors, there is a wide range of possibilities aimed at gaining a better understanding of the "why" behind a client's error. Qualitative analysis can also aid in the evaluations of responses that are correct in terms of the quantitative scoring but are still unusual, such as the client who reads a word on the C8 scale but stutters in pronouncing it, or the client who can describe an object and its uses on the C4 scale but is unable to give its name.

After a qualitative analysis has been made, it should be integrated with the quantitative analysis. It is my strong belief that neither form of data is inherently "superior" in any given case. We know from our own studies that quantitative indices do not have 100 percent hit rates. We also know that clinicians make errors and frequently disagree in their qualitative interpretations of behavior, as demonstrated by the wide range of theories in neuropsychology to explain the same phenomena. In some cases, the qualitative data help to explain inconsistencies that cannot be resolved in the quantitative results. In other cases, the quantitative data suggest an alternate approach to an observation that clears up the interpretation of a qualitative aspect of behavior. Only when the two sets of data have been integrated has a fully effective initial evaluation been completed. Full integration is, of course, a clinical task based heavily on the clinician's neuropsychological knowledge and his or her ability to use this knowledge effectively with the individual client rather than an attribute of the test that is given.

PRIOR HISTORY

Even at this point, there still remains another step in the diagnostic process: the reconciliation of the conclusions of the above techniques with the history. Historical information and the conclusions made available by others prior to the neuropsychological assessment may be right or wrong. A lesion may or may not exist as reported. The client's developmental history may be accurate or may contain serious errors. The relative accuracy of information depends on the source of that information, as well as its nature. In all cases, however, it is important to double-check all such information.

COMPARISONS WITH OTHER TESTS

An important way to gain insight on a relatively new test such as the LNNB is to examine its correlation with other, more established tests that have been discussed in other chapters.

Halstead-Reitan Comparisons

An initial comparison was made by Kane, Sweet, Golden, Parsons, and Moses (1981). The authors compared diagnostic accuracy of the LNNB and the Halstead-Reitan in classifying as brain damaged or non-brain damaged 45 difficult-to-diagnose individuals. The authors found that the batteries (interpreted by an expert at each procedure) agreed on 37 of the cases.

Golden, Kane, et al. (1981) examined 108 subjects who had taken both the LNNB and the Halstead-Reitan. The 14 major LNNB scores were compared against the 15 major Halstead-Reitan scores, as selected from Russell, Neuringer, and Goldstein (1970). Multiple correlations were then run between each test and all the tests of the other battery. The multiple Rs ranged from .67 to .95, with a median in the .80s. The lowest multiple correlation was Finger Tapping (dominant hand).

Shelley and Goldstein (1982b) examined the same intercorrelations in an independent sample of 125 brain injured patients. Their results were generally comparable to those reported in the previous study. In addition, the authors reported a correlation of .82 between impairment level from the Halstead-Reitan and the LNNB average T scores. A more recent study (Kane, Parsons, Goldstein, & Moses, 1983) found that the two batteries were essentially identical in their abilities to discriminate between a sample of 50 brain injured and 50 normal subjects.

Comparisons to the WAIS and WAIS-R

McKay, Golden, Moses, Fishburne, and Wisniewski (1981) compared the intercorrelations between the WAIS and the LNNB in a sample of 280 mixed psychiatric, neurological, and normal subjects. Correlations between the C11 scale and the WAIS summary IQ measures were −.84 for Verbal IQ, −.74 for Performance IQ, and −.84 for Full Scale IQ. Picker and Schlottmann (1982) reported LNNB-WAIS correlations in a study employing only normal individuals. In this case, the higher correlations were somewhat lower than in the previous study, in the mid-.70s.

Preliminary work with the WAIS-R suggests similarly high correlations with the LNNB, with some minor differences in the correlations for specific subtests. Dill and Golden (1983) recently investigated the relationship of the original 14 LNNB scales from Form II with the 14 subtest and IQ scores for the WAIS-R.

Of particular interest are the correlations between the C11 scale and the Verbal, Performance, and Full Scale IQs ($-.86$, $-.88$, and $-.89$). On cross-validation, the correlations decreased to some extent. After correcting for age and education level, IQ accounted for about 35% of the overall variance of the LNNB scale scores.

In an ambitious study, Shelley and Goldstein (1982a) attempted to confirm the previous findings of Prifitera and Ryan (1981) and compare the LNNB, the WAIS, and the WRAT. They administered all three measures to 150 neuropsychiatric patients. Using selected T scores for the 11 basic clinical scales of the LNNB, correlations with the WAIS and WRAT subtests were computed. Correlations with the WAIS subtests ranged from $-.38$ between C8 and Digit Symbol to $-.73$ between the two Arithmetic measures. In general, the correlations were somewhat higher than those obtained by McKay et al. (1981).

Comparisons With Other Tests

Ryan and Prifitera (1982), in a population of 32 psychiatric patients, found a correlation of $-.65$ between the Wechsler Memory Scale (WMS; Wechsler, 1945) and the LNNB C10 scale. McKay and Ramsey (1981) found a similar correlation between the two measures of memory with a slightly older and less educated group of alcoholics. However, the correlation between the raw scores for the C10 and the WMS was much higher ($-.82$, $p < .001$). In addition to the concurrent validity studies reported above, preliminary correlations between the LNNB and several other measures also suggest generally high correlations of the various LNNB scales with the Peabody Individual Achievement Test (PIAT; Dunn & Markwardt, 1970), the Benton Visual Retention Test (Benton, 1955), the Wide Range Achievement Test (J. F. Jastak & S. R. Jastak, 1965), the Boston Aphasia Examination (Goodglass & Kaplan, 1972), and the

Peabody Picture Vocabulary Test (Dunn, 1970). These correlations are generally maximum in the range of .70 to .90 and follow the expected pattern of results, with PIAT and WRAT scores maximally correlated with the similar scales on the LNNB (e.g., Spelling with C7, Reading Recognition with C8, Arithmetic with C9, General Information with C11, and Reading Comprehension with C8 and C11). The Benton correlated highest with C4, and the Boston Aphasia Examination correlated highest with C6 and C5.

ADVANTAGES AND DISADVANTAGES

The Luria test offers some major advantages as a neuropsychological test battery. First, the test takes $2^{1}/_{2}$ hours to administer, as opposed to test batteries such as the Halstead-Reitan, which takes 6 or more hours to administer. The test allows the user to break general functions (e.g., Receptive Speech) into specific skills and deficits. This is of use both in detailing a patient's deficits and in diagnosing a patient's disorder. The qualitative nature of the items allows for the understanding of the patient on a more clinical level, whereas the quantitative indices allow for the use of research and the insights available from a quantitative approach (as discussed in chapter 9).

The Luria has several disadvantages as well. First, the test does not have the extensive background or use represented by the Halstead-Reitan tests and other test batteries. Second, although the test offers potentially more information, the most valuable information requires that the user be aware of the theoretical system on which the test is based. This, indeed, is a drawback of almost all tests offering qualitative observations.

The best initial readings on Luria's tests and theories can be found in Luria (1973). (Readers without any background in this area may first wish to read Golden & Anderson, 1978.) A second, but more advanced, test can be found in Luria (1966). For qualitative information on the specific test items contained in the standardized battery, the best source is Christensen (1975), whose manual details both Luria's theories and the intended role of each item. With this background, the reader should have sufficient theoretical information to appreciate the integrated standardized-qualitative approach used in the interpretation of the Luria battery.

There is a strong relationship between the advantages and disadvantages of the Luria techniques. The test's comprehensiveness, ease of use, accuracy, and administration time are based upon the combined standardized and qualitative interpretative system. Use of the test without considering both aspects of the interpretation results in a significant loss of information, which interferes considerably with the clinical efficacy of the battery.

CLINICAL EXAMPLES

Because of the length of a Luria protocol, it is not possible to reproduce an entire test record to give the reader a full feeling for the potential of the test, as well as for the problems in dealing with a large set of items. Consequently, the case examples included here examine only the conclusions that can be reached from the more formal quantitative aspects of the test. The reader should remember, however, that in actual clinical practice, such an evaluation would consist of a qualitative evaluation as well. In addition, the final report would integrate the results from the two methods in order to fully describe the patient's problems.

Case 1. As can be seen in Figure 10-1, the Right Hemisphere score is significantly elevated over the Left Hemisphere score, suggesting lateralization to the right hemisphere, although both hemispheres appear impaired. The Tactile score is significantly higher than the Motor score, suggesting a parietal rather than a frontal focus. Receptive Language is greater than Expressive Language, as is usually seen in right hemisphere injuries; and Rhythm, Reading, Writing, and Memory are the best scores in the profile. Overall, this is highly suggestive of a clear focus in the right parietal area including the sensory strip in the postcentral gyrus. This was subsequently confirmed by CAT scan.

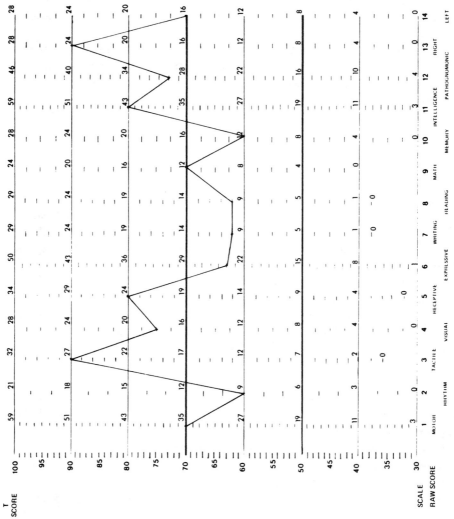

Figure 10-1. Luria profile for Case 1.

314

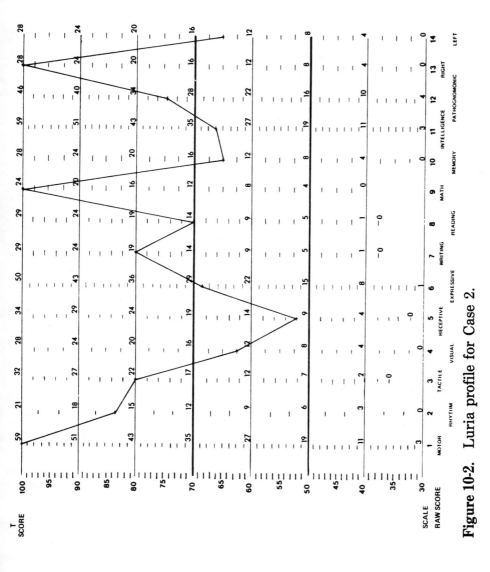

Figure 10-2. Luria profile for Case 2.

315

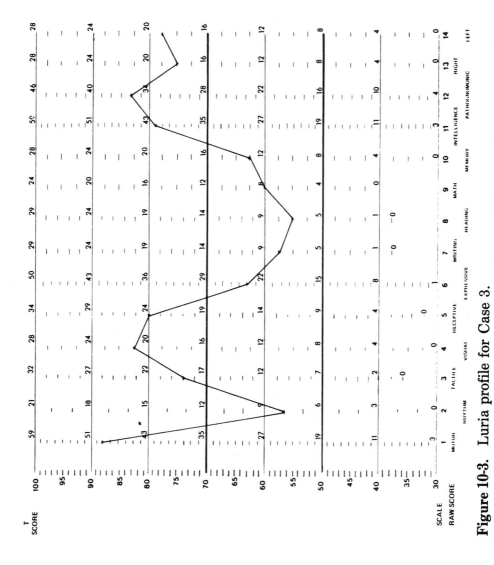

Figure 10-3. Luria profile for Case 3.

316

Case 2. This second case (Figure 10-2) presents a clear lateralization to the right hemisphere. In addition, the Motor score is significantly higher than the Tactile score, and Expressive Language is elevated above Receptive Language (somewhat rare in right hemisphere injuries). There is an elevation in Arithmetic as well. Overall, this points to a clear serious involvement of the right frontal area, with possibly a great deal of injury to motor speech structures either in the left hemisphere or in the lower brain areas. (The case was a 14-year-old with a serious gunshot wound involving the right frontal lobe and some lower cortical structures, the latter injury causing a partial paralysis of the speech musculature.)

Case 3. The third case (Figure 10-3) does not show a clear lateralization, because the Left and Right Hemisphere scores are quite close (one raw score point). Motor functions are more impaired than tactile functions, suggesting some frontal localization. Since the pattern does not suggest direct sensorimotor involvement, this would have to be in the prefrontal areas. There is significant visual impairment, suggesting a right hemisphere focus, as well as considerable loss on Receptive as opposed to Expressive Language, consistent with a right hemisphere focus. Relatively good scores on Reading, Writing, Math, and Memory are also consistent with this diagnosis. The Pathognomonic score is somewhat elevated for a lesion limited to the right frontal/temporal area, however, suggesting either a fast-growing tumor or some bilateral involvement. The lack of difference between the Right and Left Hemisphere scores, however, argue against an acute, lateralized disorder, as generally one side of the body is significantly more impaired. As a result, the pattern suggests a bilateral injury, but with the worst effects and primary focus in the right hemisphere. (The patient had a right frontal, slow-growing tumor that was extended into the left hemisphere as well.)

References

Aita, J. A., Armitage, S. C., Reitan, R. M., & Rabinowitz, A. (1947). The use of certain psychological tests in the evaluation of brain injury. *Journal of General Psychology, 37*, 25.

Bach, P. J., Harowski, K., Kirby, K., Peterson, P., & Schulein, M. (1981). The interrater reliability of the Luria-Nebraska Neuropsychological Battery. *Clinical Neuropsychology, 3*, 19.

Bachrach, H., & Mintz, J. (1974). The Wechsler Memory Scale as a tool for the detection of mild cerebral dysfunction. *Journal of Clinical Psychology, 30*, 58.

Balthazar, E. E. (1963). Cerebral unilateralization in chronic epileptic cases: The Wechsler Object Assembly Subtest. *Journal of Clinical Psychology, 19*, 169.

Balthazar, E. E., & Morrison, D. H. (1961). The use of Wechsler Intelligence Scales as diagnostic indicators of predominant left, right, and indeterminate unilateral brain damage. *Journal of Clinical Psychology, 17*, 161.

Barron, F. (1953). An ego strength scale which predicts response to psychotherapy. *Journal of Consulting Psychology, 17*, 327.

Bartz, W. R. (1968). Relationship between Wechsler, Beta, and Shipley-Hartford scores. *Psychological Reports, 22*, 676.

Bender, L. A. (1938). Visual Motor Gestalt Test and its clinical use. *American Orthopsychiatric Association Research Monograph, 3*, New York: American Orthopsychiatric Association.

Benton, A. L. (1945). A visual retention test for clinical use. *Archives of Neurology and Psychiatry, 54*, 212.

Benton, A. L. (1955) *Benton Visual Retention Test.* New York: Psychological Corporation.

Benton, A. L. (1968). Differential behavioral effects in frontal lobe disease. *Neuropsychologia, 6*, 53.

Benton, A. L. (1974). *The Revised Visual Retention Test* (4th ed.). New York: Psychological Corporation.

Benton, A. L., & Spreen, O. (1961a). Visual Memory Test: The simulation of mental incompetence. *Archives of General Psychiatry, 4,* 79.

Benton, A. L., & Spreen, O. (1961b). Zur Simulation intellektueller Leistungsdefekte im Benton-Test. *Psychologische Beitraege, 7,* 147.

Black, F. W. (1974). The utility of the Shipley-Hartford as a predictor of WAIS Full Scale IQ for patients with traumatic head injuries. *Journal of Clinical Psychology, 30,* 168.

Boerger, A. R., Graham, J. R., & Lilly, R. S. (1974). Behavioral correlates of single-scale MMPI code types. *Journal of Consulting and Clinical Psychology, 42,* 398.

Boller, F. (1968) Latent aphasia: Right and left "nonaphasic" brain damaged patients compared. *Cortex. 4,* 245.

Boller, F., & Vignolo, L. A. (1966). A latent sensory aphasia in hemisphere-damaged patients: An experimental study with the Token Test. *Brain. 89,* 815.

Bonner, L. W. (1969). Comparative study of the performance of Negro seniors of Oklahoma City High Schools on the WAIS and the PPVT. *Dissertation Abstracts. 30,* 921A.

Borgatta, E. F., & Corsini, R. T. (1960). The Quick Word Test and the WAIS. *Psychological Reports. 6,* 201

Brilliant, P. J., & Gynther, M. D.(1963). Relationships between performance on three tests for organicity and selected patient variables. *Journal of Consulting Psychology, 27,* 474.

Bruhn, A. R., & Reid, M. R. (1975). Simulation of brain damage on the Bender-Gestalt Test by college students. *Journal of Personality Assessment. 39,* 244.

Canter, A. H. (1976). *The Canter Background Interference Procedure for the Bender-Gestalt Test.* Nashville: Counselor Recordings.

Carson, R. C. (1969). Interpretative manual to the MMPI. In J. N. Butcher (Ed.), *MMPI research developments and clinical applications.* New York: McGraw-Hill.

Cattell, R. B. (1957). *Personality and motivation structure and measurement.* Yonkers-on-Hudson, New York: World Book.

Cattell, R. B. (1973). *Personality and mood by questionnaire.* San Francisco: Josey-Bass.

Cattell, R. B., Eber, H. W., & Tatsuoka, M. M. (1970). *Handbook for the Sixteen Personality Factor Questionnaire* (16PF). Champaign, IL Institute for Personality and Ability Testing.

Cattell, R. B., & Warburton, F. W. (1967). *Objective personality and motivation tests.* Champaign, IL. University of Illinois Press.

Christensen, A. L. (1975). *Luria's neuropsychological investigation.* New York: Spectrum.

Cohen, J. (1950). Wechsler Memory Scale performance of psychoneurotic, organic, and schizophrenic groups. *Journal of Consulting Psychology, 14,* 371.

Cohen, J. A. (1960). Coefficient of agreement for nominal scales. *Educational and Psychological Measurement. 20,* 37.

Colonna, A., & Faglioni, P. (1966). The performance of hemisphere-damaged patients on spatial intelligence tests. *Cortex. 2,* 293.

Costa, L. D., & Vaughan, H. G., Jr. (1962). Performance of patients with lateralized cerebral lesions: I. Verbal and perceptual tests. *Journal of Nervous and Mental Disease. 134,* 162.

Costa, L. D., Vaughan, H. G., Jr., Levita, E., & Farber, N. (1963). Purdue Pegboard as a predictor of the presence and laterality of cerebral lesions. *Journal of Consulting Psychology, 27,* 133.

Crochelet, Y. (1970). Considérations sur L'apport de L'exarien médicopsychologique dans l'expertise du syndrome postcommotionnel subtectif des traumatisés craniens. *Acta Psychiatrique Belgian. 70,* 233.

Cronholm, B., & Schalling, D. (1963). Intellectual deterioration after focal brain injury. *Archives of Surgery. 86,* 670.

Dahlstrom, W. G. (1954). Prediction of adjustment after neurosurgery. *American Psychologist. 9,* 353.

Dahlstrom, W. G., Welsh, G. S., & Dahlstrom, L. E. (1972). *An MMPI handbook: Volume I. Clinical interpretation.* Minneapolis: University of Minnesota Press.

Dahlstrom, W. G., Welsh, G. S., & Dahlstrom, L. E. (1975). *An MMPI handbook: Volume II. Research applications.* Minneapolis: University of Minnesota Press.

Davis, W. E., & Dizonne, M. F. (1970). Relationships between the Quick Test and the WAIS. *Psychological Reports. 26,* 457.

Delprato, D. J., & Jackson D. E. (1975). The effects of seating arrangement upon WAIS Digit Span and Digit Symbol performance. *Journal of Clinical Psychology, 31,* 88.

Dennerll, P. D. (1964). Prediction of unilateral brain dysfunction using Wechsler Test scores. *Journal of Consulting Psychology, 28,* 278.

Dill, R., & Golden, C. (1983). *The relationship of the LNNB and WAIS-R.* Unpublished manuscript.

Doehring, D. G., Reitan, R. M., & Klove, H. (1961). Changes in patterns of intelligence test performance associated with homonymous visual field defects. *Journal of Nervous and Mental Disease. 132,* 227.

Donahue, D., & Sattler, J. M. (1971). Personality variables affecting WAIS scores. *Journal of Consulting and Clinical Psychology, 36,* 441.

Drake, L. E., & Oetting, E. R. (1959). *An MMPI codebook for counselors.* Minneapolis: University of Minnesota Press.

Dunn, L. M. (1970). *Peabody Picture Vocabulary Test.* Circle Pines, MN: American Guidance Service.

Dunn, L. M., & Markwardt, F. C. (1970). *Peabody Individual Achievement Test.* Circle Pines, MN. American Guidance Service.

Edinger, J. D. (1976). WAIS Picture Arrangement and premorbid social competence among process schizophrenics. *Journal of Personality Assessment. 40,* 52.

Ernhart, C. B. (1970). The correlation of PPVT and WAIS Scores for adult psychiatric patients. *Journal of Clinical Psychology, 26,* 470.

Fedio, P., & Mirsky, A. F. (1968). Selective intellectual deficits in children with temporal lobe or centrencephalic epilepsy. *Neuropsychologia. 7,* 287.

Fernald, L. D., Fernald, P. S., & Rines, W. B. (1966). Purdue Pegboard and differential diagnosis. *Journal of Consulting Psychology, 30,* 279.

Fields, F. R. J., & Whitmyre, J. W. (1969). Verbal and performance relationships with respect to laterality of cerebral involvement. *Diseases of the Nervous System. 30,* 177.

Finlayson, M. A. J., Johnson, K. A., & Reitan, R. M. (1977). Relationship of level of education to neuropsychological measures in brain-damaged and non-brain-damaged adults. *Journal of Consulting and Clinical Psychology, 45,* 536.

Firetto, A. C., & Davey, H. (1971). Subjectively reported anxiety as a discriminator of digit span performance. *Psychological Reports. 28,* 98.

Fisher, M. (1956). Left hemiplegia and motor impersistence. *Journal of Nervous & Mental Disease, 123,* 201.

Gilberstadt, H., & Duker, J. A. (1965). *A handbook for clinical and actuarial MMPI interpretation.* Philadelphia: Saunders.

Goldberg, L. R. (1965). Diagnosticians vs. diagnostic signs: The diagnosis of psychosis vs. neurosis from the MMPI. *Psychological Monographs, 9,* 79.

Goldberg, L. R. (1974). Objective diagnostic tests and measures. *Annual Review of Psychology, 25,* 343.

Golden, C. J. (1976). The identification of brain damage by an abbreviated form of the Halstead-Reitan Neuropsychological Battery. *Journal of Clinical Psychology, 32,* 821.

Golden, C. J. (1977). Validity of the Halstead-Reitan Neuropsychological Battery in a mixed psychiatric and brain-injured population. *Journal of Consulting and Clinical Psychology, 45,* 1043.

Golden, C. J. (1978a). *Diagnosis and rehabilitation in clinical neuropsychology.* Springfield, IL: Charles C Thomas.

Golden, C. J. (1978b). *Learning disabilities and brain dysfunction.* Springfield, IL: Charles C Thomas.

Golden, C. J., & Anderson, S. M. (1977). Short form of the Speech-Sounds Perception Test. *Perceptual and Motor Skills. 45,* 485.

Golden, C. J., Hammeke, T. A., & Purisch, A. D. (1978). Diagnostic validity of a standardized neuropsychological battery derived from Luria's neuropsychological tests. *Journal of Consulting and Clinical Psychology, 46,* 1258–1265.

Golden, C. J., Kane, R., Sweet, J., Moses, J. A., Cardellino, J. P., Templeton, R., Vicente, P., & Graber, B. (1981). Relationship of the Halstead-Reitan Neuropsychological Battery to the Luria-Nebraska Neuropsychological Battery. *Journal of Consulting and Clinical Psychology, 49,* 410–417.

Golden, C. J., Moses, J. A., Fishburne, F. J., Engum, E., Lewis, G. P., Wisniewski, A. M., Conley, F. K., Berg, R. A., & Graber, B. (1981). Cross-validation of the Luria-Nebraska Neuropsychological Battery for the presence, lateralization, and localization of brain damage. *Journal of Consulting and Clinical Psychology, 49,* 491.

Golden, C. J., Moses, J. A., Graber, B., & Berg, R. A. (1981). Objective clinical rules for interpreting the Luria-Nebraska Neuropsychological Battery: Derivation, effectiveness, and validation. *Journal of Consulting and Clinical Psychology, 49,* 616.

Golden, C. J., Purisch, A. D., & Hammeke, T. A. (1981). *Luria-Nebraska Neuropsychological Battery: Manual.* Los Angeles: Western Psychological Services.

Golden, C. J., Purisch, A. D., & Hammeke, T. A. (1986). *Luria-Nebraska Neuropsychological Battery: Forms I and II.* Los Angeles: Western Psychological Services.

Golden, C. J., Sweet, J. J., & Osmon, D. C. (1979). The diagnosis of brain damage by the MMPI: A comprehensive evaluation. *Journal of Personality Assessment. 43,* 138.

Goldstein, G. (1974). The use of clinical neuropsychological methods in the lateralization of brain lesions. In J. Dimond & J. G. Beaumont (Eds.), *Hemisphere function in the brain.* New York: Wiley.

Goldstein, G., & Neuringer, C. (1966). Schizophrenic and organic signs on the Trail Making Test. *Perceptual and Motor Skills, 22,* 347.

Goldstein, G., & Shelley, C. H. (1973). Univariate vs. multivariate analysis in neuropsychological test assessment of lateralized brain damage. *Cortex, 9,* 204.

Goldstein, G. & Shelley, C. H. (1974) Neurodiagnosis of multiple sclerosis in a neuropsychiatric setting. *Journal of Nervous and Mental Disease, 158,* 280.

Good, P. K. E., & Brantner, J. B. (1974). *The physician's guide to the MMPI.* Minneapolis: University of Minnesota Press.

Goodglass, H., & Kaplan, E. (1972). *Boston Diagnostic Aphasia Examination.* Philadelphia: Lea & Febiger.

Gough, H. G. (1950). The F minus K dissimulation index for the MMPI. *Journal of Consulting Psychology, 14.* 408.

Graham, F. K., & Kendall, B. S. (1960). Memory-for-Designs Test: Revised general manual. *Perceptual and Motor Skills. Monograph Supplement, 11*(2, Pt. 8), 147.

Graham, J. R. (1977). *The MMPI: A practical guide.* New York: Oxford University Press.

Granick, S. (1971). Brief tests and their interrelationships as intellectual measures of aged subjects. *American Psychological Association Proceedings, 7,* 599.

Grossman, H. J. (1973). *Manual on terminology and classification in mental retardation* (rev. ed.). Baltimore: American Association on Mental Deficiency, Garamond/Pridemark Press.

Grundvig, J. L., Ajax, A. E., & Needham, W. E. (1973). Screening organic brain impairment with the Memory-for-Designs Test. Validation of comparison of different scoring systems and exposure times. *Journal of Clinical Psychology, 29,* 350.

Grundvig, J. L., Needham, W. E., & Ajax, A. E. (1970). Comparison of different scoring and administration procedures for the Memory-for-Designs Test. *Journal of Clinical Psychology, 26,* 353.

Gudeman, H. E., Craine, J. F., Golden, C. J., & McLaughlin, D. (1977). Higher cortical dysfunction associated with long-term alcoholism. *International Journal of Neuroscience, 8,* 33.

Gudeman, H. E., Golden, C. J., & Craine, J. F. (1978). The role of neuropsychological evaluation in the rehabilitation of the brain-injured patient. A program in neurotraining. *JSAS Catalogue of Selected Documents in Psychology, 8,* 30. (Ms. No. 1693)

Hain, J. D. (1964). The Bender-Gestalt Test: A scoring method for identifying brain damage. *Journal of Consulting Psychology, 28,* 34.

Halstead, W. C. (1947). *Brain and intelligence.* Chicago: University of Chicago Press.

Hammeke, T., Golden, C. J., & Purisch, A. (1978). A standardized, short, and comprehensive neuropsychological test based on the Luria Neuropsychological Evaluation. *International Journal of Neuroscience, 8,* 135–141.

Hammer, E. F. (1955). An experimental study of symbolism on the Bender-Gestalt. *Journal of Projective Techniques, 18,* 335.

Hanvik, L. J. (1949). *Some psychological dimensions of low back pain.* Unpublished doctoral dissertation, University of Minnesota.

Hanvik, L. J. (1951). MMPI profiles in patients with low back pain. *Journal of Consulting Psychology, 15,* 350.

Hartje, W., Kerstechensteiner, M., Poeck, K., & Orgass, B. (1973). A cross validation study on the Token Test. *Neuropsychologia, 11,* 119.

Hathaway, S. R., & Meehl, P. E. (1951). *An atlas for the clinical use of the MMPI.* Minneapolis: University of Minnesota Press.

Hedlund, J. L. (1977). MMPI clinical scale correlates. *Journal of Consulting and Clinical Psychology, 45,* 739.

Heilbrun, A. B. (1959). Lateralization of cerebral lesion and performance on spatial-temporal tasks. *Archives of Neurology, 1,* 282.

Heimburger, R. F., Demyer, W., & Reitan, R. M. (1964). Implications of Gerstmann's Syndrome. *Journal of Neurology, Neurosurgery, and Psychiatry, 27,* 52.

Holland, T. R. (1974). Wechsler Memory Scale paired associate learning in discrimination of brain-damaged and non-brain-damaged psychiatric patients. *Perceptual and Motor Skills, 39,* 227.

Hooper, H. E. (1983). *Manual for the Hooper Visual Organization Test.* Los Angeles: Western Psychological Services.

Hovey, H. B. (1964). Brain lesions and five MMPI items. *Journal of Consulting Psychology, 28,* 78.

Howard, A. R. (1950). Diagnostic value of the Wechsler Memory Scale with selected groups of brain-damaged patients. *Journal of Consulting Psychology, 14,* 395.

Hulicka, I. M. (1966). Age differences in Wechsler Memory Scale scores. *Journal of Genetic Psychology, 109,* 135.

Hunt, W., Quay, H., & Walker, R. E. (1966). Validity of diagnostic judgment as a function of amount of test information. *Journal of Clinical Psychology, 22,* 154.

Hutt, M. L. (1968). The projective use of the Bender-Gestalt Test. In A. I. Rabin (Ed.), *Projective techniques in personality assessment.* New York: Springer.

Hutt, M. L. (1969). *The Hutt Adaptation of the Bender-Gestalt Test* (2nd ed.). New York: Grune & Stratton.

Isenberg, S. J., & Bass, B. A. (1974). Effects of verbal and nonverbal reinforcement on the WAIS performance of normal adults. *Journal of Consulting and Clinical Psychology, 42,* 467.

Jastak, J. F., & Jastak, S. R. (1965). *The Wide Range Achievement Test: Manual of instructions.* Wilmington, DE: Guidance Associates.

Jastak, S. & Wilkinson, G. (1984). *Wide Range Achievement Test-Revised.* Wilmington, DE: Jastak Associates.

Kane, R. L., Parsons, O. A., Goldstein, G., & Moses, J. A., Jr. (1983, February). *Further comparisons of the relative diagnostic accuracy of the Halstead-Reitan and Luria-Nebraska neuropsychological test batteries.* Paper presented at the meeting of the International Neuropsychological Society, Mexico City.

Kane, R. L., Sweet, J. J., Golden, C. J., Parsons, O. A., & Moses, J. A. (1981). Comparative diagnostic accuracy of the Halstead-Reitan and standardized Luria-Nebraska neuropsychological batteries in a mixed psychiatric and brain-damaged population. *Journal of Consulting and Clinical Psycholoay, 49,* 484.

Karson, S. (1958). Second-order personality factors and the MMPI. *Journal of Clinical Psychology, l4,* 313.

Karson, S. (1959). The Sixteen Personality Factor Test in clinical practice. *Journal of Clinical Psychology, 15,* 174.

Karson, S. (1960). Validating clinical judgments with the 16 PF test. *Journal of Clinical Psychology, 16,* 394.

Karson, S. (1961). Second-order personality factors in positive mental health. *Journal of Clinical Psychology, 17,* l4.

Karson, S., & O'Dell, J. W. (1976). *A guide to the clinical use of the l6 PF.* Champaign, IL: Institute for Personality and Ability Testing.

Karson, S., & Pool, K. B. (1957). The construct validity of the Sixteen Personality Factors Test. *Journal of Clinical Psychology, l3,* 245.

Keiser, T. W. (1975). Schizotype and the Wechsler Digit Span Test. *Journal of Clinical Psychology, 3l,* 303.

Kieffer, D. M., & Golden, C. J. (1978). The Peabody Individual Achievement Test with normal and special school populations. *Psychological Reports, 42,* 395.

Kiernan, R. J., and Matthews, C. G. (1976). Impairment index versus T score averaging in neuropsychological assessment. *Journal of Consulting and Clinical Psychology, 44,* 951.

Kljajic, I. (1975). Wechsler Memory Scale indices of brain pathology. *Journal of Clinical Psychology, 3l,* 698.

Klove, H., & Matthews, C. G. (1966). Psychometric and adaptive abilities in epilepsy. *Epilepsia, 7,* 330.

Klove, H., & Matthews, C. G. (1969). Neuropsychological evaluation of the epileptic patient. *Wisconsin Medical Journal, 68,* 296.

Klove, H., & Matthews, C. G. (1974). Neuropsychological studies of patients with epilepsy. In R. M. Reitan & L. S. Davison (Eds.), *Clinical neuropsychology: Current status and applications.* Washington, DC: Winston.

Knox, W. J., & Grippaldi, R. (1970). High levels of state or trait anxiety and performance on selected verbal WAIS subtests. *Psychological Reports, 27,* 375.

Koppitz, E. M. (1963). *The Bender-Gestalt Test for young children.* New York: Grune & Stratton.

Koppitz, E. M. (1975). The Bender-Gestalt Test and Visual Aural Digit Span Test and reading achievement. *Journal of Learning Disabilities, 8,* 154.

Kratochwill, T. R., & Brody, G. H. (1976). Effects of verbal and self-monitoring feedback on Wechsler Adult Intelligence Scale performance in normal adults. *Journal of Consulting and Clinical Psychology, 44,* 879.

Krug, S. E. (1977). *Psychological assessment in medicine.* Champaign, IL: Institute for Personality and Ability Testing.

L'Abate, L., Vogler, R. E., Friedman, W. N., & Chusid, T. M. (1972). The diagnostic usefulness of two tests of brain damage. *Journal of Clinical Psychology, 39,* 508.

Ladd, C. E. (1964). WAIS performances of brain damaged and neurotic patients. *Journal of Clinical Psychology, 20,* 114.

Levine, J., & Feirstein, A. (1972). Differences in test performance between brain damaged, schizophrenic, and medical patients. *Journal of Consulting and Clinical Psychology, 39,* 508.

Lewinsohn, P. M. (1965). Dimensions of MMPI change. *Journal of Clinical Psychology, 21,* 37.

Lewis, G., Golden, C. J., Moses, J. A., Jr., Osmon, D. C., Purisch, A. D., & Hammeke, T. A. (1979). Localization of cerebral dysfunction with a standardized version of Luria's Neuropsychological Battery. *Journal of Consulting and Clinical Psychology, 47,* 1001.

Lezak, M. D. (1976). *Neuropsychological assessment.* New York: Oxford University Press.

Logue, P. E., & Allen, K. (1971). WAIS predicted Category Test score with the Halstead Neuropsychological Battery. *Perceptual and Motor Skills, 33,* 1095.

Luria, A. R. (1963). *Restoration of function after brain injury.* New York: MacMillan.

Luria, A. R. (1966). *Higher cortical functions in man.* New York: Basic.

Luria, A. R. (1973). *The working brain.* New York: Basic.

Mack, J. L. A. (1970). A comparative study of group test estimates of WAIS verbal, performance and full scale IQs. *Journal of Clinical Psychology, 26,* 177.

Mahan, H. (1976). *Sensitivity of WAIS tests to focal lobe damage.* Privately mimeographed.

Maloney, M. P., & Ward, M. P. (1976). *Psychological assessment: A conceptual approach.* New York: Oxford University Press.

Marks, P. A., & Seeman, W. (1963). *Acturial description of abnormal personality.* Los Angeles: Western Psychological Services.

Marvel, G., Golden, C. J., Hammeke, T., Osmon, D. C., & Purisch, A. (1979). *The effects of age and education on a standardized version of Luria's neuropsychological tests.* Manuscript submitted for publication.

Marvel, G.A., Golden, C.J., Hammeke, T., Purisch, A., & Osmon, D. (1979). Relationship of age and education to performance on a standardized version of Luria's neuropsychological tests in different patient populations. *International Journal of Neuroscience, 9,* 63-70.

Matthews, C. G., Cleeland, C. S., & Hopper, C. L. (1970). Neuropsychological patterns in multiple sclerosis. *Diseases of the Nervous System, 31,* 161.

Matthews, C. G., & Klove, H. (1967). Differential psychological performance in major motor, psychomotor and mixed classifications of known and unknown etiology. *Epilepsia, 8,* 117.

Maxwell, E. (1957). Validities of abbreviated WAIS scales. *Journal of Consulting Psychology, 21,* 121.

McAndrews, C. (1965). The differentiation of male alcoholic outpatients from nonalcoholic psychiatric patients by means of the MMPI. *Quarterly Journal of Studies on Alcohol, 26,* 238.

McFie, J. (1969). The diagnostic significance of disorders of higher nervous activity. In P. J. Vinken & G. W. Bruyn (Eds.), *Handbook of clinical neurology* (Vol. 3). New York: Wiley.

McFie, J. (1975). *Assessment of organic intellectual impairment.* New York: Academic Press.

McGuire, F. L. (1960). A comparison of the Bender-Gestalt and Flicker Fusion as indicators of CNS involvement. *Journal of Clinical Psychology, 16,* 276.

McIver, D., McLaren, S. A., & Phillip, A. E. (1973). Inter-rater agreement on Memory-for-Designs Test. *British Journal of Social and Clinical Psychology, 12,* 194.

McKay, S. E., Golden, C. J., Moses, J. A., Fishburne, F., & Wisniewski, A. (1981). Correlation of the Luria-Nebraska Neuropsychological Battery with the WAIS. *Journal of Consulting and Clinical Psychology, 49,* 940.

McKay, S., & Ramsey, R. (1981). Correlation of the Wechsler Memory Scale and the Luria-Nebraska Memory scale. *Clinical Neuropsychology, 5,* 168.

McKeever, W. F., May, P. R. A., & Tuma, A. H. (1965). Prognosis in schizophrenia: Prediction of length of hospitalization from psychological test variables. *Journal of Clinical Psychology, 21,* 214.

McManis, D. M. (1974). Memory-for-Designs performance of brain damaged and non-brain damaged psychiatric patients. *Perceptual and Motor Skills, 38,* 47.

Meier, M. J. (1974, September). *Neuropsychological predictors of motor recovery after cerebral infarction.* Paper read at the 82nd Annual Convention of the American Psychological Association, New Orleans.

Meier, M. J., & French, L. A. (1966). Longitudinal assessment of intellectual function following unilateral temporal lobectomy. *Journal of Clinical Psychology, 22,* 22.

Meyer, V., & Jones, H. G. (1957). Patterns of cognitive test performance as functions of the lateral localization of cerebral abnormalities in the temporal lobe. *Journal of Mental Science, 103,* 758.

Monroe, K. L. (1966). Note on the estimate of the WAIS full-scale IQ. *Journal of Clinical Psychology, 22,* 79.

Nikols, J. (1963). Mental deficit, schizophrenia and the Benton Test. *Journal of Nervous and Mental Disease, 136,* 279.

Norman, R. P., & Wilensky, H. (1961). Item difficulty of the WAIS Information subtest for a chronic schizophrenic sample. *Journal of Clinical Psychology, 17,* 56.

Norton, J. C., & Matthews, C. G. (1972). Psychological test performance in patients with subtentorial versus supratentorial CNS disease. *Diseases of the Nervous System, 33,* 312.

O'Dell, J. W. (1971). Method for detecting random answers on personality questionnaires. *Journal of Applied Psychology, 55,* 380.

Ogilvie, R. D. (1965). Correlation between the Quick Test and the WAIS as used in a clinical setting. *Psychological Reports, 16,* 497.

Orgass, B., & Poeck, K. (1966). Clinical validation of a new test for aphasia: An experimental study on the Token Test. *Cortex, 2,* 222.

Orme, J. E. (1962). Bender design recall and brain damage. *Diseases of the Nervous System, 23,* 329.

Osmon, D.C., & Golden, C. J. (1978). Minnesota Multiphasic Personality Inventory correlates of neuropsychological deficits. *International Journal of Neuroscience,* 112.

Osmon, D. C., Golden, C. J., Purisch, A. D., Hammeke, T. A., & Blume, H. G. (1979). The use of a standardized battery of Luria's tests in the diagnosis of lateralized cerebral dysfunction. *International Journal of Neuroscience, 9,* 1.

Parker, J. W. (1957). The validity of some current tests for organicity. *Journal of Consulting Psychology, 21,* 425.

Pascal, G. R., & Suttel, B. J. (1951). *The Bender-Gestalt Test: Its quantification and validity for adults.* New York: Grune & Stratton.

Paulsen, M. J., & Lin, T. (1970). Predicting WAIS IQ from Shipley-Hartford scores. *Journal of Clinical Psychology, 26,* 453.

Peck, D. F. (1970). The conversion of Progressive Matrices and Mill Hill Vocabulary raw scores into deviation IQs. *Journal of Clinical Psychology, 26,* 67.

Pedrini, D. T., & Pedrini, L. N. (1970). *The Pedrini Supplementary Aid to the administration of the Stanford-Binet Intelligence Scale (Form L-M): A handbook.* Los Angeles: Western Psychological Services.

Pennington, H., Galliani, C. A., & Voegele, G. E. (1965). Unilateral electroencephalographic dysrhythmia and children's intelligence. *Child Development, 36,* 539.

Perret, E. (1974). The left frontal lobe of man and the suppression of habitual responses in verbal categorical behavior. *Neuropsychologia, 12,* 323.

Picker, W. R., & Schlottmann, R. S. (1982). An investigation of the Intellectual Processes scale of the Luria-Nebraska Neuropsychological Battery. *Clinical Neuropsychology, 4,* 120.

Pool, D. A., & Brown, R. (1970). The PPVT as a measure of general adult intelligence. *Journal of Consulting and Clinical Psychology, 34,* 8.

Prifitera, A., & Ryan, J. J. (1981). Validity of the Luria-Nebraska Intellectual Processes scale as a measure of adult intelligence. *Journal of Consulting and Clinical Psychology, 49,* 755.

Prifitera, A., & Ryan, J. J. (1983). WAIS-R/WAIS comparisons in a clinical sample. *Clinical Neuropsychology, 5,* 97.

Pringle, R. K., & Haanstad, M. (1971). Estimating WAIS IQs from Progressive Matrices scores. *Journal of Clinical Psychology, 27,* 479.

Purisch, A. D., Golden, C. J., & Hammeke, T. A. (1978). Discrimination of schizophrenic and brain damaged patients by a standardized version of Luria's neuropsychological tests. *Journal of Consulting and Clinical Psychology, 34,* 661.

Quattlebaum, L. F., & White, W. F. (1969). Relationships between two quick screening measures of intelligence for neuropsychiatric patients. *Psychological Reports, 24,* 691.

Rapaport, D., Gill, M. M., & Schafer, R. (1970). *Diagnostic psychological testing.* New York: International Universities Press.

Raven, J. C. (1960). *Guide to the Standard Progressive Matrices.* London: Lewis.

Reed, H. B., Reitan, R. M., & Klove, H. (1965). Influence of cerebral lesions on psychological test performance of older children. *Journal of Consulting Psychology, 29,* 247.

Reitan, R. M. (1955a). Affective disturbances of brain damaged patients. *Archives of Neurology and Psychiatry, 73,* 530.

Reitan, R. M. (1955b). Investigation of the validity of Halstead's measures of biological intelligence. *A.M.A. Archives of Neurology and Psychiatry, 73,* 28.

Reitan, R. M. (1959). *The effect of brain lesions on adaptive abilities in human beings.* Unpublished manuscript.

Reitan, R. M. (undated). *Neuropsychological methods of inferring brain damage in adults and children.* Unpublished manuscript.

Reitan, R. M., & Boll, T. J. (1971). Intellectual & cognitive functions in Parkinson's disease. *Journal of Consulting and Clinical Psychology, 37,* 364.

Reitan, R. M., Reed, J. C., & Dyken, M. L. (1971). Cognitive, psychomotor and motor-correlates of multiple sclerosis. *Journal of Nervous and Mental Disease, 153,* 218.

Robbins, S. L. (1974). *Pathologic basis of disease.* Philadelphia: Saunders.

Russell, E. W. (1972). WAIS factor analysis with brain damaged subjects using criterion measures. *Journal of Consulting and Clinical Psychology, 39,* 133.

Russell, E. W. (1975). Validation of a brain damage versus schizphrenia MMPI key. *Journal of Clinical Psychology, 31,* 659.

Russell, E. W., Neuringer, C., & Goldstein, G. (1970). *Assessment of brain damage: A neuropsychological key approach.* New York: Wiley-Interscience.

Ryan, J. J., Nowak, T. J., & Geisser, M. E. (1987). On the comparability of the WAIS and WAIS-R: Review of the research and implications for clinical practice. *Journal of Psychoeducational Assessment, 5,* 15–30.

Ryan, J. J., & Prifitera, A. (1982). Concurrent validity of the Luria-Nebraska Memory scale. *Journal of Clinical Psychology, 38,* 378.

Ryan, J. J., Prifitera, A., & Rosenberg, S. J. (1983). Interrelationships between and factor structures of the WAIS-R and WAIS in a neuropsychological battery. *International Journal of Neuroscience, 21,* 191.

Ryan, J. J., & Rosenberg, S. J. (1983). Relationship between WAIS-R and WRAT in a sample of mixed patients. *Perceptual and Motor Skills, 56,* 623.

Ryan, J. J., Rosenberg, S. J., & Heilbronner, R. L. (1984). Comparative relationships of the WAIS-R and the WAIS to the Wechsler Memory Scale. *Journal of Behavioral Assessment, 6,* 37.

Sattler, J. M. (1969). Effects of cues and examiner influence on two Wechsler subtests. *Journal of Consulting and Clinical Psychology, 33,* 716.

Sattler, J. M. (1974). *Assessment of children's intelligence.* Philadelphia: Saunders.

Savage, R. D. (1970). Intellectual assessment. In P. Mittler (Ed.), *The psychological assessment of mental and physical handicaps.* London: Methuen.

Shaw, D. J., & Matthews, C. G. (1965). Differential MMPI performance of brain damaged versus pseudoneurologic group. *Journal of Clinical Psychology, 21,* 405.

Shearn, C. R., Berry, D. F., & Fitzgibbons, B. (1974). Usefulness of the Memory-for Designs Test in assessing mild organic complications in psychiatric patients. *Perceptual and Motor Skills, 38,* 1099.

Shelley, C., & Goldstein, G. (1982a). Intelligence, achievement, and the Luria-Nebraska Battery in a neuropsychiatric population: A factor analytic study. *Clinical Neuropsychology, 4,* 164.

Shelly, C., & Goldstein G. (1982b). Psychometric relations between the Luria-Nebraska and Halstead-Reitan Neuropsychological Test Batteries in a neuropsychiatric setting. *Clinical Neuropsychology, 4,* 128.

Silverstein, A. B. (1970). Reappraisal of the validity of a short form of Wechsler's scales. *Psychological Reports, 26,* 559.

Smith, A. (1964). Changing effects of frontal lesions. *Journal of Neurology, Neurosurgery, and Psychiatry, 27,* 511.

Smith, A. (1966a). Intellectual functions in patients with lateralized frontal tumors. *Journal of Neurology, Neurosurgery, and Psychiatry, 29,* 52.

Smith, A. (1966b). Verbal and nonverbal test performances of patients with "acute" lateralized brain lesions (tumors). *Journal of Nervous Mental Deficiency, 70,* 595.

Smith, A. (1975). Neuropsychological testing in neurological disorders. In W. J. Friedlander (Ed.), *Advances in neurology* (Vol. 7). New York: Raven Press.

Spreen, O., & Benton, A. L. (1969). *Neurosensory Center Comprehensive Examination for Aphasia.* Victoria, BC: University of Victoria, Department of Psychology, Neuropsychology Laboratory.

Sterne, D. M. (1969). The Benton, Porteus, and WAIS Digit Span Tests with normal and brain-injured subjects. *Journal of Clinical Psychology, 25,* 173.

Sterne, D. M. (1973). The Hooper Visual Organization Test and the Trail Making Test as discriminants of brain damage. *Journal of Clinical Psychology, 29,* 212.

Sydiaha, D. (1967). Prediction of WAIS IQ for psychiatric patients using the Ammons Full Range Picture Vocabulary and Raven Progressive Matrices. *Psychological Reports, 20,* 823.

Todd, J., Coolidge, F., & Satz, P. (1977). The Wechsler Adult Intelligence Scale discrepancy index: A neuropsychological evaluation. *Journal of Consulting and Clinical Psychology, 45,* 450.

Tymchuk, A. J. (1974). Comparison of the Bender error and time scores from groups of epileptic, retarded, and behavior problem children. *Perceptual and Motor Skills, 39,* 71.

Urbina, S. P., Golden, C. J., & Ariel, R. (1982). WAIS/WAIS-R: Initial comparisons. *Clinical Neuropsychology, 4,* 145.

Von Kerekjarto, M. (1961). Wahrnehmungstests zur Diagnose und Differentialdiagnose der Multiplen Sklerose, Eine Untersuchung mit dem Benton Visuellen Merkfaehigkeitstest, dem Goldstein-Scheerer Mosaiktest und dem Halstead Taktilen Leistungstest. *Zeitung Experimentalen und Angelwalten Psychologie, 8,* 369.

Walker, R. E., Sannito, T. C., & Firetto, A. C. (1970). The effect of subjectively reported anxiety on intelligence test performance. *Psychology in the Schools, 7,* 241.

Walker, R. E., & Spence, J. T. (1964). Relationship between digit span and anxiety. *Journal of Consulting Psychology, 28,* 220.

Watson, C. G. (1968). The separation of NP hospital organics from schizophrenics with three visual motor screening tests. *Journal of Clinical Psychology, 24,* 412.

Watson, C. G. (1971). An MMPI scale to separate brain damaged from schizophrenic men. *Journal of Consulting and Clinical Psychology, 36,* 121.

Watson, C. G., & Klett, W. G. (1968). Prediction of WAIS IQs from the SH, AGCT, and Revised Beta Examination. *Journal of Clinical Psychology, 24,* 338.

Watson, C. G., & Thomas, R. W. (1968). MMPI profiles of brain damaged and schizophrenic patients. *Perceptual and Motor Skills, 27,* 567.

Wechsler D. A. (1945). A standardized memory scale for clinical use. *Journal of Psychology, 19,* 87.

Wechsler, D. (1955). *Wechsler Adult Intelligence Scale: Manual.* New York: Psychological Corporation.

Wechsler, D. (1958). *The measurement and appraisal of adult intelligence.* Baltimore, MD: Williams & Wilkins.

Wechsler, D. (1981). *Wechsler Adult Intelligence Scale – Revised.* New York: Psychological Corporation.

Wechsler, D. (1987). *Wechsler Memory Scale – Revised.* New York: Psychological Corporation.

Weiner, L. B. (1966). *Psychodiagnosis in schizophrenia.* New York: Wiley.

Welsh, G. S. (1948). An extension of Hathaway's MMPI profile coding system. *Journal of Consulting Psychology, 12,* 343.

Welsh, G. S., & Dahlstrom, W. G. (Eds.). (1956). *Basic readings on the MMPI in psychology and medicine.* Minneapolis: University of Minnesota Press.

Wheeler, L., Burke, C. H., & Reitan, R. M.(1963). An application of discriminant functions to the problems of predicting brain damage using behavioral variables [Monograph]. *Perceptual and Motor Skills, 16,* 417.

Wheeler, L., & Reitan, R. M. (1963). Predictions of brain damage from an aphasia screening test, an application of discriminant functions and a comparison of a nonlinear method of analysis. *Perceptual and Motor Skills, 17,* 63.

Williams, R. L. (1975). The BITCH-100: A culture specific test. *Journal of Afro-American Issues, 3,* 103.

Willis, J., & Ehrlick, S. (1975). Tangible reinforcement and feedback effects on the IQ scores of college students. *Journal of Clinical Psychology, 31,* 463.

Winder, P., O'Dell, J. W., & Karson, S. (1975). New motivational distortion scales for the 16-PF. *Journal of Personality Assessment, 39,* 532.

Yates, A. J. (1954). The validity of some psychological tests of brain damage. *Psychological Bulletin, 51,* 359.

Zimmerman, I. L., & Woo-Sam, J. M. (1973). *Clinical interpretation of the Wechsler Adult Intelligence Scale.* New York: Grune & Stratton.

Zwann, E. J., De Vries, E., & Van Dijk-Bleker, H. (1967). De Benton Test: Aspecten bedoeld en onbedoeld. *Nederl. Tijdschr. Psychol. Grens., 22,* 427.

Index